HISTORICAL DICTIONARIES OF
RELIGIONS, PHILOSOPHIES, AND MOVEMENTS
Edited by Jon Woronoff

Historical Dictionary of Hegelian Philosophy

John W. Burbidge

*Historical Dictionaries of Religions,
Philosophies, and Movements, No. 34*

The Scarecrow Press, Inc.
Lanham, Maryland, and London
2001

SCARECROW PRESS, INC.

Published in the United States of America
by Scarecrow Press, Inc.
4720 Boston Way
Lanham, Maryland 20706
www.scarecrowpress.com

4 Pleydell Gardens, Folkestone
Kent CT20 2DN, England

British Library Cataloguing-in-Publication Information Available

Library of Congress Cataloging-in-Publication Data

Burbidge, John W., 1936-
    Historical dictionary of Hegelian philosophy / John W. Burbidge.
      p. cm.—(Historical dictionaries of religions, philosophies, and movements ; no. 34)
    Includes bibliographical references.
    ISBN 0-8108-3878-8 (alk. paper)
      1. Hegel, Georg Wilhelm Friedrich, 1770-1831—Dictionaries.   I. Title.   II. Series.

B2901 .B87 2001
193—dc21   00-041285

For Bruce

Contents

Editor's Foreword

G. W. F. Hegel is one of the most influential philosophers ever, his ideas and concepts having so thoroughly permeated our view of reason, right, freedom, and many other things that we are all a bit Hegelian. But he is also one of the more difficult philosophers to fathom, partly because of his language (and the translation thereof) and partly because of his thought. This explains, among other things, why so many different interpretations have been given by so many successors, sometimes ranged in opposing groups such as the Right Hegelians and the Left Hegelians, sometimes just borrowing what interested them, such as Karl Marx. These are compelling motives for compiling a dictionary: the obscurity of the language and thought, the widespread and continuing influence, and, most important, the intrinsic value of the ideas of Hegel and his successors.

This *Historical Dictionary of Hegelian Philosophy* merits its name more than any other volume in the series. The dictionary aspect is essential as regards the translation and meaning of the original German terms. The historical aspect is also vital, placing Hegel in his historical context but also tracing the historical line through his successors. Moreover, given the large number of successors, it is more Hegelian philosophy than just Hegel's philosophy that must be described. This is done primarily through the dictionary section, with entries on terms and concepts, books and lectures, Hegel and his time, his successors, and their contributions. The terms themselves are noted in a glossary, the historical sequence is followed through a chronology, and the bibliography directs readers to further literature on Hegelian philosophy as a whole and its many components.

The author of this volume is John W. Burbidge, longtime professor of philosophy and also chair of the Department of Philosophy of Trent University in Ontario, Canada. Dr. Burbidge's education, covering both philosophy and theology and undertaken at Heidelberg University in Germany as well as Canada and the United States, was particularly relevant to his study of Hegel, which included, among other things, a year at the Centre de Recherche et de Documentation sur Hegel et Marx in Poitiers, France. One of the leading authorities on Hegel, he has written numerous articles, translated several books, and authored three books of his own on Hegel. He was also president of the Hegel Society of America and a member of the editorial board of *Owl of Minerva*. This background provided a very solid basis for a historical dictionary on one of the world's great philosophers.

Jon Woronoff
Series Editor

Chronology

1815	Napoleon finally defeated at Waterloo.
1816	*Science of Logic*: The Doctrine of Concept.
	Hegel appointed Professor in Heidelberg, Baden.
	Winter semester: lectures on *Encyclopedia* and history of philosophy.
1817	*Encyclopedia of the Philosophical Sciences.*
	In the *Heidelberg Yearbooks* Hegel publishes a review of Jacobi's third volume and a critique of the refusal of the Württemberg estates to accept a constitution proposed by the king.
	Summer semester: lectures on logic and metaphysics.
	Winter semester: lectures on natural law and history of philosophy.
1818	Summer semester: lectures on aesthetics and *Encyclopedia*
	Hegel becomes professor in Berlin, Prussia.
	Winter semester: lectures on *Encyclopedia* and natural law
	Karl Marx born.
1819	Summer semester: lectures on logic and history of philosophy.
	Winter semester: lectures on philosophy of nature and natural law.
1820	Summer semester: lectures on logic and philosophy of subjective spirit.
	Winter semester: lectures on aesthetics and history of philosophy.
1821	Summer semester: lectures on logic and philosophy of religion
	Philosophy of Right.
	Winter semester: lectures on philosophy of nature and philosophy of right.
1822	Summer semester: lectures on logic and philosophy of subjective spirit.
	Winter semester: lectures on philosophy of right and philosophy of world history.
1823	Summer semester: lectures on aesthetics and logic.
	Winter semester: lectures on philosophy of nature and history of philosophy.
1824	Summer semester: lectures on logic and philosophy of religion.
	Winter semester: lectures on philosophy of right and philosophy of world history.
1825	Summer semester: lectures on logic and philosophy of subjective spirit.

	Winter semester: lectures on philosophy of nature and history of philosophy.
1826	Summer semester: lectures on aesthetics and logic. *Journal for Scientific Criticism* founded. Winter semester: lectures on *Encyclopedia* and philosophy of world history.
1827	Summer semester: lectures on logic and philosophy of religion. Second expanded edition of *Encyclopedia of the Philosophical Sciences.* Winter semester: lectures on history of philosophy and philosophy of subjective spirit.
1828	Summer semester: lectures on logic and philosophy of nature. Winter semester: lectures on aesthetics and philosophy of world history.
1829	Hegel becomes rector of the University of Berlin. Summer semester: lectures on logic and proofs for the existence of God. Winter semester: lectures on history of philosophy and philosophy of subjective spirit.
1830	Summer semester: lectures on logic and philosophy of nature. Third edition of *Encyclopedia of the Philosophical Sciences*. Winter semester: lectures on philosophy of world history.
1831	Summer semester: lectures on logic and philosophy of religion. Second edition of *Science of Logic*: The Doctrine of Being. Winter semester: lectures announced on philosophy of right and history of philosophy. Hegel dies of cholera on November 14.
1832–40	First edition of the *Collected Works* prepared by Hegel's students and friends: Ludwig Boumann, Friedrich Förster, Eduard Gans, Leopold von Henning, Heinrich G. Hotho, Philipp Marheineke, Karl L. Michelet, and Johannes Schulze.
1835–36	David F. Strauss's *The Life of Jesus.*
1838	Arnold Ruge founds the *Hallische Jahrbücher für deutsche Wissenschaft und Kunst*, which later becomes the *Deutsche Jahrbücher* (1841), and then the *Deutsche-Französische Jahrbücher* (1844). August Cieszkowski's *Prolegomena to Historiosophy.*
1840–47	Second edition of the *Collected Works* edited by Hegel's students and friends.

1841	Bruno Bauer's *The Trumpet of the Last Judgment against Hegel the Atheist and Antichrist.*
	Schelling called to Berlin to combat Hegelian philosophy. Søren Kierkegaard, Michael Bakunin, Friedrich Engels, and Jakob Burckhardt all attend his lectures.
1843	Ludwig Feuerbach's *Essence of Christianity.*
1844	Karl Rosenkranz's *G. W. F. Hegels Leben* (G. W. F. Hegel's Life).
	Benjamin Jowett travels to Germany to meet with J. E. Erdmann and learn about Hegelian philosophy.
1845	Max Stirner's *The Ego and Its Own.*
1848	J. B. Stallo's *General Principles of the Philosophy of Nature* published in Cincinnati, Ohio.
	The failure of the Revolution of 1848 scattered German emigrants, imbued with Hegelian philosophy, to the United States and elsewhere.
1857	Rudolf Haym's *Hegel und seine Zeit* (Hegel and His Time) accuses the Hegelian philosophy of theoretically undergirding the Prussian post-Napoleonic restoration.
1858	Henry C. Brokmeyer meets William T. Harris in St. Louis, Missouri, and they form what later becomes the St. Louis Philosophical Society, which publishes the *Journal of Speculative Philosophy* (1867–93).
1865	J. Hutchinson Stirling's *The Secret of Hegel.*
1867	Karl Marx's *Capital.*
1874	William Wallace's English translation of the *Encyclopedia Logic.*
1876	Francis H. Bradley's *Ethical Studies.*
1883	Edward Caird's *Hegel.*
1885	Josiah Royce's *The Religious Aspects of Philosophy.*
1888	Bernard Bosanquet's *Logic or the Morphology of Knowledge.*
1896	James M. E. McTaggart's *Studies in Hegelian Dialectic.*
	Samuel W. Dyde's English translation of the *Philosophy of Right.*
1905	Wilhelm Dilthey's *Die Jugendgeschichte Hegels* (Hegel's Early Years), the book that initiated the study of Hegel's development.
1906	Benedetto Croce's *What Is Living and What Is Dead in Hegel's Philosophy.*
1907	Hermann Nohl publishes *Hegel's Theologische Jugendschriften* (Hegel's Early Theological Writings).

1910	James B. Baillie's English translation of the *Phenomenology of Mind*.
1913	Giovanni Gentile's *La riforma della dialettica hegeliana* (The Reform of the Hegelian Dialectic).
1920	Franz Rosenzweig's *Hegel und der Staat* (Hegel and the State).
1924	Walter Stace's *The Philosophy of Hegel: A Systematic Exposition*.
1929	W. H. Johnston and L. B. Struther's English translation of the *Science of Logic*.
	Theodor L. Häring's *Hegel: Sein Wollen und sein Werk* (Hegel: His Willing and His Work).
	Jean Wahl's *Le malheur de la conscience dans la philosophie de Hegel* (The Unhappiness of Consciousness in the Philosophy of Hegel).
1933	Alexandre Kojève begins his seminars on Hegel in the École Pratique des Hautes Études, Paris, France. Among his students are Jean-Paul Sartre, Maurice Merleau-Ponty, Jean Hyppolite, Eric Weil, Raymond Aron, Georges Bataille, Jacques Lacan, and Alexandre Koyré.
	Enrico De Negri's Italian translation of the *Phenomenology of Spirit*.
1940	Geoffrey R. G. Mure's *An Introduction to Hegel*.
1941	Jean Hyppolite's French translation of the *Phenomenology of Spirit*.
	Herbert Marcuse's *Reason and Revolution: Hegel and the Rise of Social Theory*.
1946	Jean Hyppolite's *Genesis and Structure of the Phenomenology of Spirit*.
1948	György Lukács's *The Young Hegel*.
1950	Eric Weil's *Hegel and the State*.
1951	Ernst Bloch's *Subjekt-Objekt: Erläuterungen zu Hegel* (Subject-Object: Comments on Hegel).
1953	Wilhelm R. Beyer founds the Deutsche Hegel-Gesellschaft (German Hegel Society) in Nürnberg, Germany.
1958	The Hegel Archiv is established in Bonn, Germany, and undertakes the preparation of a critical edition of Hegel's works. At the Second International Congress of the German Hegel Society in Frankfurt am Main, the name is changed to the Internationale Hegel Gesellschaft (International Hegel Society). John N. Findlay's *Hegel: A Reexamination*.

1961	*Hegel-Studien* first appears.
1962	At a congress held in Heidelberg, Germany, the Internationale Hegel Vereinigung (International Hegel Association) is founded. Hans-Georg Gadamer is elected president, and Alexandre Koyré and Joachim Ritter are elected assessors.
1965	Walter Kaufmann's *Hegel: Reinterpretation, Texts, and Commentary*.
1967	Emil Fackenheim's *The Religious Dimension of Hegel's Thought*.
1968	The Hegel Archiv transferred from Bonn to Bochum, Germany.
	Hegel Society of America founded at the Wofford Symposium, held at Wofford College, South Carolina, United States. *Owl of Minerva* first appears in 1969.
1970	Centre de Recherche et de Documentation sur Hegel et Marx established at the Université de Poitiers, France, by Jacques D'Hondt; name later changed to Centre de Recherche sur Hegel et l'Idéalisme Allemand.
1972	Shlomo Avinieri's *Hegel's Theory of the Modern State*.
	Henry S. Harris's *Hegel's Development I: Toward the Sunlight*.
1975	L'Istituto Italiano per gli Studi Filosofici established in Naples, Italy, by Gerardo Marotta.
	Charles Taylor's *Hegel*.
1976	Hegel Forschungsstelle (Hegel Research Center) is established at the Univerity of Zurich, Switzerland, under the direction of R. W. Meyer and W. Zimmerli.
1979	Hegel Society of Great Britain founded in Oxford, England. *Bulletin of the Hegel Society of Great Britain* first appears in 1980.
1981	Societas Hegeliana, or the Internationale Gesellschaft für dialektische Philosophie, founded in Frankfurt am Main.
1983	Henry S. Harris's *Hegel's Development II: Night Thoughts*.
1997	Henry S. Harris's *Hegel's Ladder*.

Introduction

Not every philosopher merits inclusion in a series devoted to religions, philosophies, and movements. Even while he was still alive, however, Georg Wilhelm Friedrich Hegel evoked passionate discipleship and equally passionate opposition. His close students and associates would talk about their encounter with Hegel's thought in the language of conversion—of moving from darkness to light and from despair to salvation. At his funeral, his liberating and redeeming achievements were placed side by side with those of Jesus Christ himself. Yet he was frequently put under suspicion of heresy by some of the pastors of Berlin. A philosophical opponent observed that his "metaphysical mushroom had developed not in the garden of science but on the manure heap of boot-licking servility."[1] And the obscurity of his expression, even in social conversation, led a member of Johann Wolfgang von Goethe's household to observe, "I cannot tell whether he is brilliant or mad. He seems to me to be an unclear thinker."[2]

Adulation and revulsion have continued ever since. In *Capital* Karl Marx openly avowed himself a pupil of Hegel, even though his dialectical method "must be turned right side up again, if you would discover the rational kernel within the mystical shell."[3] John Dewey's first encounter with Hegel "operated as an immense release, a liberation." Even after he had drifted away from Hegelianism, he still found that "in the content of his ideas there is an extraordinary depth; in many of his analyses, taken out of their mechanical dialectical setting, an extraordinary acuteness. Were it possible for me to be a devotee of any system," he went on to say, "I still should believe that there is greater richness and greater variety of insight in Hegel than in any other single philosopher."[4]

On the other hand, he became the object of Karl Popper's scorn: "Hegel's intention is to operate freely with all contradictions. 'All things are contradictory in themselves,' he insists, in order to defend a proposition which means the end not only of all science, but of all rational argument."[5] And Bertrand Russell attributes the "whole imposing edifice of his system" to Hegel's mistaken belief that all the properties of a thing could be inferred by logic if one knew enough to distinguish it from everything else.[6]

1

Such responses, even the gradual falling away from an early conversion, fit easily into the typology of religious movements. What is it about this German philosopher, whose language was so convoluted that even his friends found it difficult to understand him, that he could become the focus of an almost religious attachment on the part of some and an almost religious revulsion on the part of others?

HEGEL'S TIME

Hegel lived from 1770 to 1831. Born before the American Revolution, when the ancien régime in France still held sway and Germany was a collection of almost 300 independent statelets theoretically united under the Holy Roman Emperor, he died just after the revolutions of 1830 failed to reintroduce breathing space into the post-Napoleonic restoration and just before the first tentative moves towards reforming the British House of Commons. While still a student in the seminary at Tübingen, the Bastille fell and fellow students from across the Rhine introduced him to the *Marseillaise.* As a tutor in Bern, he made contact with activists from the moderate Gironde, now exiled from a more radical Paris. As the French wars consumed Germany, he took an interest in moves toward constitutional government. He had the indignity of having his residence occupied by French troops after the battle of Jena and caught a glimpse of Napoleon I on reconnaisance in the city.

From Jena he moved to Bamberg and on to Nürnberg, both by this time in Bavaria, which Napoleon had reorganized as a kingdom after the demise of the Holy Roman Empire. Hegel thus benefited from the progressive policies of the king, Maximilian I; his prime minister, Max Josef von Montgelas; and Hegel's own friend, Friedrich Niethammer, who worked in the ministry of schools and churches. After peace was restored in 1815, Hegel soon found himself in Berlin, the capital of Prussia, where the king, Friedrich Wilhelm III, not only had promised a constitution but had also entrusted to the liberal Prince Karl von Hardenberg responsibility for government.

The years of Hegel's life did not simply span some of the most profound political changes that modern Europe has experienced. They were also years of immense intellectual ferment in Germany itself. No other period, save perhaps Athens in the fifth century before the present era, has seen such a pantheon of distinguished thinkers and artists.

Standing like a giant over the whole period was Johann Wolfgang von Goethe. Novelist, poet, natural historian, man of affairs, Goethe not only defined German identity for those living in the dispersed duchies and electorates with such works as *Wilhelm Meister's Wanderjahr* and *Faust* but, as minister of culture under Duke Karl August of Saxe-Weimar, made Weimar and its university at Jena the intellectual center of Germany until Napoleon's victory near that very city marked an end to its period of glory. Associated with him there were the dramatist Friedrich Schiller, whose tragedies integrated elements of both classical and Shakespearean drama, and the romantic, Johann Gottfried Herder, whose *Ideas for a Philosophy of the History of Mankind* initiated the quest for philosophical significance in our human past. The university attracted some of the leading figures of academic life. To be sure, Immanuel Kant, whose *Critique of Pure Reason* had explored the presuppositions of both empiricism and rationalism and thereby opened a whole new way of doing philosophy, remained in Königsberg in the far reaches of Prussia. But Jena attracted Karl Reinhold, who first popularized Kant's thought, Johann Fichte, who attempted to make it systematic, Friedrich Schelling, who balanced Kant's and Fichte's transcendental idealism with a philosophy of nature, and eventually Hegel himself.

Beyond Jena one finds other figures who have helped to define the modern world. Baron Karl Wilhelm von Humboldt not only founded the University of Berlin in 1810 but also introduced literature from India and China to German culture and speculated that languages could significantly affect thought and culture. Friedrich Schleiermacher's defense of religion set the standard for Protestant theology for the next 200 years. The poets Friedrich Hölderlin and Heinrich von Kleist broke with traditional patterns and evoked new forms of imagery. The brothers Grimm, Wilhelm and Jakob, dug into the roots of German dialects and exposed the way many Western and Eastern languages were all members of a single Indo-European family.

There were others, almost too numerous to mention: Gotthold Ephraim Lessing, Friedrich Heinrich Jacobi, Moses Mendelsohn, Johann Georg Hamaan, August Wilhelm and Friedrich von Schlegel, Friedrich von Hardenberg (better known as Novalis), and, later on, Arthur Schopenhauer. Ludwig van Beethoven was almost an exact contemporary. The operas of Wolfgang Mozart and Gioacchino Rossini were being performed in Vienna when Hegel visited in 1824. Felix Mendelsohn-Bartholdy attended his lectures on aesthetics.

Hegel took his place among these luminaries. Hölderlin and Schelling were fellow students in Tübingen and eased his way into Frankfurt and Jena. Goethe interceded on his behalf in Jena and entertained him on his return from Paris in 1827. Even though Hegel disagreed vigorously with Schleiermacher on the appropriate grounding for religion, they joined in contributing to the support of a Berlin colleague who had been summarily dismissed by the authorities.

HEGEL'S LIFE

Yet there was little in Hegel's early life that marked him out as the founder of a new philosophical tradition. He was born in Stuttgart on August 27, 1770, the son of an administrative official in the duchy of Württemberg. A state bursary, which committed him to serving its government either in the church or in education, paid his way to the theological seminary in Tübingen where, together with Hölderlin and the younger Schelling, he studied philosophy for two years and theology for three. During those years, the French Revolution broke out, and the enthusiasm of the students for constitutional reform brought them under the scrutiny of the duke and his court. Hegel did not stand out as a brilliant student, and he found the dogmatism and traditionalism of his instructors less than inspiring. At the same time, however, he began a project for a rational religion that would appeal to people's hearts while promoting an integrated society.

Not wanting to enter the bureaucracy directly, he received permission to serve as tutor for a family in the Swiss canton of Bern. Using the resources of the family library in Tschugg, he continued researches already begun into the natural sciences, wrote some drafts for his project on religion, looked into the finances of Bern, and followed from afar philosophical developments as first Fichte and then his friend Schelling pushed the Kantian revolution to its limits.

Finding himself removed from the center of German culture, he welcomed the initiative of Hölderlin and Isaac von Sinclair to find another post as tutor, this time in Frankfurt am Main. There he not only continued his writing on religion but also began to take more interest in political questions. A translation of a revolutionary tract concerning French territories controlled by Bern was his first publication. When German patriots (including his friend Sinclair), inspired by the French example, became interested in constitutional matters, he started work on an extensive discussion of the German constitution, and wrote another essay on the situation in Württemberg.

On the death of his father in 1799, Hegel came into a small inheritance that made possible a return to academic life. He joined Schelling at Jena, which (as we have seen) was the center of German intellectual life, and soon qualified as an unsalaried junior instructor by defending a set of

12 paradoxical theses and submitting a dissertation on the orbits of the planets. Until Schelling left for Würzburg, the two of them produced a *Critical Journal of Philosophy*; and Hegel began lecturing on natural law, logic and metaphysics, mathematics, philosophy of nature and spirit, and the history of philosophy. After several attempts to produce a textbook for his courses, he turned to writing an introduction to his proposed system, eventually called *Phenomenology of Spirit*.

Thanks to the good offices of Goethe, he obtained a promotion that brought with it a small honorarium. But by that time the Napoleonic wars had ruined the economy of Germany in general and Saxe-Weimar in particular, and funds were not easily forthcoming. In the aftermath of the battle of Jena, with very little resources, Hegel learned that his chambermaid was pregnant with his son. In desperation, he appealed to the good offices of his friend, Friedrich Niethammer, who found positions for him: first as editor of a newspaper in Bamberg and then as headmaster of a newly established secondary school in Nürnberg. While in Nürnberg, Hegel was responsible not only for instruction in the school, teaching courses on mathematics and philosophy, but also for the physical plant. He married Marie von Tucher and also completed the three books of his *Science of Logic*.

The return of peace to Europe with the fall of Napoleon freed resources for the state-run universities, and Hegel once again exploited contacts in Erlangen, Berlin, and Heidelberg in his quest for an academic post. Heidelberg was the first to respond with a positive offer, so Hegel spent two years there before moving on to Berlin. As a textbook for his lectures he published an outline of his system, *Encyclopedia of the Philosophical Sciences,* and he served as an editor of, and contributor to, the *Heidelberg Yearbook*.

In 1818, he took over the chair in philosophy at Berlin that had been vacant since Fichte's death in 1814. Under the chancellorship of Prince Karl August von Hardenberg and the minister of public education, Karl von Altenstein, Prussia had emerged from the patriotic wars against Napoleon with an administration that sought to introduce liberal reforms in a state still molded by the traditions of feudalism. Hegel now discovered the financial security and recognition that he had craved for so long, and he soon stood at the center of the German academic world. Johannes Schulze, the Prussian director of higher education, not only attended a complete set of Hegel's lectures, but also collaborated in the Society for Scientific Criticism and its *Journal*, which Hegel, his colleagues, and students had established. With friends in high places, Hegel was able to arrange appointments for his disciples, even for those who had fallen under suspicion for progressive activity, such as Friedrich Förster, or those who had only recently converted to Christianity, such as Eduard Gans. Students flocked to Berlin to hear his lectures (which now included the philosophy of world history and philosophy of religion), not only from other states in disunited Germany, but also from Russia, Poland, Estonia, and Denmark. The second edition of his *Encyclopedia of the Philosophical Sciences* proved to be so popular that a third edition was required within three years, and he expanded its paragraphs on political philosophy into the *Philosophy of Right*. When he died in 1831, he had just completed a term as rector of the university.

Yet there was another side to this renown. The theologian, Friedrich Schleiermacher, blocked his entry to the Prussian Academy of Sciences. A number of his students and friends, active in the national student movement, came under suspicion of the authorities, fearful of demagogues in the aftermath of the French Revolution; Hegel at times had to intervene on their behalf. When a Berlin newspaper reported a celebration over the night that separated his 56th birthday from that of Johann Wolfgang von Goethe, arranged by his students, the king took umbrage, since his own birthday had gone unnoticed, and decreed that no celebrations but his own should be reported in the press. So Hegel found it advisable to be in Paris when his birthday came around the following year. He was offended by an anonymous article that criticized his polemics in the *Philosophy of Right* against a disgraced colleague, Jakob Friedrich Fries, and sought redress from his patrons. A casual comment from the crown prince that Gans's lectures on political science endangered the state led Hegel to resume responsibility for them. Once the crown prince came to power as Friedrich Wilhelm IV, he called on Hegel's old colleague, Friedrich Wilhelm Joseph Schelling, to combat his insidious philosophy in Berlin.

A student, Heinrich Hotho, described the convoluted way in which he lectured:

> Exhausted, morose, he sat there as if withdrawn into himself, his head bent down, and while speaking kept turning pages and searching in his long folio notebooks, forward and backward, high and low. The constant clearing of his throat and coughing interrupted any flow of speech. Every sentence stood alone and came out with effort, cut in pieces and jumbled. Every word, every syllable detached itself only reluctantly to receive a strangely thorough emphasis from the metallic-empty voice with its broad Swabian dialect, as if each were the most important. Nevertheless, his whole appearance compelled such

a profound respect, such a sense of worthiness, and was so attractive through the naïveté of the most overwhelming seriousness that, in spite of all my discomfort, and though I probably understood little of what was said, I found myself captivated forever.[7]

Then, in November 1831, at the tail end of a cholera epidemic, Hegel fell ill, and on the 14th he died. The shock galvanized his students and disciples. The center of their intellectual world had vanished. But he had himself provided the blueprint for the future. Spirit, he had said, overreaches death to become universal. Quickly they assembled lecture notes from their colleagues and published them, together with his written works, in a "complete edition." They used their positions in universities and government to show that his ideas could provide the bulwark for both church and state. Many of the younger generation, however, found themselves without prospect of employment. The postwar "baby boom," combined with the repressive policies of governments, limited opportunities in universities and elsewhere. These began to find in Hegel's thought a critique of revealed religion and a challenge to feudal and autocratic regimes.

Thus, the ambiguities inherent in Hegel's life and thought became more pronounced. On the one hand, he had been an enthusiast for the French Revolution, a supporter of Napoleonic reforms, and an associate of progressive members of the nationalistic student movement. His dialectical method claimed that any position, pushed to its extreme, collapses into its opposite and dies. On the other hand, he craved security, took few risks in challenging authority, relished his renown, and sought to use his position to silence criticism. His system claimed completeness and totality, transcending all relative partiality.

These two sides to Hegel's ambiguous legacy have continued to dominate his succession. On the one side, he has been charged with being an ideologue of the post-Napoleonic restoration, defender of an illiberal and authoritarian state. On the other, his thought has been accused of instigating the revolutionary fervor of Karl Marx and Friedrich Engels, which aimed at the ultimate dissolution of the state. He inspired the conservative Bernard Bosanquet as much as the liberal T. H. Green, the bureaucrat William T. Harris, and the bohemian Francis Sedlak. He has been ostracized by a totalitarian Stalin because of his threat to stability and lionized as heralding the end of real historical change now that the liberal, democratic state has achieved its apotheosis.

The purpose of this *Historical Dictionary of Hegelian Philosophy* is to throw light on this ambiguity between stability and change, between defender of the status quo and advocate of progress. Yet each term in its title retains aspects of the two sides.

HISTORICAL

Consider the term *historical*. For some, Hegel's philosophy is a system, complete in itself. Indeed, the students and friends who published the early editions of his works called themselves "friends of the immortalized," as if the philosopher's thoughts were now eternally enshrined in heaven, never to be altered. The English and Americans who first took an interest in his thought focused on his *Science of Logic,* suggesting that it contained the fixed and immutable truth not only of thought but of the universe itself.

Yet Hegel more than anyone other than Baron Charles de Montesquieu saw the importance of geographic and historical conditions in defining what could be achieved by a nation. In his lectures on history, art, religion, and philosophy, he showed how various aspects of a culture interact to create a complex world that is so integrated that any serious challenge to its fundamental principle would bring the whole system crashing to the ground. The next nation on the world's stage would benefit from the achievements of its predecessor, but it would do so in a new way, with an entirely new integrating dynamic. Each nation, each artist, each philosopher, is a product of its age.

Those convinced that Hegel had written an "immortalized" system could only consider this description of historical emergence and decline to be itself partial, applying to the past, but not to the present or future. The phrase "the end of history," which could be saying that any present marks the end of history to that point, is read as something more profound: that once Hegel's comprehensive understanding of thought, nature, and history has come on the scene, all significant development is over. There might be change, but it is simply an eternal recurrence of the same.

It took some time for the perception that Hegel's system is a comprehensive totality subject to no alteration to be put in question. Indeed, it is still the predominant tendency in much Anglo-Saxon Hegelianism. Yet in 1905, Wilhelm Dilthey drew attention to Hegel's early writings, showing that the system had not sprung full blown from Hegel's mind like Athene from the head of Zeus but had been the product of a number of tentative ventures that were left incomplete as his thinking moved on. Hermann Nohl published some of the early manuscripts from Tübingen, Bern, and Frankfurt. Then Georg Lasson, in his edition of the *Works*, both reproduced manuscripts from the Jena period and took account of how Hegel had amended his lectures throughout his years in Berlin. Only recently, however, has a serious attempt been made to publish separately the various lecture courses to show how Hegel kept changing his mind on what constituted a proper systematic structure. Also only recently has scholarship begun to explore the reasons for Hegel's revisions in subsequent editions of the *Encyclopedia* and *Science of Logic*. Henry S. Harris has brought the attention of English-speaking scholars to Hegel's early development, spearheading the translation of a number of early texts, and Peter Hodgson has led a team who translated the various series of lectures on the Philosophy of Religion into English. But the thought that Hegel was a living thinker, never satisfied completely with what he had previously thought, is only slowly beginning to make its way.

What these texts and transcripts suggest is that Hegel was always rethinking, reworking, and revising his system. It was not a closed package with a single, fixed form. Indeed, some have argued that the Hegelian method itself, which he said was the only true method, is a dynamic process that involves constantly learning from having put ideas and convictions into practice and taking note of all the consequences, expected and unexpected alike.

From this perspective, Hegelian philosophy was not finalized at his death. New occasions teach new duties. Scientific discoveries require a rethinking of the philosophy of nature; political developments put in question the constitution proposed in the *Philosophy of Right*; the emergence of religious pluralism and modern secularism requires a new discussion of how humans respond to the ultimate essence of the universe. Indeed, one can go so far as to say that new distinctions drawn and new similarities noticed may lead to significant modifications in the *Science of Logic* itself. On this view, Hegel's philosophy expected to have a creative life even after the master's death.

So, while this version of the dictionary has tended to focus on Hegel's reading of the history of philosophy, of science, religion and art, of concepts and experience, it has also extended the project further and incorporated concepts and approaches developed by his Hegelian successors: by Karl Marx and Francis Bradley, by John Dewey and Jacques Derrida, by Søren Kierkegaard and Benedetto Croce, by Nishida Kitaro and Slavoi Zizek.

DICTIONARY

For all that *historical* is embedded in ambiguity, *dictionary* is the more so. A dictionary, like an encyclopedia, is organized on a most superficial level: by the initial letters of the words that a particular language uses to articulate the thought of its culture. Hegel himself took issue with such an approach. Even though the one complete articulation of his system was called *Encyclopedia of the Philosophical Sciences* "which could leave room for a lesser degree of rigor in the scientific method," he specifically rejected the arbitrary order used by the French *encyclopédistes* and opted for logical coherence.

According to Hegel, each stage, when explored to its full and understood in its totality, should manifest the elements of another, more intricate stage, which in its turn merits careful analysis. This, he suggested, was the way reason works. It understands a concept or term by subjecting it to conceptual analysis, each of its moments being fixed with precision. An honest evaluation of the result realizes that other terms have emerged that also need to be examined—terms that are inevitably the counterpart or opposite of the one with which reason began. This emergence of its contrary out of an original concept Hegel called the work of dialectical reason.

Then a careful investigation of the opposing terms finds that they are not simply opposed but are predicated of the same subject—that they are contradictories and that thought, in its attempt to work out all the determinations, moves back and forth from one to the other. Since reason cannot function with unresolved contradictions, it can only get out of this dilemma by reflecting on the total picture. The ground of the contradiction turns out to be a network of relations that together constitute an integrated unity—a new stage that incorporates into its meaning elements of the previous one, no longer as dominant, but as subordinate. This reflective integration is the work of speculative reason.

Understanding and dialectical and speculative reason are, says Hegel, the three sides of systematic development. Since we humans are rational, thinking beings, an encyclopedia, in offering an all-around education, needs to build on this fundamental nature of reason. By understanding how each stage is made up and how it leads conceptually into the next one, we are led into the logical coherence of the universe. In contrast, an alphabetical order presents things as simply an arbitrary collection, the order changing haphazardly when one translates into another language or when one decides to replace a term with its synonym. Meaning and comprehension are abandoned—at least at this macroscopic level.

Hegel, then, explicitly challenged the whole project of a dictionary of his philosophy. When one adds entries on his life, on his interpreters, and on those who applied his insights in new geographic and historical settings, one is in danger of succumbing to an eclecticism far removed from his systematic ideal.

Nonetheless, the dictionary format does offer advantages. Within entries on concepts and systematic stages, one can provide not simply a synonym but also a thumbnail indication of the process by which it breaks down and sows the seeds of its successor — a glimpse into the dynamic of reason. Also, the use of cross-references enables one to document connections that intersect the simple linear progress of systematic advance. In the *Encyclopedia of the Philosophical Sciences* itself, Hegel appeals back in any one paragraph to a diverse collection of concepts previously discussed. He anticipates by showing how a concept under discussion does not yet contain the full significance of a term that emerges only later in the story.

Underneath the contingent, alphabetical ordering of the dictionary, then, can lie a more intricate sense of system, in which the various moments are not just strung along a single thread (which, like a necklace, turns out to be circular) but are rather interconnected in a more complex way. A distinction between inner and outer resurfaces in the discussion of animals or of the spirit of a culture. The chemical discovery that sodium has a natural preference for some substances over others can lead back to a reconsideration of the logic of measure, in which we use such affinities to measure quantitatively some qualified entity. A fully articulated philosophy thus may benefit from a basic ordering principle that is arbitrary, in that a complete set of cross-references to many different points in the system can be developed. It becomes a hypertext, in which one clicks on any concept or term and is led into a whole range of other applications and logical developments.

HEGELIAN

A systematic structure becomes problematic once we move from Hegel's philosophy to Hegelian philosophy. For now we lack the presupposition of a single mind working through all the components with some sort of integrated vision. Yet, for all the diversity, the various applications of his insight ought to be part of the same family, even if they lead to widely diverging, if not contradictory, conclusions.

What can we use to define someone's thought as distinctively Hegelian? One feature, certainly, is the dialectic—the process mentioned before in which a concept, moment, or stage works out its implications to the full only to turn into its counterpart or opposite.

Such a regular inversion of meaning is particularly evident in the *Phenomenology of Spirit*, in which Hegel shows how, in human experience, strongly held claims to certainty and truth, once consistently put into practice, turn out to be inconsistent and self-contradictory. The appeal to *immediate* sensation learns that it constantly has to *mediate* between different times and locations. Antigone's committed loyalty to the family and Creon's conscientious efforts to maintain the integrity of the state come into a head-on collision, heralding the demise of classical Greek culture. A master's confirming his independence by subjecting a slave to his will turns out to be making himself dependent on the slave, while the slave, forced in fear of his life to transform things for the master's enjoyment, paradoxically discovers independently the truth about himself in the products of his labor.

Dialectical transitions occur, not only in logical concepts or experience but also in human history. The espousal of freedom in the French Revolution converts into the despotism of the reign of terror. The full participation of all citizens in Athenian democracy nurtures the individual self-certainty of a Socrates, an independence that threatens to undermine the cohesive community.

Dialectical development is the foundation of rational derivation according to Hegel. In this he was transforming and extending the approach taken by Johann Gottlieb Fichte, who had been the first to derive concepts one from another. Immanuel Kant had identified 12 categories, grouped in sets of three. But for Kant these were simply a given, drawn from a table of judgments found in traditional logic texts. Fichte's *Science of Knowledge* showed how one could move from identity or reality to difference or negation and on to ground or limitation. However, he did not reflect on the logical operations that underlay his derivations; so he missed the way reason functions dialectically. Nor did he notice that this dialectical pattern was not simply a function of subjective knowing and thinking but constitutive of social reality itself.

If Fichte's systematic project pointed in the right direction, his focusing on the subjective made his philosophy one-sided and partial. It was Friedrich Wilhelm Joseph Schelling who saw the need to balance the transcendental philosophy of Kant and Fichte with a philosophy of nature that takes account of the objective realm. He, too, was inspired by Kant. In the *Critique of Judgment,* Kant had recognized that organisms escaped the straightforward linear sequence of cause and effect. Each member of a living being—the heart, liver, lungs, brain, kidney, digestive system—is a contributing cause to the functioning of the others yet at the same time is the result of their activity. This mutual interaction produces the centered life of the organism as a whole, even as that whole determines the role each organ plays. So the reciprocal influence is not simply among members but also between the organs and the whole organism. Schelling adopted this model for his philosophy, the organic whole, or absolute, being the point of indifference between its constituent parts: subjective consciousness and objective nature.

If the first characteristic of Hegelian philosophy—dialectical development—built on Fichte's concern for systematic derivation, the second characteristic—speculative consideration of the total picture—capitalized on Schelling's sense of the organic. It was not that everything is dissolved into an all-encompassing totality, as tended to occur in Baruch Spinoza's absolute. One has to understand how each part of the whole functions on its own, how its unique characteristics contribute to and constitute both the other parts and the total dynamic, and how this reciprocal causality is balanced by a susceptibility to the workings of the other parts, making possible the effective working of the original constituent. This network of interconnections would become the theory of internal relations in the philosophy of the British idealists, pushing toward the view that everything is but the internal workings of some comprehensive organism or absolute.

Although Hegel was prepared to use the term *absolute,* familiar to those contemporaries who read Spinoza and Schelling, he preferred the term *absolute spirit.* For spirit is more than an organism. It does not have a simple, natural body with constituent organs. Rather, it is created by the interactions of conscious human beings, in acts of mutual recognition, in the sealing of contracts, in the division of labor, in the family, corporations, or leisure activities. Through their interactions, paradoxically enough, humans become more independent, able to determine freely their own actions, just because they are interdependent, able to rely on the customs and conventional practices of daily social intercourse.

In developing this theory of an all-encompassing spirit, Hegel was not necessarily advocating a receptive quietism. When humans rebel against the strictures of tradition, they also may contribute to a vital and dynamic society, pointing toward the future; and when they conscientiously will to do what is in the best interests of all, the result could easily turn out to be a stagnation that heralds decadence and the fall of a civilization.

If spirit could be said to have a "body," that would be not only its own past but also the world of nature. Nature, at least initially, is not defined by internal relations of mutual cause but by the external relations of spatial location and temporal sequence. Gradually, as our knowledge of nature increases, we discover the rationality inherent there: the orbits of the planets, electrical polarization, the functioning of animal organisms. But even with all of these implicit internal relations, nature is still bedeviled with contingency and powerlessness, producing aberrations and events that are dead ends, leaving no direct prospect of renewal. Renewal, if renewal there be, will be the work of spirit. For spirit, through science and technology, incorporates nature into its life, just as biological life incorporates inanimate objects into its living body.

For Hegel, the simpler in nature does not of itself produce the more complicated. Unable to accept the evolutionary theory of his day because of its inadequate scientific justification, he followed Aristotle in seeing within nature a pattern of more complicated forms and structures, each one presupposing the ones that are more elementary but not derived genetically from them. Starting with space and time, Hegel systematically moves through mechanics, physics, chemistry, geology, and botany to zoology. But each of these moves is the work of philosophical reflection, not a development inherent to nature itself. By looking at the total picture of chemical interaction, for example, thought can notice a pattern in which each chemical is both the result of some process and the presupposition for another one. In this way, that picture has some of the features of an organism. But the philosopher has to turn back to nature and study plants and animals to see how natural organisms really do function. There are, said Hegel, no metamorphoses in nature. It was not until Friedrich Engels applied the dialectic to evolutionary theory that one could begin to talk about a dialectic within nature itself.

For Hegel, spirit is centered life that uses the simpler mechanical and chemical processes and in appropriating them develops its more sophisticated forms. A full comprehension only emerges from the standpoint of the whole, from the standpoint of *absolute* spirit.

With this in mind, Hegel was omnivorous in his quest for knowledge: astronomy, physics, chemistry, geology, biology; world literature extending from the Bhagavad Gita to Shakespeare; anthropological reports from Africa and America; accounts of colonial officials in India and Jesuit missionaries in China; English newspapers on economics and politics; classical history, medicine, Egyptian temples, and psychology. His lectures were filled with details of recent discoveries and events. At times he even rethought the organization of his courses in light of new material. If speculative reason means taking the whole into account and showing how its components are interrelated, then one needs to know what those details are and how they are distinctive and unique. One must do justice to the rich diversity of the world, and not just dissolve all differences into a bland undifferentiated absolute. Spirit and life individuate their components and members into independent functions even as they connect them together into a dynamic totality.

Hegel's successors could not easily match his all-inclusiveness. In part, this was because many of them focused on only one or two aspects of his thought: religion and politics, for example, or thought and metaphysics. They did not share his curiosity for all things human. But their failure may also be endemic to more recent times. For knowledge itself has expanded and become the domain of technical specialists. In the early years of modern chemistry, one could hope to keep abreast of developments as new elements were discovered and electrolysis produced new kinds of compounds. But during the 19th and 20th centuries, each discipline probed into finer and finer details, and new discoveries presuppose more and more sophisticated knowledge. Half a lifetime may be necessary to master the intricacies of one part of modern physics alone or one aspect of molecular biology, leaving little occasion to capture all the complicated issues that make up capitalist economics, all the subtle differences between religious traditions, all the developments and cultural practices of societies ranging from Austria to Afghanistan, from Zimbabwe to the Yukon, or all the creative energy of modern art and literature through multitudes of schools and movements. One individual can no longer achieve comprehensive and detailed knowledge of all human endeavor.

So it is not easy to be a Hegelian after Hegel, to be both dialectical and comprehensive. Either one adopts the dialectic and follows its path without knowing how it contributes to the whole, or one develops a comprehensive view that offers the vision of an integrating principle without being able to document how it works in detail, much less how those details are connected to each other.

PHILOSOPHY

It would seem, then, that Hegelian philosophy will fall apart into two competing schools: a dialectical left wing and a comprehensive right wing. In that case, one could say that the genuine heir of Hegel's philosophy is not any one set of its more recent exponents, but all of them together. For they, in fact, provide the necessary corrective for each other. The challenge is not simply to leave them as a diverse and disparate collection but to explore the implicit rational connections that bind them together. One takes each position and understands its distinctive determinations. That leads us to recognize how other positions are their counterpart, exploring what has been ignored or deliberately excluded. Together they would then represent a complete Hegelian picture of how modern culture understands itself and its natural environment.

Such an endeavor might go further to include not just the two "schools" who have explicitly appropriated Hegelian themes, but also those whose theories have nothing at all to do with Hegel: Bertrand Russell's knowledge by acquaintance; Gottlob Frege's rejection of psychologism in logic; Martin Heidegger's dread as the intuitive moment of truth; Gilles Deleuze's repudiation of any kind of comprehensive philosophy as repressive. They, too, could turn out to be part of the total reality that Hegelian thought must come to terms with during the 21st century. For they also have intricate connections with the strands that have emerged more directly from Hegel.

Ultimately, there may not be different and diverse philosophies of which one is Hegelian. Rational thought may be ultimately integrated in a complex dynamic in which reaction creates radical differences and reflection recognizes implicit connections. Hegel, in fact, made this claim himself. There is only one philosophy, all of it the work of human reason, coming to terms with the ultimate essence of the cosmos. He did not see himself as producing a new arbitrary theory, unique to himself and his disciples. He was, rather, exposing to view the way human reason as such functions when it isolates and analyzes particular moments (understanding), reacts to that partiality by affirming equally partial counterweights (dialectic), and integrates those diffuse moments into comprehensive pictures (speculative reason).

Even the comprehensive pictures will not be the last word. For Hegel also says that philosophy only comes on the scene when a culture has become fully mature, enabling its reflective thinkers to comprehend how its various conflicting and competing features belong together in a single community. By understanding its character and analyzing its constituents, however, and by making the integrating principle explicit, they set the stage for a new reaction. Dialectical reason, implicitly or explicitly, will attack the achieved consensus and initiate a decline that leads to the fall of that world culture and the possibility for another to take its place.

For the movement through understanding, dialectic, and speculation back to understanding is, as we have seen, not simply the pattern of logical thinking. Hegel claims that it is just as much the way human societies function. What distinguishes humans from the rest of the animal kingdom is that they are rational, that the rhythms of logical thought are implicit in everything they do, whether intentionally or impulsively. People understand, react, reflect, and comprehend.

Does this pattern also apply to the nonhuman world of nature? Is it implicit in the way the ecosystem adapts to new circumstances? Is it inherent in the kinds of equilibrium that resulted in the solar system, in the expansion of the universe, in the emergence of new species? It could be that a more sensitive appreciation of what Hegel means by reason would throw some such light on our understanding of nature. Were that to be the result of honest research by reflective scientists, it would confirm Hegel's claim that he was not simply creating an idiosyncratic philosophy but rather bringing to consciousness the implicit truth of the conceptions that govern all our scientific research and social life. Such a response would confirm that what he produced was not a final, immortalized system but rather one further step along the pathway of human knowledge. If he is right, that realization would mark the culmination of the modern world, initiate its demise, and sow the seeds for another to inherit its mantle.

NOTES

1. Ernst Ludwig Theodor Henke, *Jakob Friedrich Fries: Aus seinem handschriftlichen Nachlasse dargestellt* (Leipzig, 1867), 224, cited in Bernd Burkhardt, *Hegels Wissenschaft der Logik im Spannungsfeld der Kritik* (Hildesheim: Olms, 1993), 188.

2. Ulrike von Pogwisch, cited in *Hegel: The Letters*, trans. Clark Butler and Christiane Seiler (Bloomington: Indiana University Press, 1984), 711.

3. Karl Marx, *Capital: A Critique of Political Economy,* vol. 1, trans. Samuel Moore and Edward Aveling (Moscow: Progress, 1954), 29.

4. John Dewey, *On Experience, Nature and Freedom: Representative Selections*, ed. Richard J. Bernstein (Indianapolis: Bobbs-Merrill, 1960), 10, 12.

5. Karl Popper, *The Open Society and Its Enemies,* vol. 2, *The High Tide of Prophecy: Hegel, Marx, and the Aftermath* (London: Routledge & Kegan Paul, 1966), 40.

6. Bertrand Russell, *History of Western Philosophy* (London: Allen & Unwin, 1961), 715.

7. From Heinrich Gustav Hotho, *Vorstudien für Leben und Kunst* (Stuttgart: Cotta, 1835), in Walter Kaufmann, *Hegel: A Reinterpretation* (Garden City, N.Y.: Doubleday, 1965), 357–58.

The Dictionary

– A –

ABSOLUTE ESSENCE (DAS ABSOLUTE WESEN). This phrase, often translated "absolute being," is the philosophical term Hegel uses when talking about God (q.v.). He is thereby suggesting that God is the ultimate essence (q.v.) of everything that is. The philosophy of religion (q.v.) explores the way various traditions have fleshed out this abstract expression in concrete form: as the ground of the natural order, as beauty or the sublime (qq.v.), and as free personality.

ABSOLUTE FREEDOM (DIE ABSOLUTE FREIHEIT). In the *Phenomenology of Spirit* (q.v.), the Enlightenment's (q.v.) appeal to utility (q.v.) vanquishes faith's (q.v.) orientation toward the absolute essence (q.v.) of the world, so that people's freedom (q.v.) is no longer limited by anything external and becomes absolute. Each person is free to use people and things for the good of all. Because these acts of will are singular and reflect the particular perspectives of the agent, however, they turn out to be opposed to the universal good and are thus condemned as both useless and evil. So absolute freedom develops into the reign of terror of the French Revolution (q.v.) where anyone who presumes authority to act for the good of all is condemned to death (q.v.).

ABSOLUTE IDEA (DIE ABSOLUTE IDEE). The culminating chapter of the *Science of Logic* (q.v.) describes the method (q.v.) that underlies the preceding logical development: A beginning (q.v.), when examined carefully, leads to its contrary or opposite. Focusing on that opposition (q.v.) reveals relations that connect the contrasting terms to a point where, because of a total interconnection, they collapse into a new single term, which becomes the next immediate (q.v.) beginning. This method, suggests Hegel, is the principle of all valid reasoning whatever. As the strictly logical principle of pure thinking (q.v.), the absolute idea is to be distinguished from the absolute spirit (q.v.), which incorporates the natural and social world as well into a comprehensive, and reasonable, totality. *See also* DIALECTIC; LOGIC; SPECULATIVE REASON; UNDERSTANDING.

ABSOLUTE KNOWING (DAS ABSOLUTE WISSEN). As the culminating chapter of the *Phenomenology of Spirit* (q.v.), absolute knowing brings together the subjective process of the beautiful soul (q.v.) (in which the condemnation of self-confident action [q.v.] leads to reconciliation) with an objective process described in revealed religion (Christianity [q.v.]) in which God self-confidently creates a world that then falls into sin, is condemned, and is in due course reconciled. Common to both is the process through which one learns through experience (q.v.) from the unfortunate results of one's confident actions. Since this self-correcting pattern of knowing underlies the entire experience of spirit's development, whether human or divine, it is not liable itself to being called in question and so is absolute. Based on Hegel's claim that absolute knowing integrates subjective certainty and objective truth (q.v.), some interpreters take absolute knowing to be our knowledge of the absolute (qq.v.).

ABSOLUTE SPIRIT (DER ABSOLUTE GEIST). In the final section of the *Encyclopedia of the Philosophical Sciences* (q.v.), spirit (q.v.) is considered not from partial perspectives but as valid in all respects. The three domains where human subjectivity explores absolute spirit are art, religion, and philosophy (qq.v.). Art, particularly in Greek religion (q.v.), offers an intuitive insight into spirit as such. Revealed religion recounts the details of spirit's nature in a form that remains somewhat contingent and anecdotal. Philosophy comprehends these details conceptually within a single, integrated perspective. The further development of absolute spirit involves three mediated relationships or syllogisms (q.v.). In the first, pure thought moves through the givens of the natural world to reach the life of spirit. In the second, spirit as mediator reflects on the givens of nature (q.v.) to determine the underlying logical principles. In the third, philosophical thought explains how nature and spirit are not only distinct from each other, but also presuppose and require each other. Because absolute spirit incorporates the full range of nature and human experience, it is to be distinguished from the strictly logical principles of the absolute idea (q.v.). *See also* AESTHETICS;

CHRISTIANITY; HISTORY OF PHILOSOPHY; LOGIC; PHILOSO-
PHY OF RELIGION; *PHILOSOPHY OF SPIRIT*.

ABSOLUTE, THE (DAS ABSOLUTE). In the *Science of Logic* (q.v.),
"absolute" names the empty unity of inner subjectivity (q.v.) and outer
objectivity (q.v.), in which all predicates are canceled. Reflection (q.v.)
thinks about it from the outside and fleshes out its determinations (q.v.)
by using the language of attributes and modes. This chapter thus provides the framework for Hegel's discussion of Baruch Spinoza's (q.v.)
nature or god. But this term had also been taken over by Friedrich
Schelling (q.v.) to name the undifferentiated unity of the subjective and
the objective. Since Hegel was working in a philosophical context in
which the audience would be familiar with Schelling's use of the term,
he frequently uses it as well in his lectures, prefaces, and remarks to
refer to an ultimate, but otherwise undefined, ontological reality. But
neither Spinoza's nor Schelling's absolute has any principle of self-
determination. So, in the culminating chapters of his main systematic
works, Hegel prefers to use *absolute* as an adjective, and the most comprehensive reality is called *absolute spirit* (q.v.). Inspired by Francis
Bradley and Josiah Royce (qq.v.), the later tradition has nonetheless
adopted this term to name Hegel's ultimate metaphysical principle. *See
also* ABSOLUTE IDEA; ABSOLUTE KNOWING; ABSOLUTE, THE
(SCHELLING); INNER/OUTER.

ABSOLUTE, THE (SCHELLING). In Friedrich Schelling's (q.v.) early
thought, "the absolute" (q.v.) referred to that which is indifferent and undifferentiated with respect to both the subjectivity of consciousness
(qq.v.) and the objectivity of nature (qq.v.). In his lectures and remarks
(qq.v.), Hegel appealed to his audience's familiarity with this usage, for
he agreed with Schelling that, if we were not already objectively embedded in that reality, we would have no hope of knowing it subjectively.
But he preferred the more concrete expression *absolute spirit* (q.v.) over
the abstract noun *absolute*.

ABSTRACT/CONCRETE (ABSTRAKT/KONKRET). These are relative terms. A concept (q.v.) is abstract when it is isolated from its
context; concrete when the network of internal relations (q.v.) are
fully articulated. So the logic (q.v.) is abstract when compared to the

full life of spirit; but within the logic, an abstract universal (q.v.) can be distinguished from the concrete singularity (q.v.) that it is supposed to describe.

ABSTRACT RIGHT (DAS ABSTRAKTE RECHT). The immediate (q.v.) way by which spirit (q.v.) becomes objective is through its willed appropriation of property (q.v.). A subjective spirit (q.v.) thereby becomes a person (q.v.) with legal rights, able to enter into contracts (q.v.). Abstract right, however, has no way of handling the fact that individual wills (q.v.) can act in an arbitrary manner, producing wrong (q.v.). This requires the consideration of morality (q.v.) as its concrete counterpoint. *See also* ABSTRACT/CONCRETE; LEGAL STATUS; OBJECTIVE SPIRIT; *PHILOSOPHY OF RIGHT*.

ACTION (DIE HANDLUNG). In his chapter on absolute knowing (q.v.), Hegel stresses the role of action. The beautiful soul (q.v.) cannot rest content in pure thinking (q.v.) but must will (q.v.), transforming its insight (q.v.) into a deed. The reciprocal relation of action and thinking recurs throughout Hegel's philosophy (q.v.): in the interconnection of cognition (q.v.) (the idea of the true) with the idea of the good, in the shift in his psychology (q.v.) from intelligence (q.v.) to will, and in the move from subjective spirit to objective spirit (qq.v.). *See also* CIRCLE OF CIRCLES.

ACTUALITY (DIE WIRKLICHKEIT). Whereas *being* (q.v.) is a general term for whatever is and *existence* (q.v.) is contrasted with *essence* (q.v.), actuality is defined as the *realization* of a possibility or essence (qq.v.). Even so, it can be used in several senses: as virtually equivalent to the simple term *being,* as one actual that excludes related possibilities, and as the total complex of whatever is essential. Together with possibility and necessity (q.v.), it is a modal category (q.v.) or concept. In the *Science of Logic* (q.v.), it offers the first stage in giving Baruch Spinoza's (q.v.) absolute (q.v.) some intrinsic determinations (q.v.). *See also* ACTUALITY OF THE RATIONAL.

ACTUALITY OF THE RATIONAL (DIE WIRKLICHKEIT DES VERNÜNFTIGEN). In the preface to the *Philosophy of Right* (q.v.), Hegel writes, "whatever is rational, that is actual, and whatever is actual, that is rational." These phrases have been used by critics such as Rudolf Haym, Karl Popper, and Bertrand Russell (qq.v.) as evidence that Hegel identified completely with the restoration monarchy of Prussia (qq.v.). In the second edition of the *Encyclopedia of the Philosophical Sciences* (q.v.), however, Hegel points out that the expression is similar to the statement that God is actual. From this perspective everything in common life is in part appearance (q.v.) and only in part actuality (q.v.). He is claiming, then, that what is ultimately reasonable will become actual and that whatever is genuinely actual is grounded in such rationality.

ADDITIONS (DIE ZUSÄTZE). Both the *Encyclopedia of the Philosophical Sciences* and the *Philosophy of Right* (qq.v.) are handbooks, made up of numbered, summary paragraphs, which Hegel would expand upon in his lectures (q.v.). After his death, his students collated and edited student transcripts from the various series of lectures on the *Encyclopedia* logic, the philosophy of nature, the philosophy of subjective spirit (qq.v.), and the philosophy of right and added them after the appropriate paragraphs. In most editions these are indicated by the use of smaller type. These additions are not to be confused with the remarks (q.v.), which are notes that Hegel himself added to the basic paragraphs (and are often not separately indicated in English translations). *See also* LECTURES ON LOGIC AND METAPHYSICS; LECTURES ON THE *ENCYCLOPEDIA*.

ADORNO, THEODOR W. (1903–1969). By immersing oneself in Hegel's thought, Adorno argues, one discovers how his dialectic (q.v.), when consistently followed, must lead to the sacrifice of consistency. As a result, when Hegel thought away the difference between the conditioned and the absolute (q.v.), he did an injustice to the experience (q.v.) on which he drew, and by making absolute the thesis of totality (q.v.), he espoused the principle of domination that is to subject everything to the mastery of the concept (q.v.). A thoroughly negative dialectic shows that reason cannot in fact comprehend the actual because actuality (q.v.) is not reason. *See also* ACTUALITY OF THE RATIONAL; NEGATION OF NEGATION.

AESTHETICS. For Hegel, philosophy (q.v.) organizes its discussion of art (q.v.) conceptually. It begins from the idea (q.v.) of beauty (q.v.) in general and explores the universal (q.v.) forms in which an ideal content becomes integrated with sensible reality: symbolic, classical, and romantic art (qq.v.). He then turns to the particular (q.v.) ways we sense reality: seeing is the basis of the plastic arts (architecture, sculpture, and painting [qq.v.]); hearing is the basis of music (q.v.), and sensible representation (q.v.) is the basis of the literary arts or poetry (q.v.). In his 1828–29 lectures Hegel called the symbolic, classical, and romantic forms of art the particular (rather than the universal) moment and then proceeded to talk about the plastic, musical, and literary arts as the singular (q.v.) moment. *See also* COMEDY; DRAMA; EPIC; *LECTURES ON AESTHETICS*; LYRIC; SUBLIME; TRAGEDY.

ALIENATED LABOR. Inspired by Hegel's discussion of master and slave (q.v.), Karl Marx (q.v.) shows how human labor inevitably generates the alienation (q.v.) of the laborer from his work, from the product of his labor, from himself, and from his human nature in general. This, he suggests, leads to the opposition between oppressor and oppressed and is an example of how the dialectic (q.v.) works in the realm of human affairs, producing the opposite of what is consciously intended. *See also* BLOCH, ERNST; CAPITALISM.

ALIENATION (DIE ENTFREMDUNG). In the *Phenomenology of Spirit* (q.v.), Hegel explores the way spirit (q.v.) becomes alienated from itself within society. Although universal (q.v.), because it overreaches the otherness of its natural environment, spirit nonetheless becomes actual only through singular actions of will (qq.v.). These two contrary moments (of universal and singular) presuppose each other, but they are broken apart into radical opposition (q.v.) and conflict: universal state power versus the singular appropriation of wealth, good versus evil, noble versus base, faith in a beyond (qq.v.) versus insight (q.v.) into the truth (q.v.) of the present. When the two sides are finally brought together as absolute freedom (q.v.), all determinate content has to be left behind. So the singular will, freed from all external restraints, simply wills what is universally useful. The result is a reign of terror in which every exercise of will, as singular, is condemned to death (q.v.). Ludwig Feuerbach (q.v.) used Hegel's analysis of the unhappy consciousness (q.v.) to claim that religion (q.v.) in general and Christianity (q.v.) in particular resulted from humans alienating their real nature into a transcendent beyond (q.v.). *See also* ALIENATED LABOR; BLOCH, ERNST; CULTURE; ENLIGHTENMENT; FRENCH REVOLUTION.

ANTHROPOLOGY (ANTHROPOLOGIE). As the first part of Hegel's *Philosophy of Spirit* (q.v.), anthropology focuses on the unmediated soul (q.v.), the most basic aspects of the human person. Starting from given natural conditions, both environmental and genetic, and the natural alterations of aging, sexual differentiation, and sleeping/waking, Hegel moves on through passive sensitivity to feeling, in which the soul begins to take possession of itself and, by developing habits, to make its immediate (q.v.) sensibility objective. Madness and other psychic diseases occur when consciousness, understanding, and reason (qq.v.) fall into abeyance and these more basic anthropological aspects of the soul become dominant. Once the feeling soul actualizes itself through embodied habits, it becomes explicitly conscious of something other, setting the stage for a second discipline that Hegel calls *phenomenology* (q.v.). *See also* BODY (DER LEIB); INSANITY.

ANTIGONE. This tragedy (q.v.) by Sophocles provides Hegel with a paradigm for the way Greek society understood itself. Antigone, as a woman (q.v.), identifies with the family (q.v.) and the family's gods. In burying her brother who had been declared an outlaw, she comes in conflict with the king, Creon, who as a man (q.v.) embodies the state (q.v.) with its human law (q.v.). Because the human grounds its authority in the divine and the divine must find expression in public life, this conflict disrupts the immediate (q.v.) union between the human and the divine, which was the genius of Greek communal life. *See also* DEATH; ETHICAL LIFE; GREEK HISTORY.

ANTINOMIES (DIE ANTINOMIEN). Immanuel Kant (q.v.) had argued for restricting the role of reason (q.v.) because it resulted in antinomies: pairs of rational arguments about the cosmos that lead to contradictory conclusions. Hegel points out that the antinomies come from analyzing essential features of space, time, and causality (qq.v.) into their component elements and then isolating those elements, taking them to be independent. Thus, the second antinomy, which sets the argument for indivisible atoms against the argument for infinite (q.v.) divisibility, isolates and opposes the two complementary aspects of quantity (q.v.): continuous and discrete magnitude (q.v.). Similarly the first antinomy, about whether the world is infinite or has a beginning in space and time, results from distinguishing the two moments of a qualitative infinity (q.v.): the limit and going beyond (or sublating [qq.v.]) the limit. For Hegel, the antinomies reflect the nature of speculative reason (q.v.). Anything, when analyzed into independent terms, will be thought of as involving a contradiction (q.v.) between those terms. The task of reason is to find the ground (q.v.) or explanation, which will show how these discrete terms are yet components of a continuous relationship. *See also* ATOMISM.

APPEARANCE (DIE ERSCHEINUNG). In the *Science of Logic* (q.v.), things (q.v.) are understood as simply appearance when their immediate existence (qq.v.) suggests, but is not identical with, their essence (q.v.). The essential that underlies appearance is first identified with persisting laws and then with an inverted world (q.v.) that is the dynamic counterpart of the immediate, appearing world. To describe this relationship between appearance and reality, reflection (q.v.) uses such terms as *whole/part, force,* and *inner/outer* (qq.v.). *See also* UNDERSTANDING.

ARCHITECTURE (DIE ARCHITEKTUR). Architecture sets limits to unlimited space (q.v.). Temples and churches are given a form that does aesthetic justice to the divine that is housed in them and the community that worships there, though that form will vary from the huge symbolic temple precincts of India and Egypt to the proper proportions of classical Greek temples and the romantic heights and decoration of Gothic churches. *See also* AESTHETICS; ART; CLASSICAL ART; ROMANTIC ART; SYMBOLIC ART.

ARISTOTLE. Aristotle was "one of the richest, most scientific, most comprehensive, and deepest geniuses that has ever appeared." Although he developed traditional formal logic (q.v.), his own reasoning was more speculative (q.v.). On the one hand, he observed widely and took account of all empirical details, natural as well as psychological and social. On the other hand, he looked for the inner purpose or rationale that transforms potentialities into actualities (q.v.) and thus integrates the many details into a unity. In the last analysis, thinking (q.v.) that thinks itself is the absolute good—the final end toward which everything moves. Aristotle's treatises, however, remain independent and unconnected with each other, since he lacked the logical framework for an integrated system (q.v.). *See also* HISTORY OF PHILOSOPHY.

ART (DIE KUNST). The beautiful and the sublime (q.v.) are ways by which humans have intuited absolute spirit (q.v.) in its simple unity.

Early art symbolized the sublime ultimate, whereas in Greek religion (q.v.), the beautiful ultimate took human form, not only in plastic statues but also in the genius of sculptors and poets. Christian art is romantic (q.v.), pointing beyond (q.v.) what is directly intuited to a reality that transcends the immediate (q.v.). *See also* AESTHETICS; ARCHITEC-TURE; BEAUTY; COMEDY; DRAMA; EPIC; INTUITION; *LEC-TURES ON AESTHETICS*; LYRIC; MUSIC; PAINTING; POETRY; RE-LIGION IN THE FORM OF ART; ROMANTICISM; SCULPTURE; TRAGEDY.

ATOMISM (DAS ATOMISMUS). Atomism is a theory that sees matter and sometimes human society as made up of self-contained ones, or be-ings for self (qq.v.). The independence of the units one from another then requires that they repel each other, even as they are attracted to each other. Because it presupposes this interrelationship but cannot really ex-plain its particular forms, Hegel rejects atomism as a viable theory both in natural philosophy and in his theory of social interaction. For all that civil society (q.v.) may appear to be atomistic, it nonetheless requires and establishes networks of interconnection. *See also* ANTINOMIES; AT-TRACTION; REPULSION.

ATTRACTION (ATTRAKTION). Immanuel Kant (q.v.) had argued that matter is not just particles in motion but constituted by attractive and re-pulsive forces. In the *Science of Logic* (q.v.), Hegel explores the logical thinking involved in this approach. When anything is thought of as made up of a number of units or ones (q.v.), not only must each repel the oth-ers but that repulsion (q.v.) must presuppose their implicit unity or at-traction for each other. Such an analysis remains on the surface of things and does not explore the specific interconnections that provide a deter-minate content. *See also* ATOMISM; BEING FOR SELF.

AVINIERI, SHLOMO. In *Hegel's Theory of the Modern State*, Avinieri presents Hegel as a perceptive student of the ambiguities of modern so-ciety, who recognizes, but has no solution for, the inevitability of poverty (q.v.) in a capitalist economy. Since personal recognition (q.v.) depends on property (q.v.), this is a critical flaw. This weakness is balanced in part by his view of the state (q.v.) as transcending the individualism of civil society (q.v.), in that patriotism leads people to work for the well-being of all and to risk their lives for the security of the political community.

The state thus envisioned, far from glorifying the kingdom of Prussia (q.v.), offers an implicit critique of its lack of constitution (q.v.). Curious is Hegel's omission of industrial workers from his review of the social classes (q.v.), despite his recognition that labor is important for personal dignity. *See also* CAPITALISM; HAYM, RUDOLF; *PHILOSOPHY OF RIGHT*.

– B –

BACCHANALIAN REVEL (DER BACCHANTISCHE TAUMEL). In the preface to the *Phenomenology of Spirit* (q.v.), Hegel not only says that the true is subject (q.v.) as well as substance but also that it is equally a Bacchanalian revel "in which no member is not drunk; yet because each member dissolves as soon as it separates itself out, the revel is just as much transparent and simple repose." When the various moments of the true are separated out and distinguished (by understanding [q.v.]), they immediately dissolve (dialectically) into something else. Yet the whole maintains itself (speculatively) in simple repose through such constant separation and dissolution. *See also* DIALECTIC; SPECULATIVE REASON.

BAILLIE, JAMES B. (1872–1940). As well as translating the *Phenomenology of Mind* (as he called it) into English, Baillie wrote *The Origin and Significance of Hegel's Logic*, in which Hegel is understood as uniting the immediacy valued by the romantics with the mediated reflection (q.v.) of Immanuel Kant and Johann Fichte (qq.v.). This strength is also his greatest weakness, since it reduces all immediate experience (qq.v.) to mediated knowledge (qq.v.) and so cannot do justice to the experienced real which transcends what we know. *See also* PHENOMENOLOGY OF SPIRIT; ROMANTICISM.

BAMBERG. In 1807 after the defeat of the Prussians had left the university of Jena (q.v.) demoralized and disorganized, Hegel accepted a position as editor of the local newspaper in Bamberg. Bavaria (q.v.), a member of the Confederation of the Rhine (1806) and thus under the hegemony of Napoleon (q.v.), was implementing a program of modernization under King Maximilian I and his prime minister, Maximilian Josef von Montgelas. Hegel's friend, Friedrich Niethammer (q.v.), arranged for the position in Bamberg but soon moved on to Munich where he became responsible for reforming the educational system of the whole kingdom. In due course, he made arrangements for Hegel's appointment as headmaster of the Protestant gymnasium (secondary school) in Nürnberg (q.v.), which was being reorganized in accordance with his program. Although Hegel performed his duties in Bamberg as editor and publisher conscientiously, he nonetheless came under investigation by the authorities for unadvisedly reporting troop movements, and (shortly after he left) the paper's publication was temporarily suspended.

BAUER, BRUNO (1808–1882). Initially an associate of Philipp Marheineke (q.v.) and defender of the orthodox Christian reading of Hegel against David Strauss's (q.v.) critique, Bauer moved to a more radical position that brought him into contact with Arnold Ruge, Ludwig Feuerbach, and the young Karl Marx (qq.v.). While working on the second edition of Hegel's *Lectures on the Philosophy of Religion* (q.v.) with Marheineke, he found that Hegel did not resolve the tensions between traditional Christian dogma and conceptual comprehension. For Bauer, the historical expressions of faith (q.v.) needed to be recognized as the creations of a mythic consciousness, rather than the work of a transcendent subject. In the coming dawn, people would consciously affirm the revolutionary power of self-determining, active self-consciousness. *See also* CHRISTIANITY; LEFT-WING HEGELIANS; RELIGION IN THE YOUNG HEGELIANS; YOUNG HEGELIANS.

BAVARIA. In 1799, Maximilian IV became elector of Bavaria at a time when it was caught in the rivalry of Austria with revolutionary France. He appointed as minister Maximilian Josef von Montgelas, who followed a pro-French policy leading to the incorporation of a number of small bishoprics and independent cities, including Bamberg (q.v.), into the electorate. With the termination of the Holy Roman Empire in 1806, the elector became King Maximilian I. Under the influence of Napoleon (q.v.), the king with his minister replaced the medieval system of privileges and exemptions with equality before the law (q.v.), universal taxation, abolition of serfdom, security of person and property, and liberty of conscience and of the press. Hegel's friend, Friedrich Immanuel Niethammer (q.v.), was put in charge of public instruction soon after Hegel moved to Bamberg and arranged for Hegel's appointment as rector of the gymnasium (secondary school) in Nürnberg (q.v.) in 1808.

When Montgelas refused to implement constitutional reforms in 1817, he was dismissed, but Maximilian continued to rule as a model constitutional monarch until his death in 1825.

BEAUTIFUL SOUL (DIE SCHÖNE SEELE). Hegel uses this term for the community where, disillusioned by the failure of moral principles to make unambiguous decisions, conscientious individuals together know what is right with immediate self-certainty. Whenever such individuals act, however, the action (q.v.) turns out to be the opposite of what was intended and is condemned by those who have refrained from acting. The admission of failure by the one and the offering of forgiveness by the others lead to reconciliation. In his discussion of absolute knowing (q.v.), Hegel takes this dynamic of self-certain action to be the subjective *form* of truth (q.v.). Friedrich Hölderlin (q.v.), Novalis (Friedrich von Hardenberg), and Friedrich Jacobi's (q.v.) novel *Woldemar* have been proposed as models for this section. *See also* CONSCIENCE; *PHENOMENOLOGY OF SPIRIT*; ROMANTICISM.

BEAUTY (DAS SCHÖNE). In his *Lectures on Aesthetics* (q.v.), Hegel defines the beautiful as presenting to eyes and ears intuitions (q.v.) into a unity that incorporates disparate things. By uniting an integrating concept (q.v.) with sensible reality, beauty can be called an idea (q.v.). *See also* AESTHETICS; ART; CLASSICAL ART; EARLIEST SYSTEM-PROGRAM.

BECOMING (DAS WERDEN). This is the third term in Hegel's *Science of Logic* (q.v.) after being (q.v.) results from thinking nothing (qq.v.), and nothing results from thinking being. When logical thought puts those two moves together, it recognizes how important is the *movement* or transition (q.v.) from one term to the other and identifies this "becoming" as a new concept. There are two forms of becoming: being *passes away* into nothing; nothing *comes to be*. When these are taken together in thought as a recurrent cycle, the whole pattern collapses into a simple being or Dasein (q.v.). The dynamic of becoming (or transition) is thus fundamental to all logical thinking. *See also* CIRCLE OF CIRCLES; HERACLITUS; SUBLATE.

BEGINNING (DER ANFANG). Since philosophy works with concepts (q.v.) and not with representations (q.v.), its task is to find the way pure thinking (q.v.) derives one concept from another. Its starting point, then, needs to be the most indeterminate thought, one that is not mediated by, or derived from, any other. This, suggests Hegel, is the thought of pure being (q.v.). He recognizes, however, that our ability to think such pure concepts is itself mediated by the full range of human experience (q.v.) over the ages. The *Phenomenology of Spirit* (q.v.) analyzes that experience and so provides an introduction to the philosophical sciences as such: *Science of Logic*, *Philosophy of Nature*, and *Philosophy of Spirit* (qq.v.). It in turn begins from the most immediate (q.v.) form of knowledge (q.v.), which Hegel calls *sense certainty* (q.v.). *See also ENCYCLOPEDIA OF THE PHILOSOPHICAL SCIENCES.*

BEING (DAS SEIN). The first term in Hegel's logic serves as a predicate that can be ascribed to anything whatsoever and has no distinguishing characteristic of its own. As such a simple term, *being* offers thought no determinate information, so it really tells us nothing (q.v.), which thus becomes the second term that has to be discussed. Being also names the first book of the *Science of Logic* (q.v.), devoted to the immediate transitions (qq.v.) of thought: quality, magnitude (quantity), and measuring (qq.v.). *See also* BECOMING; BEGINNING.

BEING FOR SELF (DAS FÜRSICHSEIN). Based on the idiomatic German sense of "for itself" (q.v.), this term refers to self-contained being or being on its own account. The self-determining dynamic of the true or valid infinite (q.v.), in which both the finite (q.v.) and that which is beyond (q.v.) the finite mutually condition each other, collapses in thought into the simple concept of that which is simply related to itself or being for self. Such a being is a unit or one (q.v.) that repels others, even though attracted by them. Self-consciousness (q.v.) is the most fully developed example of this concept (q.v.). *See also* ATOMISM; ATTRACTION; CIRCLE OF CIRCLES; MAGNITUDE; REPULSION; *SCIENCE OF LOGIC*; SUBLATE.

BELIEF. *See* **FAITH.**

BERLIN. In 1818, the Prussian minister responsible for education, Karl von Altenstein, reissued Kaspar Friedrich von Schuckmann's invitation for Hegel to take over Johann Gottlieb Fichte's (q.v.) chair in the recently founded University of Berlin. Prussia (q.v.) was the leading Protestant state in the nationalistic wars against Napoleon (q.v.), and its king had mustered support by promising constitutional reform and appointing a chancellor with liberal inclinations, Karl August von Hardenberg. Hegel moved not only to the center of German intellectual life but also to what (in 1818) appeared to be the most progressive state in Germany. He attracted students from other German states, as well as from abroad, introducing lectures on the philosophy of religion and the philosophy of world history (qq.v.), as well as continuing with lectures on aesthetics, the history of philosophy (qq.v.), and the various parts of his system (q.v.). He expanded the chapter in the *Encyclopedia of the Philosophical Sciences* (q.v.) on natural law (q.v.) and political science into the *Philosophy of Right* (q.v.) (1821), revised the *Encyclopedia* extensively in 1827 and more modestly in 1830, and completed a revision of the first book of the *Science of Logic* (q.v.) just before his death. He spent several years as examiner for the Brandenberg school system and in 1829–30 served as rector of the university, in which role he gave a formal address on the Augsburg Confession. One of his key disciples, Johannes Schulze (q.v.), was director of higher education under von Altenstein, so Hegel had some influence with the government. At the same time, he had as students and associates many of the leaders of the *Burschenschaft* (q.v.), a student federation suspected of demagoguery, and his final essay, on the British Reform Bill, was censored when it appeared in the *Prussian State Gazette.* In 1827, his colleagues founded the *Journal for Scientific Criticism* (q.v.), in which Hegel wrote essays on Karl Wilhelm von Humboldt, Karl Wilhelm Ferdinand Solger, Johann Georg Hamaan, and Karl Friedrich Göschel. Stricken with cholera in the aftermath of an epidemic, he died suddenly on November 14, 1831.

BERN. When he left the seminary at Tübingen (q.v.) in 1793, Hegel, as a student supported by the government of Württemberg (q.v.), had to obtain permission to accept a position as private tutor with the von Steiger family of Bern, Switzerland. During the summers, he had access to the library of the family estate at Tschugg, which he used to further his education. He continued to work on his project for a religion of the people, writing a life of Jesus (q.v.) and an explanation of how Jesus' moral teaching was transformed into positive doctrine. He also took an interest in the political affairs of Bern, translating a text advocating the liberation of the land of Vaud in France, which was under Bern's control. In 1796, his friend Friedrich Hölderlin (q.v.) found a similar position for him with a Frankfurt am Main (q.v.) family, which brought him closer to the center of German intellectual life. *See also* CONSTITUTION; FREEMASONRY; FRENCH REVOLUTION; THEOLOGICAL WRITINGS.

BEYOND (DAS JENSEITS). When faced with any limit (q.v.), thought projects a beyond that lies on the other side of the finite (q.v.) barrier. Such a beyond is the first form of the infinite (q.v.), although it will itself become the focus of thought and so become determinate and finite. A new move beyond is the second shift in an indefinite regress, which thus becomes a second (bad) form of the infinite. Once the finite limit and the infinite beyond are seen as two contrary moments that mutually imply each other, thought arrives at a valid third form of the infinite. *See also* CIRCLE OF CIRCLES; *SCIENCE OF LOGIC*.

BLOCH, ERNST (1885–1977). The key to understanding Hegel, says Bloch, is the ancient Greek formula: "Know thyself." But in Hegel this becomes "Grasp conceptually the way the subject has become objectified historically." The self is a laboring person, who finally grasps his own production and thus emerges from his self-estrangement. While Hegel explores this process idealistically, it should be followed through in the material world of production, where it becomes both dissatisfaction with a present alienation (q.v.) and hope in an anticipated freedom (q.v.) of self-contained being. *See also* ALIENATED LABOR; CAPITALISM; MARX, KARL.

BODY (DER KÖRPER). *Body* in this sense is a concept (q.v.) from the *Philosophy of Nature* (q.v.) and names a mass of matter that has spatial and temporal unity. *See also* BODY (DER LEIB); MECHANICS; SPACE; TIME.

BODY (DER LEIB). Soul (q.v.), or unmediated spirit, is conditioned by its body; as well, its own feelings come to be embodied through habits. The effort to learn about persons by simply observing their skulls or faces, however, fails to discover their living truth (q.v.). *See also* ANTHROPOLOGY; OBSERVING REASON; *PHILOSOPHY OF SPIRIT*; PHRENOLOGY; PHYSIOGNOMY.

BOSANQUET, BERNARD (1848–1923). A student of Benjamin Jowett and Thomas Hill Green (qq.v.) at Balliol College, Oxford, Bosanquet drew no sharp distinction between logic (q.v.), on the one side, and epistemology and metaphysics (qq.v.), on the other. Knowledge (q.v.) advances through the discovery by inference of the systematic connections that hold facts together. Individuals (q.v.) are the concrete integration of sets of facts. On this basis, society and the state (q.v.) are more comprehensive individuals than particular persons. *See also* BRITISH IDEALISM.

BOTANY (DIE VEGETABILISCHE NATUR). Vegetable nature (as Hegel calls it) is a part of Hegel's discussion of organics (q.v.). While integrating the internal dynamic of life (q.v.) with the objective structure of an organism (q.v.), plants do not have fully differentiated organs or members in the way animals do, even though roots, leaves, buds, and seeds all perform different functions. In his lectures on this text from the *Philosophy of Nature* (q.v.), Hegel quotes extensively from the botanical research of his day. *See also* LECTURES ON THE PHILOSOPHY OF NATURE; ZOOLOGY.

BRADLEY, FRANCIS H. (1846–1924). Influenced by Thomas Hill Green (q.v.) while a student at Oxford, Bradley argued polemically against the utilitarian ethics, empiricist epistemology (q.v.), and atomistic metaphysics (q.v.) of his contemporaries. His most Hegelian work was *Ethical Studies* (1876, 1927), in which he argues that a person's moral obligations were determined by his or her concrete station in society. In *Principles of Logic* (1883, 1922), he argues for an (un-Hegelian) distinction between meaning (the what) and reality (the that). On this basis, in *Appearance and Reality* (1893, 1897), he concludes that the conceptual distinctions between substance and accident, quality and relation are self-contradictory and so unreal, while reality is the absolute (q.v.): a consistent, harmonious, and all-inclusive experience (q.v.), which transcends thought. *See also* ATOMISM; EMPIRICISM; INTERNAL RELATIONS; MORALITY; UTILITY.

BRITISH IDEALISM. In the 19th century, the British interest in Hegel focused on his logic (q.v.) and the way both concepts (q.v.) and social reality are interconnected by a network of internal relations (q.v.). The movement largely centered on Oxford, although it extended to Cambridge, Scotland, Wales, and Canada and included, in addition to Bernard Bosanquet, Francis H. Bradley, Edward Caird, Thomas H. Green, John M. E. McTaggart, Geoffrey R. G. Mure, J. Hutchinson Stirling, William Wallace, John Watson (qq.v.), Brand Blanshard, John Caird, Richard B. and John S. Haldane, Henry Jones, Harold H. Joachim, John S. Mackenzie, John H. Muirhead, and Andrew S. Pringle-Pattison. Attacked by both Bertrand Russell's (q.v.) logical atomism (q.v.) and the ordinary language philosophy of conceptual analysis, Hegelian studies went into decline in Britain. However, in 1979, Zbigniew A. Pelczynski, Raymond Plant, William H. Walsh, and Charles Taylor (qq.v.) sponsored the formation of the Hegel Society of Great Britain (q.v.), which now holds annual meetings in Oxford and publishes the *Bulletin of the Hegel Society of Great Britain*. *See also* COLLINGWOOD, ROBIN; HOULGATE, STEPHEN; PETRY, MICHAEL; THESIS.

BROKMEYER, HENRY CONRAD (1826–1906). Living as a hermit in rural Missouri, Brokmeyer's "deep insights and his poetic power of setting them forth with symbols and imagery" stimulated William Torrey Harris and the St. Louis Hegelians (qq.v.) in their study of Hegel and German philosophy generally. He prepared a translation of Hegel's *Science of Logic* (q.v.) that received wide circulation, but was never published. In due course, he became lieutenant governor of Missouri.

BUDDHISM. In his *Lectures on the Philosophy of Religion* (q.v.), Hegel places his discussion of Buddhism between his discussions of Chinese and Indian religion (qq.v.). Whereas magic highlights the immediate (q.v.) (Chinese) spiritual power over nature, Buddhism turns this power in towards the self, offering spiritual control over the will and the passions (qq.v.) to achieve peace and obedience. Hegel shows familiarity with the literature about Tibet, Burma, and India, as well as the religion of Fo in China. *See also* JAPAN; NATURAL RELIGION; NISHIDA KITARO; PHILOSOPHY OF RELIGION; TANABE HAJIME.

BURBIDGE, JOHN. Burbidge sees the development within the *Science of Logic* (q.v.) as a thinking (q.v.) that is aware of its own processes: the simple transitions (q.v.) from one thought to its counterpart, reflection (q.v.) on how the two are related to each other, and conceptual understanding (q.v.) of its determinate significance. In the *Philosophy of Nature* (q.v.), thought sets each stage; then reflectively integrates how empirical evidence actualizes that stage. *See also* CANADA; CONCEPT.

BURSCHENSCHAFT. Inspired by German patriotism in the wars against Napoleon (q.v.), students from the German universities organized societies to promote nationalism and advocate liberal reforms. A speech by Hegel's colleague from Jena (q.v.), Jakob Fries (q.v.), given at a student festival at the Wartburg, came under severe attack in the preface to Hegel's *Philosophy of Right* (q.v.) because it appealed to sentiment rather than reason (q.v.). Nonetheless, Hegel attended a number of student gatherings and counted among his disciples and friends many *Burschenschaftler*: Friedrich Carové, Friedrich Förster, Leopold Henning (qq.v.), Julius, the son of his colleague Friedrich Niethammer (q.v.), and his own brother-in-law Gottlieb von Tucher. A number of these came under official suspicion, particularly after a student from Jena assassinated a well-known playwright, August Kotzebue, and some were imprisoned. Hegel is known to have taken steps in support of a number of the accused. *See also* BERLIN.

BUTLER, CLARK. In Butler's reading, not only religion (q.v.) but also Hegel's philosophical comprehension of it are a concrete organic whole through which the absolute (q.v.) becomes conscious of itself. In Christianity (q.v.), the absolute has come to be defined as essentially related to nature (q.v.), so that the knowing mind shares a common nature with the physical world, and the cosmos is a community of independent, self-productive things-in-themselves. *See also* UNITED STATES.

– C –

CAIRD, EDWARD (1835–1908). A student of Benjamin Jowett and associate of Thomas Hill Green (qq.v) at Balliol College, Oxford, Caird succeeded the former as master in 1893 after 27 years as professor of moral philosophy at Glasgow. In his introduction to the thought of Hegel (*Hegel*) and his expositions of Immanuel Kant's critical philosophy (q.v.), he argued that there was a center of unity to which the mind must return out of all the oppositions between subject and object, religion (q.v.) and science, freedom (q.v.) and determination, reason and desire (qq.v.). He influenced a generation of students, including Henry Jones, John H. Muirhead, J. S. Mackenzie and John Watson (q.v.), and his brother, John Caird, became a leading Hegelian theologian.

CANADA. Hegelian philosophy was introduced into Canada by John Clark Murray and John Watson (q.v.), who lectured at McGill and Queen's Universities. James Doull in Halifax; Theo F. Geraets in Ottawa; Emil Fackenheim, Henry S. Harris (qq.v.), and Kenneth Schmitz in Toronto; and Charles Taylor (q.v.) and George di Giovanni in Montreal maintained the tradition in the latter part of the 20th century. *See also* BURBIDGE, JOHN.

CAPITALISM (DER KAPITALISMUS). In his discussion of civil society (q.v.) within the *Philosophy of Right* (q.v.), Hegel builds on his studies of Sir James Steuart's (q.v.) political economy. Individualism grounded on the possession of property (q.v.) would produce a division of labor (q.v.), the concentration of wealth, and the emergence of poverty (q.v.) among the unemployed, corporations (q.v.), and colonialism; but the only prescription Hegel could propose to handle the evils of capitalism was the state (q.v.) as an institution concerned for the totality (q.v.) of the body politic. Friedrich Engels and Karl Marx (qq.v.) extended this analysis by predicting a revolution by the exploited workers that would destroy private property and produce a communist society in which the state would wither away. *See also* AVINIERI, SHLOMO; WEIL, ERIC.

CAROVÉ, FRIEDRICH W. (1789–1852). Educated in French universities during the French occupation of Trier, Carové went to Heidelberg (q.v.) after the Napoleonic wars to study medieval German literature and culture. While there, he came under the influence of Hegel and followed him to Berlin (q.v.). Active in organizing the Burschenschaft (q.v.), he worked unsuccessfully to open it to Jews and foreigners. After a member of the movement assassinated the dramatist August von Kotzebue in 1819, Carové wrote a pamphlet, seeing in this event the first signs of a new "heaven of actualized freedom and peace." This publication brought him under the suspicion of the Prussian authorities, so that Hegel was unsuccessful in having him appointed as teaching assistant. Carové had to return to the Rhineland where he became a publicist, arguing for the advent of an ethical community that would transcend the limitations of the state (q.v.) altogether. *See also* LEFT-WING HEGELIANS.

CATEGORY. Immanuel Kant (q.v.) had argued that we understand our intuitions of the world in terms of 12 categories, which he derived from the table of logical judgments (q.v.). Hegel points out that many more concepts come into play, and the *Science of Logic* (q.v.) can be seen as an elaboration of the large range of categories used by thought to understand and interpret the world. Kant's categories of quality and quantity (qq.v.) are developed in key sections of Hegel's doctrine of being (q.v.), whereas the categories of relation and modality emerge at the end of the doctrine of essence (q.v.). In the *Phenomenology of Spirit* (q.v.), the chapter on reason (q.v.) explores knowledge (q.v.) claims in which categories common to thought and reality are used to discover the truth (q.v.) of the observed world, human motivation, and social activity. *See also* ACTUALITY; CAUSALITY; CONTINGENCY; LAW-GIVING REASON; LAW OF THE HEART; LAW-TESTING REASON; NECESSITY; OBSERVING REASON; PHRENOLOGY; PHYSIOGNOMY; PLEASURE; POSSIBILITY; RECIPROCITY; SPIRITUAL ANIMAL KINGDOM; SUBSTANTIALITY; VIRTUE.

CAUSALITY (DIE KAUSALITÄT). In principle, a cause is a substance that acts to posit its determination necessarily in another substance. But when this formal structure is applied to any concrete content, it leads to an infinite (q.v.) series of causes that are in turn effects or of effects that become causes. The causality relation thus comes to be distinguished from other attributes of the thing (q.v.). Isolated in this way, causality is understood as something distinct, working on a passive substance. At the same time, this passive substance can be acted on only if it allows that to happen; as a result, it is equally a cause in bringing the causal relationship about. On the basis of this analysis of mutual implication, Hegel makes the logical move to the concept of reciprocity (q.v.). *See also* CATEGORY; CIRCLE OF CIRCLES; NECESSITY; *SCIENCE OF LOGIC*; SUBSTANTIALITY.

CENTER HEGELIANS. This term can be used for those Hegelians in the decade after Hegel's death who espoused neither the Prussian resistance to reform (right-wing Hegelians [q.v.]) nor the need for a revolutionary transformation of society (left-wing Hegelians [q.v.]). Eduard Gans (q.v.) argued that the Prussian regime was a transition stage to a more equitable future, while Karl Michelet (q.v.) and Karl Bayrhoffer held that Hegel's "only legitimate method" would gradually penetrate the cultural world with Hegelian principles. This progressive, liberal approach represented the dominant Hegelian position in German academic circles during the 1830s and 1840s. As Prussia (q.v.) reverted to a more traditional and repressive regime under Friedrich Wilhelm IV in the 1840s, the center Hegelians (who held academic and administrative posts) tended to accommodate themselves to the changed circumstances rather than adopt the critique of society espoused by the young Hegelians (q.v.).

CENTRE DE RECHERCHE SUR HEGEL ET L'IDÉALISME ALLE-MAND. Founded by Jacques D'Hondt (q.v.) in 1970 as the Centre de Recherche et de Documentation sur Hegel et Marx at the Université de Poitiers, the center has a basic research library, holds regular colloquia, and publishes bulletins. With the fall of the communist regimes of Eastern Europe, the center adjusted its focus, although it retains its library holdings on Marx and Marxism. *See also* FRANCE.

CHEMICAL PROCESS (DER CHEMISCHE PROZESS). For Hegel, the key chemical processes are galvanism, combustion, neutralization, and the exchange of radicals among salts (or elective affinity [q.v.]). Although primarily used to effect chemical combinations, these four can also serve to isolate or separate chemicals. In the *Philosophy of Nature* (q.v.), the discussion of these phenomena provides the bridge between physics and organics (geology, botany, and zoology) (qq.v.). *See also* CHEMISM.

CHEMISM (DER CHEMISMUS). In the *Science of Logic* (q.v.), this is the term Hegel uses for a way of thinking about the objective world in which independent objects in polar tension come to be united in a compound through a middle term or catalyst or in which a compound can be analyzed into its constitutive elements. Chemical processes (q.v.) in nature (q.v.) instantiate this logical structure, though it can be found elsewhere as well. *See also* CONCEPT; ELECTIVE AFFINITY; OBJECTIVITY.

CHINA. Although some studies of Hegel appeared in the 1920s and 1930s, Hegel's work only began to be translated into Chinese in 1953 with the *Encyclopedia Logic* (q.v.). There followed translations of the lectures on aesthetics, philosophy of history, history of philosophy, the

Phenomenology of Spirit, the *Philosophy of Nature*, and the *Philosophy of Right* (qq.v.). These have been accompanied by a number of monographs and articles on all aspects of his thought and development.

CHINESE HISTORY. Although China has records that go back over many millennia, Hegel finds little historical development. Rather Chinese life was built around a patriarchy: everything was centered on the will (q.v.) of the emperor, who alone is free and who stands at the pinnacle of an elaborate hierarchy. Even though dynasties changed over the centuries, the societal structure remained static. *See also* CHINESE RELIGION; FREEDOM; *LECTURES ON THE PHILOSOPHY OF WORLD HISTORY*; PHILOSOPHY OF WORLD HISTORY; WORLD HISTORY.

CHINESE RELIGION. In his *Lectures on the Philosophy of Religion* (q.v.), Hegel considers the religion (q.v.) of imperial China as a developed form of magic in that the emperor, at one with heaven, has authority not only over the living but also over the dead. He recognizes Buddhism (q.v.) as a second Chinese tradition and in 1827 distinguishes it from Taoism. *See also* CHINESE HISTORY; NATURAL RELIGION.

CHRISTIANITY. In early manuscripts from his time in Bern and Frankfurt am Main (qq.v.), Hegel developed his understanding of Jesus (q.v.) as a moral teacher and of the processes by which Christianity became a positive religion instead of a force for moral education. By the time he wrote the *Phenomenology of Spirit* (q.v.), however, Christianity, as the "manifest religion," marks the culmination of Hegel's discussion of religion (q.v.). The incomplete versions of unhappy consciousness and faith (qq.v.) give way to an understanding by the Christian community of itself as the end result of a cosmic process, in which a triune God (q.v.) creates a world where creatures fall away from what was intended. Accounts of the death of the god-man trigger agony and self-abandonment on the part of believers. These feelings convert into the ongoing life of the community as spirit (q.v.) and set the stage for absolute knowing (q.v.). Similarly, in the *Encyclopedia of the Philosophical Sciences* (q.v.), "revealed religion" contains the representation (q.v.) of absolute spirit (q.v.), standing between the immediate intuition of art (qq.v.) and the conceptual integration of philosophy (q.v.). In the *Lectures on the Phi-*

losophy of Religion (q.v.), Christianity, as the "consummate religion," receives a thorough exposition of its doctrines and cultic practices, as making explicit what is implicit in the concept (q.v.) of religion. *See also* ABSOLUTE SPIRIT; BAUER, BRUNO; BUTLER, CLARK; CHURCH FATHERS; FACKENHEIM, EMIL; FEUERBACH, LUDWIG; STRAUSS, DAVID; WESTPHAL, MEROLD.

CHURCH FATHERS (DIE KIRCHENVÄTER). The church fathers performed two important functions. They brought philosophy into religion (qq.v.), and they introduced into philosophy the recognition that the idea (q.v.) cannot remain abstract but must become concrete in "this" individual man. As a result, Christianity (q.v.) showed that the trinitarian conceptions of Proclus (q.v.) were true. *See also* ABSTRACT/CONCRETE; HISTORY OF PHILOSOPHY.

CIESZKOWSKI, AUGUST VON (1814–1894). Returning to Poland from Berlin (q.v.) where he studied under Hegel, Cieszkowski published in 1838 his *Prolegomena to Historiosophy*. By applying Hegel's dialectical laws to history, he argued that the proper threefold schema was past (antiquity, based on feeling and producing art and beauty [qq.v.]), present (Christianity [q.v.], based on thought and producing philosophy [q.v.] and wisdom), and future (based on action [q.v.] and producing social institutions). Although he anticipated the direction young Hegelians (q.v.) would take, this Polish Catholic aristocrat did not easily fit into the anti-Protestant, democratic factions that were emerging in Germany (q.v.) during the 1830s. *See also* MICHELET, KARL; PHILOSOPHY OF WORLD HISTORY; RUGE, ARNOLD.

CIRCLE OF CIRCLES (DER KREIS VON KREISEN). Hegel says that his method (q.v.) is a circle made up of circles. At the most basic level, the dialectic (q.v.) moves thought back and forth from one opposite to another in an ongoing or infinite (q.v.) progress, and speculative reason (q.v.) reflects on this circle in its totality (q.v.), leading on to a new starting point. But the circles recur at higher levels, so that in the *Phenomenology of Spirit* (q.v.), the singularity (q.v.) of observing reason (q.v.) leads to the social interaction of law-testing reason and spirit (qq.v.), while spirit as social concludes with the singularity of conscience and the beautiful soul (q.v.). In the *Science of Logic* (q.v.), the immediacy of being (qq.v.) leads to mediated essence (q.v.), which in turn leads back to reciprocity (q.v.) as the immediacy of being. In the *Philosophy of Right* (q.v.), the cohesion of the family (q.v.) leads to the independence of the children, while the independence of civil society (q.v.) leads to mutual dependence within corporations (q.v.) and the institutions of public order (police [q.v.]). At the highest level, the *Science of Logic* starts from pure thinking (q.v.) only to end with a surrender to nature (q.v.) as other than thought; the *Philosophy of Nature* (q.v.) shows how nature develops into living organisms, who manifest the internal relations (q.v.) characteristic of thought; and the *Philosophy of Spirit* (q.v.) explores the integration of centered beings who become fully self-aware through philosophy, or the discipline of pure thinking. The *Phenomenology*, which starts from immediate consciousness to lead to the standpoint of absolute knowing (q.v.) or pure thought, has its own starting point established within the system (q.v.) as anthropology (q.v.) moves from animals to embryonic consciousness (q.v.). *See also* BECOMING; KAINZ, HOWARD; MAGNITUDE; RECIPROCITY; ROCKMORE, TOM; SUBLATE.

CIVIL SOCIETY (DIE BÜRGERLICHE GESELLSCHAFT). Hegel was one of the first to distinguish between civil society, where economic individualism reigns supreme, creating division of labor, classes, corporations (qq.v.), the sharp contrast between rich and poor, and the need for public structures, on the one hand; and the state (q.v.), which, through its constitution (q.v.) and the patriotism of its citizens, maintains the unity of the community, on the other. This focus on the middle class (which stands between the agricultural and the governing classes) was then taken up in Karl Marx's (q.v.) discussions of the modern bourgeoisie. By overcoming the individualism of civil society, says Marx, a communist society would surrender the need for a state. *See also* CAPITALISM; INDIVIDUAL; *PHILOSOPHY OF RIGHT*; POLICE; POVERTY.

CLASSES (DIE STÄNDE). In Hegel's theory of civil society (q.v.), participation in the "social capital" that the division of labor (q.v.) generates depends on the role one plays within that society. He distinguishes three classes that compare with the traditional "estates": an agricultural, hereditary class grounded in the family (q.v.); a commercial class made up of craftspeople, manufacturers, and merchants, which works to satisfy individual needs and desires within civil society; and a "universal" (q.v.)

class of civil servants, who provide service to the whole community and are employed by the state (q.v.). This division of classes is then enshrined in the executive and legislature of the state's constitution (qq.v.). *See also* AVINIERI, SHLOMO.

CLASSICAL ART (DIE KLASSISCHE KUNSTFORM). In Greek religion (q.v.) and culture, beauty (q.v.) finds its most complete expression. The diverse particularity of the gods finds appropriate expression in particular works of art (q.v.). Sculptures (q.v.) of the human form capture in stone the ideal unity of spirit (q.v.). Epic, lyric, and drama (qq.v.) transform static beauty into something dynamic, incorporating subjectivity (q.v.). *See also* AESTHETICS; *LECTURES ON AESTHETICS*; RELIGION IN THE FORM OF ART.

COGNITION (DAS ERKENNEN). In the *Science of Logic* (q.v.), cognition is a way of thinking (q.v.) that recognizes how subjective thought interacts with actual objects. On the one hand, the subject submits to the object under the idea (q.v.) of the true; on the other hand, the subject overreaches (q.v.) the object under the idea of the good. In this way the implicit union of the subjective and the objective in life (q.v.) is broken up into its distinct components. Absolute idea (q.v.) then outlines the method (q.v.) that combines the unity of life with the discreteness of cognition. Hegel uses a different term (*knowledge* [q.v.] or *das Wissen*) when he develops his epistemology (q.v.) within the *Phenomenology of Spirit* (q.v.). *See also* ACTION; OBJECTIVITY; SUBJECTIVITY.

COHERENCE. Taking their clue from the way Hegel systematically interconnects all the various parts of philosophy, the British idealists (q.v.) argue that truth (q.v.) is found in the coherence of claims and experience (q.v.) rather than in the correspondence of our ideas (q.v.) with reality. Not only is coherence a test of the truth of our convictions and beliefs; some argue that it also characterizes the way the world itself is an interconnected whole.

COLLINGWOOD, ROBIN GEORGE (1889–1943). Although educated in Oxford under realists who were opposed to the British idealists (q.v.), Collingwood maintained Hegel's distinction between nature (q.v.) and history, while recognizing that, through evolution, nature did develop over time in a way that Hegel had rejected. Hegel was right in trying to bring about a synthesis between the conception of nature as a machine and the conception of all reality as permeated by process, though wrong in the synthesis he proposed. While nature is concerned with events, history is concerned with acts, the result of rational motivation; so the ultimate task of historical research is to reproduce the reasoning that interconnects the "inside" of actions. Similarly, the task of metaphysics (q.v.) is to investigate the "absolute presuppositions" that determine the way people think about the world. While admiring Hegel's lectures on the history of art, religion, and philosophy (qq.v.), Collingwood questioned the way he isolated political history from its context in intellectual and cultural life. *See also PHILOSOPHY OF NATURE;* PHILOSOPHY OF WORLD HISTORY; WORLD HISTORY.

COMEDY (DIE KOMÖDIE). In comedy, self-consciousness (q.v.) gains the upper hand. The dramatic action (q.v.) focuses on the contradiction (q.v.) between serious intention and ineffective character, or between purposeful action (q.v.) and frivolous personality—ultimately between what is absolutely true and its realization in a specific individual. The partiality of individual action is brought to naught, however, by the individual subjects themselves, rather than by the substantial destiny that underlies tragedy (q.v.). *See also* ABSOLUTE KNOWING; AESTHETICS; ART; DRAMA; POETRY; RELIGION IN THE FORM OF ART.

CONCEPT (DER BEGRIFF). Conceiving, for Hegel, is a type of thinking (q.v.) that begins from a general or universal (q.v.) concept, distinguishes or particularizes (q.v.) its components and its contraries, and then integrates these various moments into something singular (q.v.). The third and final book of Hegel's *Science of Logic* (q.v.) focuses on the way thought thinks concepts. Conceiving spells out the differences and connections between universal and particular concepts, between concepts and singulars, between different forms of judgments (q.v.) or propositions (in which concepts are connected to singulars), and between different forms of arguments or syllogisms (q.v.) (which are used to justify judgments). Hegel applies conceiving as well to the way we organize our thoughts of objects—when we understand them in a mechanical, chemical, or teleological way. He concludes by exploring how thought integrates into a single perspective the subjective activity of conceiving with an objective realm that is conceived. To this integration of concept and reality he gives the special name "idea" (q.v.). In the section on the Enlightenment (q.v.) within the *Phenomenology of Spirit* (q.v.), a concept is insight's (q.v.) rational comprehension of why things are the way they are and is opposed to faith's representation (qq.v.). *See also* ABSOLUTE IDEA; CHEMISM; COGNITION; LIFE; MECHANISM; NOTION; OBJECTIVITY; PHILOSOPHY; PHILOSOPHY OF RELIGION; RELIGION; TELEOLOGY; UNDERSTANDING.

CONCEPTION. *See* **REPRESENTATION.**

CONCRETE. *See* **ABSTRACT/CONCRETE.**

CONSCIENCE (DAS GEWISSEN). In contrast to the moral point of view, in which an abstract sense of duty (q.v.) governs one's instincts and desires (q.v.) and is indifferent to context, conscience is certain of a concrete obligation, defined by the particular circumstances in which one is to act. It is thus the attitude of the beautiful soul (q.v.), who has incorporated into its self-certainty all its experience (q.v.) of the world and who articulates publicly its conscientious conviction. In that the moral point of view is the modern response to the reign of terror in the French Revolution (q.v.), and conscience is a subsequent response to the ambiguities of morality (q.v.), Hegel in the *Phenomenology of Spirit* (q.v.) sets conscience and the beautiful soul at the culmination of the pilgrimage of modern culture (q.v.) toward absolute knowing (q.v.). Pure conscience, he points out in the *Philosophy of Right* (q.v.), is in danger of taking its subjective certainty to be the objective good, producing hypocrisy and evil. So it needs to be embodied in a concrete social order. In his *Lectures on the Philosophy of World History* (q.v.) Hegel argues that the authority of conscience as instructed by the indwelling spirit (q.v.) is the work of the Protestant reformation (q.v.). *See also* ABSTRACT/CONCRETE; ACTION; ETHICAL LIFE; MORALITY.

CONSCIOUSNESS (DAS BEWUSSTSEIN). We are conscious when we are aware of something. For Hegel, the quest for knowledge (q.v.) starts when consciousness senses, perceives, and understands objects presented to it. But it lacks an awareness of its own role in this process, requiring the move to self-consciousness (q.v.). *See also* PERCEPTION; *PHENOMENOLOGY OF SPIRIT*; SENSE CERTAINTY; UNDERSTANDING.

CONSTITUTION (DIE VERFASSUNG). From his first contact with the French Revolution (q.v.) while a student in Tübingen (q.v.), Hegel remained interested in political and constitutional matters. He analyzed the finances of Bern (q.v.) and in Frankfurt am Main (q.v.) wrote a pamphlet about the constitution of Württemberg (q.v.). When, in response to the invasion of French revolutionary armies, German patriots (including his friend Isaac von Sinclair) assembled in the Rastatter Congress, Hegel began work on a study of the German constitution, tracing the influences that prevented Germany from becoming a state in anything more than name. After the Napoleonic wars, in Heidelberg (q.v.), he published an article defending the action of the king in offering a constitution to the Württemberg estates. In his systematic discussion within the *Philosophy of Right* (q.v.), the substantial unity of the state (q.v.) is maintained by a constitution, which institutionalizes the customs that integrate a people. It must ensure three main functions, which follow from the nature of the rational concept (q.v.): the *universal* (q.v.) features of the state are maintained in the legislature (q.v.), the application of these universals to *particular* (q.v.) circumstances is done by the executive (q.v.), while the integrated unity of the state rests in the monarch's *singular* (qq.v.) decisions. Hegel has been accused of being the apologist for the Prussian regime, but his constitution in the *Philosophy of Right* (q.v.) contains more elements of the English and Württemberg institutions than of those currently in place in Berlin (q.v.). Although the king of Prussia (q.v.), Frederick William III (1770–1840), had promised a constitution during the Napoleonic wars, he never implemented one, and the *Philosophy of Right* of 1821 could be seen as Hegel's attempt to influence the kind of constitution that would be put in place. *See also* AVINIERI, SHLOMO; WEIL, ERIC.

CONSUMMATE RELIGION (DIE VOLLENDETE RELIGION). *See* **CHRISTIANITY.**

CONTINGENCY (DIE ZUFÄLLIGKEIT). Something is contingent when it could equally well not have been, so its possibility (q.v.) is not sufficient to explain its actuality (q.v.). Hegel argues that contingency and chance are necessary features of all reality and so must be incorporated into any logical description of nature and world history (qq.v.). It is because details of the future are contingent that the philosopher cannot tell activists what they should do. *See also* NECESSITY; OWL OF MINERVA; *SCIENCE OF LOGIC*.

CONTRACT (DER VERTRAG). In his construction of the concept of justice from its most basic elements, Hegel moves from the possession of property (q.v.) to the exchange of goods either through a gift or through a trade. The will (q.v.) to enter into a contract must be shared by two individual persons (q.v.), so this provides the first legal constituents of society. Because such acts of will must be specific and determinate, however, Hegel rejects the use of contract to explain the grounding of the state as Thomas Hobbes, John Locke, and Jean-Jacques Rousseau (qq.v.) had done. *See also* ABSTRACT RIGHT; *PHILOSOPHY OF RIGHT.*

CONTRADICTION (DER WIDERSPRUCH). A contradiction results when differences (q.v.) are isolated by the understanding (q.v.) and pushed to their logical extreme. Two opposite characteristics come to be affirmed of the same thing in the same respect. A contradiction, however, cannot be thought and collapses into the search for its ground (q.v.). Hegel thus affirms that contradictions are the inevitable result of understanding both concepts (q.v.) and things, but that they are not the last word. They serve as intermediate stages on the way toward a more complete explanation. *See also* ANTINOMIES; LAWS OF THOUGHT; OPPOSITION; *SCIENCE OF LOGIC.*

CORPORATIONS (DIE KORPORATION). The dispersed individualism of civil society (q.v.) organizes itself into corporations, whose members are given specific tasks appropriate to their skills within an institutional structure but at the same time receive respect, security of tenure, and protection from the contingencies (q.v.) of economic life. For Hegel the diverse interests of the middle class would best find expression in the lower house of the legislature (q.v.) by having them represented through the corporations to which they belong, rather than having constituencies based simply on geography. In taking this position, Hegel appears to be thinking of the English constitution (q.v.), where incorporated boroughs and universities elected the House of Commons, or possibly the traditional constitution of Württemberg (q.v.).

COUSIN, VICTOR (1792–1867). In 1818 on a trip to Munich, the French philosopher, Victor Cousin, met Hegel in Heidelberg (q.v.). In 1824, when Cousin was arrested in Dresden at the request of the Prussian authorities, Hegel intervened on his behalf; and they met again in Paris in

1827. Cousin's philosophy, however, owed more to Friedrich Schelling (q.v.) than to Hegel.

CRITICAL JOURNAL OF PHILOSOPHY (KRITISCHES JOURNAL DER PHILOSOPHIE). Attempts by Friedrich Schelling (q.v.) to establish a philosophical journal finally bore fruit in 1802 once Hegel arrived in Jena (q.v.). Because he was also involved in the *Zeitschrift für spekulative Physik*, Schelling left much of the editorial work to his collaborator. Hegel's contributions include essays on skepticism, faith and knowledge, natural law, and Wilhelm Traugott Krug's (qq.v.) common sense. When Schelling left for Würzburg in 1803, the journal folded. *See also* SCHULZE, GOTTLOB.

CROCE, BENEDETTO (1866–1952). Inspired by Francesco De Sanctis and introduced to Karl Marx (q.v.) and then Hegel by Antonio Labriola, Croce, in collaboration with Giovanni Gentile (q.v.), founded the journal *La Critica* and initiated a program of translating Hegel's works into Italian. In *What Is Living and What Is Dead in the Philosophy of Hegel* (1906), he argues that Hegel, through the dialectical logic of opposites (qq.v.), established a new notion of reality as history. He rejects, however, Hegel's panlogism, and his dialectic of the empirical; for natural things that are simply distinct from each other cannot become caught up in the conflict of opposites. *See also* ITALY; PHILOSOPHY OF WORLD HISTORY.

CULTURE (DIE BILDUNG). In the *Phenomenology of Spirit* (q.v.), culture names the society that emerges from legal status (q.v.), in which subjects objectify their individuality and thereby produce an actual social world through language (q.v.). However, the social realm breaks into two parts that are alienated from each other. Those who adopt the universal interests of the state (q.v.) are noble, whereas the wealthy who look out for their own singular interests are base. When this conceptual structure is put into practice, what starts out as noble turns out to be hypocritical and so evil, while the network of base interests produces willy-nilly a good, viable society. Denis Diderot's (q.v.) *Rameau's Nephew* captures what happens next, when the wealthy dispense their wealth to the ne'er-do-wells. The virtuous are reduced to speaking monosyllables, while the irresponsible chatter of those who live off the wealthy defines the conditions of discourse. Over against this secular dichotomy, now reduced to triviality, lies a second one, concerned with the substantial ground of culture: a struggle between faith and insight (qq.v.). *See also* ALIENATION; CIVIL SOCIETY; ENLIGHTENMENT; SPIRIT.

CUNNING OF REASON (DIE LIST DER VERNUNFT). To achieve its goal of freedom (q.v.) through world history (q.v.), reason (q.v.) cunningly uses the passions (q.v.), allowing them to work out their own peculiar destiny. In rubbing against each other and wearing each other down, the passions produce the customs and laws of society that can then become enshrined in the constitution of a state (qq.v.), providing the framework for free action (q.v.). *See also* PHILOSOPHY OF WORLD HISTORY.

– D –

DASEIN. This German word is often translated "determinate being" or on occasion "existence" (q.v.). Lacking the indeterminacy of pure being (q.v.), it names a being that has come to be and will pass away; it emerges as a logical concept (q.v.) when the repetitive cycle of coming to be and passing away collapses into a quiescent unity. It thus provides the framework for Hegel's logical discussion of such terms as something, other, quality, determination, finitude, as well as infinity (qq.v.). *See also* BACCHANALIAN REVEL; BECOMING; CIRCLE OF CIRCLES; *SCIENCE OF LOGIC*.

DAUB, KARL (1765–1836). Professor of theology in Heidelberg (q.v.), Daub was converted to Hegelianism through a close reading of the *Phenomenology of Spirit* and the *Science of Logic* (qq.v.) around 1820. He was then instrumental in introducing a number of theological students to Hegelian thought, including Karl Rosenkranz and Ludwig Feuerbach (qq.v.). While he was vice rector of the university in 1816, Daub issued the invitation for Hegel to become professor of philosophy there.

DEATH (DER TOD). In discussing the most primitive form of recognition (q.v.), Hegel describes a struggle to the death in which two protagonists become aware of themselves through striving to destroy each other and so risking their own lives. Once they realize that death proves to be self-defeating, the weaker combatant surrenders, becoming the slave of the stronger. As a result, spirit (q.v.) is defined as the living being that faces up to, and incorporates, death into its own life. Death continues to play a major role in the *Phenomenology of Spirit* (q.v.): Antigone (q.v.) assumes the obligation of burying her dead brother; the risk of death in war (q.v.) is used by the state (q.v.) to engender patriotism; in absolute freedom (q.v.), singular acts of will (q.v.) are condemned to death; Christianity (q.v.) not only tells the story of a dying god-man but also leads the believer into an experience (q.v.) of the death of God. *See also* DESIRE; MASTER/SLAVE.

DERRIDA, JACQUES. Adopting a format reminiscent of Talmudic texts, Derrida, in *Glas*, sets his reflections on Hegel's absolute knowing (q.v.) parallel to a discussion of the novelist Jean Genet, along with inserted marginalia. Resisting system (q.v.) and organization, he explores themes implicit in, but unasserted by, Hegel through discussions of family, religion and Christianity (qq.v.).

DESCARTES, RENÉ (1596–1650). Descartes established the basic idealistic principle of modern philosophy: that thinking (q.v.) on its own is capable of comprehending reality. The "cogito" thus affirms the identity of thinking and being (q.v.). *See also* HISTORY OF PHILOSOPHY; IDEALISM.

DESIRE (DIE BEGIERDE). In Hegel's *Phenomenology of Spirit* (q.v.), desire offers the most primitive form of self-knowledge. Objects are not regarded as independent but are to be incorporated into the self, providing a sense of self in the moment of satisfaction. As transient, satisfaction only awakens further desire, initiating the need for a more enduring form of self-satisfaction that is found in being recognized (q.v.) by other selves. *See also* DEATH; SELF-CONSCIOUSNESS.

DESMOND, WILLIAM. In *Art and the Absolute*, Desmond shows that, even though Hegel sees art as completed in religion and philosophy (qq.v.), it nonetheless plays a positive role in making the absolute (q.v.) present in human life. Hegel's dialectic (q.v.) is more profound than the univocity of logical analysis and the equivocity of Ludwig Wittgenstein;

but in resolving difference (q.v.) into a comprehensive unity, it cannot do justice to human existence (q.v.), which continues to be lived in a "between" that is never sublated (q.v.). *See also* UNITED STATES.

DETERMINATE BEING. *See* **DASEIN.**

DETERMINATION (DIE BESTIMMUNG). To do justice to the logical interplay between "something" and "other" (qq.v.), thought introduces the concept of determination as that which distinguishes them and indeed defines each one's limit or finitude (qq.v.). A determination may be intrinsic, or it may be a product of the other (constitution, or *die Beschaffenheit*). *See also* DASEIN, *SCIENCE OF LOGIC*.

DEWEY, JOHN (1859–1952). Introduced to Hegel by George Sylvester Morris, Dewey found his synthesis of subject and object, matter and spirit, the divine and the human to be a liberation. While he came to reject Hegel's artificial schematism, he nonetheless retained in his own philosophy the dynamic sense of interaction that gave to Hegel's thought "greater richness and variety of insight than any other philosopher save Plato." *See also* UNITED STATES.

D'HONDT, JACQUES. D'Hondt demonstrates that world history (q.v.), for Hegel, is bedeviled by contingency (q.v.). Events simply happen; people react; events and reactions create a complex social network; finally, the philosopher shows how all are interconnected in a totality (q.v.). But, by standing back to achieve this comprehension, the philosopher introduces a rupture into society, which can trigger new contingent events. D'Hondt shows as well how Hegel was situated within his own time: associated with the freemasons (q.v.), supporting liberal causes, anxious about personal security in the tumultuous years of the French wars, and on occasion in trouble with Prussian authorities. *See also* BERLIN; BURSCHENSCHAFT; FRANCE; FRENCH REVOLUTION; PRUSSIA.

DIALECTIC (DIE DIALEKTISCHE VERNUNFT). Rooted in the Greek word for "dialogue," dialectic describes the Hegelian view of reasoning: whenever thinking (q.v.) pushes its clear understanding (q.v.) of a term or state of affairs to its limits (q.v.), its contrary is evoked. The opposition (q.v.) that results can be resolved only by some kind of reflective or speculative consideration of the total picture. It is this capacity of finite (q.v.) things to go beyond (q.v.) their limits (q.v.) to their opposites that reveals the immanent connections that are the basis of logical necessity (q.v.). While Hegel understood this primarily as a characteristic of reason (q.v.) and reasoning beings, Karl Marx (q.v.) claimed that it is the primary motor that drives all economic and political development, and Friedrich Engels (q.v.) extended its reign to nature (q.v.) as well. *See also* ADORNO, THEODOR; D'HONDT, JACQUES; GADAMER, HANS-GEORG; GENTILE, GIOVANNI; KAINZ, HOWARD; KAUFMANN, WALTER; McTAGGART, JOHN M. E.; METHOD; REASON; REFLECTION; SARTRE, JEAN-PAUL; SPECULATIVE REASON; TRANSITION.

DIDEROT, DENIS (1713–1784). A posthumous work of Diderot's, *Rameau's Nephew*, was first published in 1805 by Johann von Goethe (q.v.) in a German translation. Its dialogue between a philosopher and a ne'er-do-well who lives off the benevolence of the wealthy sets a monosyllabic interest in virtue (q.v.) against an irresponsible chatter that challenges all conventions. Two years later Hegel used the dialogue in the *Phenomenology of Spirit* (q.v.) to illustrate the life of culture (q.v.) once the wealthy have assumed the mantle of secular society. Spiritual life is divided against itself and finds that its interest in the good is trivialized into a play of contradictory opinions and assertions. Yet a work of literature can capture both sides of this alienation (q.v.). *See also* ENLIGHTENMENT; SPIRIT.

DIFFERENCE (DER UNTERSCHIED). Because it presupposes some form of identity (q.v.) that is to be differentiated, difference can take various forms: where the identity is quite unrelated, we have diversity (q.v.); a shared but partial identity gives opposition (q.v.); where the differences hold between two exhaustive descriptions of the same thing we have a contradiction (q.v.). *See also* ESSENCE; LAWS OF THOUGHT; REFLECTION; *SCIENCE OF LOGIC*.

DIFFERENCE BETWEEN FICHTE'S AND SCHELLING'S SYSTEM OF PHILOSOPHY. Apart from an unsigned translation of J. J. Cart's *Confidential Letters*, the *Differenzschrift* (as it is called) was Hegel's first publication, appearing shortly after he arrived in Jena (q.v.). In response to Karl Leonhard Reinhold's (q.v.) review of recent philosophy, he spells out how understanding, reflection, and reason (qq.v.) work together to produce the philosophical tradition, and then he goes on to show how Johann Fichte's system (qq.v.) is not able to overcome a one-sided subjectivity. Friedrich Schelling's (q.v.) use of the philosophy of nature (q.v.) to counterbalance transcendental idealism (q.v.) does greater justice to both the objective and the subjective side of the absolute (q.v.) as well as to the transcendental intuition (q.v.) that grasps their identity.

DILTHEY, WILHELM (1833–1911). Although not strictly a Hegelian philosopher, Dilthey, in 1905, published *Die Jugendgeschichte Hegels* (Hegel's Early Years), in which he challenges the tradition that read Hegel's system (q.v.) as a final totality (q.v.) by showing how Hegel's thought had developed. One of his students, Hermann Nohl, then brought out in 1907 a selection of the early theological writings (q.v.). *See also* BERN; FRANKFURT AM MAIN; GERMANY; JESUS; TÜBINGEN.

DISSERTATION. To qualify as a private instructor at Jena (q.v.), Hegel had to get his degrees from Tübingen (q.v.) accredited, defend publicly a set of 12 theses, and present a dissertation: *On the Orbits of the Planets*. In it he challenged Isaac Newton's (q.v.) abstract derivation of the orbits from a parallelogram of forces, since this could only explain circular motion. Johannes Kepler's discovery of the exact elliptical orbits based on careful observation was preferable. Hegel also examined the principles thought to govern the distance of the planets from the sun, pointing out with reference to Plato's (q.v.) Timaeus that the mathematical series governing the contemporary search for a planet between Mars and Jupiter (and which had, in fact, just resulted in the discovery of Ceres) was not the only one that could be used. Hegel's rejection of Newtonian explanatory principles and his apparent ignorance of recent astronomical discoveries have led some to discredit his philosophy generally, and his philosophy of nature (q.v.) in particular. A translation by P. Adler was published in the New School *Graduate Faculty Philosophy Journal* in 1987. *See also* POPPER, KARL.

DIVERSITY (DIE VERSCHIEDENHEIT). Thinking of difference (q.v.) presupposes some kind of identity (q.v.). Where the identity is quite unrelated to the differences we have a diversity, the product of external reflection (q.v.). Since, through comparison, reflection sets the like over against the unlike, it then turns to consider the explicit opposition (q.v.) that is found between those two determinations. *See also* LAWS OF THOUGHT.

DIVISION OF LABOR (DIE TEILUNG DER ARBEITEN). In civil society (q.v.), the satisfaction of desires (q.v.) leads to a multiplication of needs, which means that individual persons find themselves relying on the labor of others to meet all their requirements. The division of labor that results increases the overall capital of a society, although the distribution of that wealth to its members may be quite unequal. Hegel is here relying on the work of the political economists Adam Smith, Jean Baptiste Say, David Ricardo, and in particular Sir James Steuart (q.v.). *See also* ALIENATED LABOR; CAPITALISM; CLASSES; MARX, KARL; *PHILOSOPHY OF RIGHT*; POVERTY.

DRAMA (DAS DRAMA). Dramatic poetry (q.v.) brings together the subjective inwardness of lyric (q.v.) with the objectivity (q.v.) of events, characteristic of epic (q.v.). The actions (q.v.) are specific to individuals, and they are given meaning by their particular intentions and purposes. The unity of a play comes from the working out of a single action and its consequences, even though many subplots may contribute to the full resolution. To achieve his purpose, the dramatist must abstract from the full panoply of life (q.v.) but then balance this partiality by introducing conflict between different individuals, each with a contrasting goal and character. While tragedy (q.v.) pits the one-sided action of an individual against the substantive framework of universal justice, in comedy (q.v.) the subject is himself the agent by which his one-sided partiality is exposed. *See also* AESTHETICS; ART; CLASSICAL ART; RELIGION IN THE FORM OF ART.

DUTY (DIE PFLICHT). Immanuel Kant's (q.v.) definition of duty as the categorical imperative is too abstract for Hegel. It cannot tell us specifically what we ought to do. Concrete duty is determined by the place where we are situated within the institutions of family, civil society, and the state (qq.v.). It is thus intimately bound up with the rights (q.v.) we enjoy within those bodies. *See also* CONSCIENCE; ETHICAL LIFE; KANT'S MORAL PHILOSOPHY; MORALITY.

– E –

EARLIEST SYSTEM-PROGRAM OF GERMAN IDEALISM (DAS ÄLTESTE SYSTEMPROGRAMM DES DEUTSCHEN IDEALIS-MUS). In 1914, Franz Rosenzweig (q.v.) published a fragment in Hegel's handwriting dating from 1795 to 1797 and outlining a plan for a philosophical system (q.v.) that would move from self, through nature (q.v.) and humanity, to beauty (q.v.) and rational mythology. Rosenzweig concluded that it was the copy of a text by Friedrich Schelling (q.v.), but subsequent researchers have claimed it for Friedrich Hölderlin (q.v.) as well as for Hegel himself. The text is frequently cited by its first two words: *eine Ethik* (an ethics). *See also* BERN; FRANKFURT AM MAIN.

EGYPTIAN HISTORY. Because the Egyptian hieroglyphics were not yet deciphered, Hegel had no access to indigenous written documents. So his discussion of Egyptian history in the *Lectures on the Philosophy of World History* (q.v.) concentrates on Egyptian religion (q.v.). *See also* WORLD HISTORY.

EGYPTIAN RELIGION. In Hegel's *Lectures on the Philosophy of Religion* (q.v.), ancient Egyptian religion moves beyond the Parsee religion (q.v.) in that it integrates darkness and death (q.v.) into an incipient subjectivity (q.v.). Although the dying and rising god (Osiris) embodies the natural rhythms of the sun and of the Nile, death remains a riddle, finding expression in the construction of tombs, labyrinths, and sphinxes. Because the spiritual is not yet fully free in the development of its cultic forms, Egyptian religion represents only the first anticipation of the religion of beauty (q.v.). In an earlier discussion of natural religion (q.v.) in the *Phenomenology of Spirit* (q.v.) of 1807, the central motif of this tradition is understood to be the master craftsman or artificer. *See also* ARCHITECTURE; EGYPTIAN HISTORY; RELIGION; SCULPTURE.

ELECTIVE AFFINITY (DIE WAHLVERWANDTSCHAFT). This term was used by chemistry to name the preference a chemical shows for combining with one substance rather than another. Hegel suggests it also applies to harmonies in sound (and Johann von Goethe [q.v.] extended it to interpersonal relations in one of his novels). The concept appears twice in the *Science of Logic* (q.v.). It refers to the use of such preferences for measuring (q.v.) the quality (q.v.) of a thing. And it reflects the way a chemical object, though independent, is oriented toward some other object. *See also* CHEMICAL PROCESS; CHEMISM; NODAL LINE.

EMPIRICISM (DER EMPIRISMUS). Empiricism correctly recognizes the need to base philosophical reflection (q.v.) on what is actual and given through perception (q.v.). But it starts from the assumption that every experience (q.v.) is individual and independent, while thinking (q.v.) is abstract and unreal; universal (q.v.) terms are only collections based on temporal or spatial conjunction and lack conceptual necessity (q.v.). Even so, empiricism unreflectively uses metaphysical terms such as *force, one, universal, infinite* (qq.v.), *matter,* and *many* to establish its conclusions. Aristotle (q.v.) offers a more wholesome empiricism, in that he takes account of all details of experience and looks for the rational principles that are implicit in them. *See also* ACTUALITY; CONCEPT; HUME, DAVID; KANT'S CRITICAL PHILOSOPHY; METAPHYSICS.

ENCYCLOPEDIA LOGIC. As the first part of the *Encyclopedia of the Philosophical Sciences* (q.v.), the "shorter Logic" initially (1817) summarized the argument of the full *Science of Logic* (q.v.) into succinct theses for Hegel's lectures (q.v.). In later editions, Hegel added an extensive introduction that set his philosophical system (q.v.) in the context of the contemporary philosophical scene. The 1830 version, together with lecture notes taken by Hegel's students, has been translated into English by William Wallace and Theodore F. Geraets et al., into French by Bernard Bourgeois, and into Italian by Valerio Verra. *See also* ADDITIONS; EMPIRICISM; HUME, DAVID; JACOBI, FRIEDRICH; KANT'S CRITICAL PHILOSOPHY; LECTURES ON LOGIC AND METAPHYSICS; LOGIC; METAPHYSICS; REMARKS.

ENCYCLOPEDIA OF THE PHILOSOPHICAL SCIENCES. When Hegel returned to the academic world after his eight years in Nürnberg (q.v.), he took up a position at the university of Heidelberg (q.v.). As a framework for his lectures (q.v.), he prepared a set of theses in numbered paragraphs, organized into a Science of Logic, a Philosophy of Nature, and a Philosophy of Spirit (qq.v.). He then expanded on and illustrated a number of the core theses by adding Remarks (q.v.). These were published as *Encyclopedia of the Philosophical Sciences in Outline*. The first edition of 1817 was revised quite extensively and given a much longer introduction during his years in Berlin (q.v.) (1827). Further changes were made for a third edition in 1830. After he died, his disciples incorporated into the 1830 text selections from lecture notes taken by students over the years (called Additions [q.v.]) and gave the total package the name "System of Philosophy " (qq.v.). The 1817 edition has been translated into English by S. A. Taubeneck. The 1830 edition with additions is usually published in three separate volumes. *See also ENCYCLOPEDIA LOGIC*; LECTURES ON LOGIC AND METAPHYSICS; LECTURES ON THE *ENCYCLOPEDIA*; LECTURES ON THE PHILOSOPHY OF NATURE; LECTURES ON THE PHILOSOPHY OF SUBJECTIVE SPIRIT.

END OF HISTORY. Alexandre Kojève (q.v.) argued that, in writing the *Phenomenology of Spirit* (q.v.), Hegel was marking the end of significant history. At the battle of Jena (q.v.), the human species had achieved its full development in principle, and whatever happens thereafter is but a working out of details. Appearing in the twilight of the day's end, the owl of Minerva or philosophy (qq.v.) could only paint its gray on gray. This idea was taken up by Francis Fukuyama (q.v.), who claims that the fall of the communist regimes in Eastern Europe in 1989 marked the fulfillment of Hegel's prophesy. *See also* WORLD HISTORY.

ENGELS, FRIEDRICH (1820–1895). Associated with Karl Marx (q.v.) in the *Communist Manifesto* (1848), Engels returned in 1850 to running the family business in Manchester, in part to support Marx in exile. In *Anti-Dühring* and the posthumous *Dialectics of Nature,* he argues that natural and historical laws are dialectical (q.v.) rather than mechanical, and he reduces them to three: the transformation of quantity into quality (qq.v.) and vice versa, the interpenetration of opposites (q.v.), and the negation of negation (q.v.). *See also* NATURE; *PHILOSOPHY OF NATURE*.

ENLIGHTENMENT (DIE AUFKLÄRUNG). In the *Phenomenology of Spirit* (q.v.), Hegel's discussion of the Enlightenment focuses on its struggle with superstition (or faith [q.v.]). Pure insight (q.v.) challenges the contingency (q.v.) of faith's representations (q.v.) and proofs, explaining them rationally as the appeal to an empty "beyond" (q.v.) whose actuality (q.v.) is nothing but the immediate givens of sense. Faith, on the other hand, relying on representations, lacks the resources to demonstrate that it is affirming not the contingent but rather the absolute essence (q.v.) of reality. While faith succumbs to simply feeling this ultimate deity, insight looks behind the givens of sense and thinks of them as all grounded in an indeterminate matter. In Hegel's analysis, the two are but versions of the same story from different perspectives. Because in both the ultimate is so indeterminate, the Enlightenment ends up understanding the determinate, actual world of experience (q.v.) in terms of utility (q.v.), in which each independent thing or person acquires its value simply from its usefulness for others. In his *Lectures on the Philosophy of World History* (q.v.), Hegel points out that the radical conflict between insight and faith was characteristic of France, Spain, and Italy, where Roman Catholicism and absolute monarchy resisted the advance of self-determining reason (q.v.), but in Germany, thanks to the Protestant reformation (q.v.) and enlightened monarchs such as Friedrich the Great (q.v.), the two were integrated more concretely into the social fabric. Nonetheless, even in Germany, the understanding (q.v.) could easily find contradictions (q.v.) in the speculative truths of religion (q.v.). *See also* ABSOLUTE FREEDOM; CONCEPT; CULTURE; FRENCH REVOLUTION.

EPIC (DAS EPOS). Epic poetry (q.v.) focuses on a single action (q.v.) that incorporates the whole breadth of a culture (q.v.) before the more formal institutions of state and civil society (qq.v.) have emerged. War (q.v.) provides the setting, because people then subordinate their individual wills (q.v.) to the well-being of the whole. Since the personality of the poet disappears into the objectivity of the subject matter, the epic, with its use of iambic hexameters, can become the religious scripture of a people. *See also* AESTHETICS; ART; CLASSICAL ART; DRAMA; RELIGION IN THE FORM OF ART.

EPISTEMOLOGY (DIE ERKENNTNISTHEORIE). Hegel explores the theory of how humans know in his *Phenomenology of Spirit* (q.v.). Various kinds of knowledge (q.v.) claims are implemented in practice, and the philosopher watches how experience (q.v.) produces the opposite of what was expected, forcing the adoption of more sophisticated theories. Absolute knowing (q.v.)—a knowledge that cannot be controverted in this way—is the theory that any confident knowledge claim, when put into practice, will discover that it has to be corrected in light of experience. *See also* ACTION; COGNITION.

ERDMANN, JOHANN EDUARD (1805–1892). As a theological student in Berlin (q.v.), Erdmann attended Hegel's lectures. After a stint in a parish, he returned to philosophy, becoming professor in the Prussian university of Halle. Through his writings and lectures, he became one of the leading exponents of right-wing Hegelianism (q.v.). *See also* JOWETT, BENJAMIN.

ESSENCE (DAS WESEN). When thought reflects on existing reality, it distinguishes what is unimportant from what is essential. The second book of Hegel's *Science of Logic* (q.v.) discusses the various strategies thought uses in drawing this distinction between essence and the inessential: the traditional laws of thought; existence and appearance; inner and outer; necessity and contingency; substance and accident (qq.v). In each case, it turns out that the two opposing concepts mutually require and presuppose each other, so both are in fact essential. *See also* AB-SOLUTE ESSENCE; REFLECTION.

ESTATES (DIE STÄNDE). *See* CLASSES.

ETHICAL LIFE, ETHICAL ORDER (DIE SITTLICHKEIT). The root of the German word suggests ethos rather than ethics, mores rather than morals. Hegel refers to the fabric of custom that forms the inherent substance of a society and thus becomes second nature. Ethical life's most basic form is the family (q.v.), but social customs provide the foundation for civil society and the state (qq.v.) as well. In the *Phenomenology of Spirit* (q.v.), the ethical order names cultures where people identify directly with the laws (q.v.), both human and divine, that determine social life. Sophocles' Antigone (q.v.) describes the destiny of a society where these principles are put into practice, come into direct conflict, and thus lose their power. What emerges is a social order that regards individuals simply as legal persons (q.v.) because their particular interests take precedence over their commitment to human or divine law. Universal empire replaces the integrated community. *See also* ACTION; DUTY;

GREEK HISTORY; LEGAL STATUS; MAN; *PHILOSOPHY OF RIGHT*; ROMAN HISTORY; SOCRATES; SPIRIT; WOMAN.

EXECUTIVE (DIE REGIERUNGSGEWALT). Responsibility for implementing the universal laws and constitution of the state (qq.v.) in particular (q.v.) circumstances belongs to the executive (which includes the judiciary and the police [q.v.]). To ensure impartiality, candidates for positions must be tested for knowledge and proof of ability and provided with an adequate income. The state is protected from the misuse of powers in that civil servants are held responsible for their actions, while corporations (q.v.) and communities are legally assigned an independent sphere for action (q.v.). *See also* LEGISLATURE; MONARCH; *PHILOSOPHY OF RIGHT*.

EXISTENCE (DIE EXISTENZ). In the *Science of Logic* (q.v.), Hegel distinguishes existence from the simple immediacy of being (q.v.). Although what exists is immediate (q.v.), it is at the same time understood to be mediated by its ground or essence (qq.v.) and distinguished from appearance (q.v.). In the *Encyclopedia Logic* (q.v.), what exists is further defined as a world of mutually dependent, existing things (q.v.). At times the German word *Dasein* (q.v.) is also translated by "existence," even though its sense is much closer to that of simple being. *See also* ACTUALITY; GOD; MEDIATION.

EXPERIENCE (DIE ERFAHRUNG). Although Hegel rejects the approach of British empiricism (q.v.) because it atomizes our human interaction with the world around us into independent and discrete units, he nonetheless saw his *Phenomenology of Spirit* (q.v.) as a science (q.v.) of the experience of consciousness (q.v.). When a knowledge (q.v.) claim is put into practice, one learns through experience that it produces the opposite of what was intended. What consciousness learns from this failure is then incorporated into the next knowledge claim. *See also* ATOMISM; EPISTEMOLOGY.

EXTERNAL RELATIONS (DIE ÄUSSERLICHKEIT). Hegel defines nature (q.v.) as the realm of externality, whose basic forms are space and time (qq.v.). As the basis for external relations, these contrast with the internal (or conceptual) relations (q.v.) intrinsic to thought. Thinking (q.v.)

comprehends nature philosophically by finding the conceptual relations that are implicit within, and do justice to, its external diversity. *See also* EMPIRICISM; INNER/OUTER; LOGIC; *PHILOSOPHY OF NATURE.*

– F –

FACKENHEIM, EMIL L. In *The Religious Dimension of Hegel's Thought*, Fackenheim argues that Hegel needs not only an actual reconciliation with the cosmos as found in Protestant Christianity (q.v.) but also the self-confident freedom (q.v.) found in the institutions of the modern world as well as the comprehensive grasp of self-conscious philosophical thought. This reconciliation has broken down, not least because of the eruption of radical evil in the Nazi Holocaust. Nonetheless, a Hegelian form of philosophical thinking that has abandoned the goal of full comprehension offers a means of doing conceptual justice to the inner logic of Judaism (q.v.). *See also* CANADA; PHILOSOPHY; PHILOSOPHY OF RELIGION.

FACT (DIE SACHE). *See SACHE SELBST.*

FAITH (DER GLAUBE). In the world of culture (q.v.), consciousness (q.v.) withdraws from the turmoil of a society where what is good turns out to be evil and vice versa, into a pure faith in the world's underlying truth (q.v.). It believes that the absolute essence or God (qq.v.) sacrifices itself to actuality (q.v.) while still maintaining itself as spirit (q.v.) in this alienation (q.v.). The rationale for this structure, however, remains hidden from the believing consciousness, so that the various moments are held in the form of representations (q.v.) that are simply given and events that simply happen. Believers are then challenged by people enmeshed in the actual world who have insight (q.v.) into the fundamental role of conceptual reason (q.v.) and the self in determining social reality and who thus explain away the transcendent. The Enlightenment's (q.v.) struggle with superstition is the result. *See also* BEYOND; CHRISTIANITY; *PHENOMENOLOGY OF SPIRIT;* PROTESTANT REFORMATION.

FAITH AND KNOWLEDGE (GLAUBEN UND WISSEN). The first part of the second volume of the *Critical Journal of Philosophy* (q.v.) is an essay entitled "Faith and Knowledge," in which Hegel examines the philosophies of Immanuel Kant, Friedrich Jacobi, and Johann Fichte (qq.v.), all of whom limit the capacity of reason with regard to things as they are in themselves, leaving the absolute beyond knowledge (qq.v.). Faith (q.v.) thus becomes the moment of objective reason for Kant, subjective immediacy for Jacobi, and the subjective affirming of the objective for Fichte.

FAMILY (DIE FAMILIE). Hegel was the eldest son of an administrative official in the Duchy of Württemberg (q.v.). His mother died when he was 13, leaving a sister, who remained a concern throughout his life, being subject to fits of depression; and a younger brother, who died in Napoleon's (q.v.) Russian campaign. The death of his father in 1799 provided an inheritance that enabled Hegel to return to the academic world. While in Jena (q.v.), a liaison with his chambermaid resulted in an illegitimate son, Ludwig Fischer, for whom he continued to accept responsibility. In 1811, he married Marie von Tucher, who became the mother of his two legitimate sons, Karl and Immanuel, and a daughter who died in infancy. In the *Philosophy of Right* (q.v.), Hegel identifies the family as the most basic form of institutional ethical life (q.v.). The natural sexual relationship is enriched by the subjective feeling of love and objectively established through a public marriage ceremony. In this context, property (q.v.) becomes the family's capital and is used for the education of children until they are able to assume their independent, free place in the wider civil society (q.v.). *See also* ANTIGONE; MAN; NÜRNBERG; STUTTGART; WOMAN.

FEUERBACH, LUDWIG (1804–1872). Introduced to Hegel's thought by the theologian, Karl Daub (q.v.) in Heidelberg (q.v.), Feuerbach went on to study in Berlin (q.v.) before completing his dissertation in Erlangen. Disappointed in his quest for a tenured academic position, he became an independent writer, producing his groundbreaking *Essence of Christianity*. In this study, he uses Hegel's dialectical (q.v.) method to show that religion (q.v.) and speculative theology are the work of human alienation (q.v.) where the ultimate reconciliation of frustrated emotions and thoughts is projected onto a transcendent world. This critique leads to an affirmation that the human sensuous species-being—that is, the relation with another "thou"—should be cultivated to achieve genuine self-fulfillment. *See also* BEYOND; MARX, KARL; RELIGION IN THE YOUNG HEGELIANS; UNHAPPY CONSCIOUSNESS; YOUNG HEGELIANS.

FICHTE, JOHANN GOTTLIEB (1762–1814). Hailed as the successor of Immanuel Kant (q.v.) on the publication of his *Critique of All Revelation*, Fichte was offered the chair of philosophy in Jena (q.v.) on Karl Reinhold's (q.v.) departure but was forced to resign over charges that he was an atheist. Although still working within the subjectivity of Kant's critical philosophy (q.v.), Fichte in his *Science of Knowledge* sees that categories of the understanding (qq.v.) cannot just be taken over from the forms of logical judgments (q.v.) but must be derived philosophically from the primordial identity of the I (or ego). As Hegel saw it, the diversity of experience (q.v.) and ethical duties in Fichte's thought is simply opposed to the subjectivity of the ego, and whatever identity one achieves is nothing but a belief, postulated by will (q.v.). So his philosophy remains subjective and partial. Fichte later became the first professor of philosophy in the new university of Berlin (q.v.), but his early death created the vacancy that Hegel filled in 1818. *See also DIFFERENCE BETWEEN FICHTE'S AND SCHELLING'S SYSTEMS OF PHILOSOPHY; FAITH AND KNOWLEDGE;* HISTORY OF PHILOSOPHY; SCHULZE, GOTTLOB.

FINDLAY, JOHN NIEMEYER (1903–1987). In 1958, Findlay, at that time at King's College, London, but later situated at Yale and Boston Universities, published *Hegel: A Reexamination*. This work became the harbinger of the Hegelian renaissance in the Anglo-Saxon world. Unlike the earlier school of British idealists (q.v.) who concentrated primarily on the *Science of Logic* (q.v.), Findlay recognized the importance of the *Phenomenology of Spirit* and the *Philosophy of Nature* (qq.v.). In Hegel's "principle of idealism" (q.v.), things tend toward certain consummating experiences (q.v.) in which barriers are broken down between self and others and between the thinking mind and the world confronting it. Initially suspicious of Hegel's triadic method, Findlay later saw it as involving the movement to higher level comment on previously entertained notions and positions. *See also* UNITED STATES.

FINITE, FINITUDE (ENDLICH, DIE ENDLICHKEIT). Since a determinate being or Dasein (q.v.) is qualitatively limited, it is finite. While its determinate quality (q.v.) is a barrier that it cannot break through, thought nonetheless considers what is beyond, or the infinite (qq.v.). So Hegel's logic understands the finite to be a necessary component in a full infinity. *See also* LIMIT; *SCIENCE OF LOGIC*.

FLAY, JOSEPH C. In *Hegel's Quest for Certainty*, Flay interprets the *Phenomenology of Spirit* (q.v.) as a development in which the claims of natural consciousness (q.v.) to absolute knowing (q.v.) become presuppositions that are then put into practice on the basis of its own interests. When its quest for totality (q.v.) is satisfied by a fully intelligible reality, absolute knowing is achieved. However, the project fails because the subjective quest for totality cannot be coordinated with the objective principle of intelligibility, as Hegel had supposed. *See also* UNITED STATES.

FOR CONSCIOUSNESS, FOR IT (FÜR DAS BEWUSSTSEIN, FÜR ES). In the *Phenomenology of Spirit* (q.v.), Hegel distinguishes between what someone within a particular knowledge (q.v.) claim is aware of ("for consciousness" or "for it") and our philosophical reflection on what is going on behind the scenes ("for us" or "in itself" [qq.v.]).

FOR ITSELF (FÜR SICH). Although often confused with "for consciousness" (q.v.), Hegel uses this phrase in its German idiomatic sense of "on its own account" or "self-contained." *See also* BEING FOR SELF.

FOR US (FÜR UNS). In the *Phenomenology of Spirit* (q.v.), we as philosophers understand what is implicit or "in itself" (q.v.) but not noticed by the consciousness (q.v.) making the various knowledge (q.v.) claims discussed. What is thus "for us" is contrasted with the way things are for consciousness (q.v.).

FORCE (DIE KRAFT). In the *Science of Logic* (q.v.), the relation of a force to its expression more adequately captures how essential reality is related to appearance (q.v.) than that of a whole (q.v.) to its part. A force must be solicited to express itself, yet that solicitation is the product of its own initiative. Force can thus be seen as an inner (q.v.), whose outer is the immediate realm of appearance. A similar analysis is found in the chapter on the Understanding (q.v.) in the *Phenomenology of Spirit* (q.v.). *See also* ESSENCE.

FÖRSTER, FRIEDRICH (1791–1868). A patriot who had been wounded in the wars of liberation against Napoleon (q.v.), Förster was lecturer in modern history at the Royal Academy of Military Engineers and Artillery Officers in Berlin (q.v.) but lost his appointment when he published an article attacking the failure of the Prussian regime to produce a constitution (q.v.). He was introduced to Hegel through friends in the Burschenschaft (q.v.) and became a staunch disciple, making impassioned tributes at Hegel's birthday party in 1826 and funeral service in 1831. Through Karl von Altenstein and Johannes Schulze (q.v.), he obtained an editorial position in the Prussian state newspaper in 1823, thereby becoming more reconciled with the regime. With Ludwig Boumann, he edited two volumes of miscellaneous writings in the first edition of Hegel's works. *See also* FREEMASONRY; PRUSSIA.

FRANCE. Although Victor Cousin (q.v.) was acquainted with Hegel, he did not actively introduce Hegelian thought to the French academic world. In the latter part of the 19th century, Augusto Vera translated the various parts of the *Encyclopedia of the Philosophical Sciences* and the *Philosophy of Religion* (qq.v), but it was not until Jean Wahl's (q.v.) *Le Malheur de la conscience dans la philosophie de Hegel* that modern French Hegelian scholarship began to develop. Alexandre Kojève's (q.v.) lectures, and Jean Hyppolite's (q.v.) translation of the *Phenomenology of Spirit* (q.v.) provided the stimulus for the next generation of Hegelian scholars, including Eric Weil, Jacques D'Hondt (qq.v.), Eugène Fleischman, Pierre J. Labarrière, Bernard Bourgeois, and Roger Garaudy. *See also* CENTRE DE RECHERCHE SUR HEGEL ET L'IDÉALISME ALLEMAND; DERRIDA, JACQUES.

FRANKFURT AM MAIN. In the fall of 1796, Hegel's friends from Tübingen (q.v.), Friedrich Hölderlin (q.v.) and Isaac von Sinclair, found him a position as tutor with the Gogel family in Frankfurt, freeing him from the isolation of Bern (q.v.). En route to the new post, he spent some time in Stuttgart (q.v.) with his father and sister, making the acquaintance of Nanette Endel, a young Roman Catholic woman with whom he corresponded briefly. In Frankfurt, he continued working on studies related to his project of a religion (q.v.) of the people. But he also translated, and published anonymously, the *Letters of J. J. Cart*, a revolutionary tract advocating the cause of the Vaud region of France against the dominion of the city of Bern; he wrote a pamphlet urging constitutional changes in Württemberg (q.v.), which, on the advice of friends, he left unpublished; he commented on the *Principles of Politi-*

cal Economy of Sir James Steuart (q.v.), a work that traces the evolution of human society "from perfect simplicity to complicated refinement"; and he began a treatise on the German constitution (q.v.). On the death of his father in early 1799, he came into a small inheritance, and took steps to return to the academic world in Jena (q.v.), where Friedrich Schelling (q.v.) was active.

FREEDOM (DIE FREIHEIT). Freedom is the predominant theme of the *Philosophy of Right* (q.v.). The will (q.v.) is free in that it determines itself by appropriating property; but this abstract freedom must become self-conscious in morality (q.v.) and then be integrated with the concrete structures of social or ethical life (q.v.) before the will is able fully to participate in its own self-determination. Individual arbitrary decisions (Willkur) are always a part of freedom, so at each stage of abstract right (q.v.), morality, and ethical life, decisions can produce wrong (q.v.) and evil as well as justice and the good. For Hegel, freedom as self-determination is the intended aim of world history (q.v.): in the Oriental world only one was free, in Greece some were free, but in the modern world all are free. *See also* ABSOLUTE FREEDOM; CHINESE HISTORY; GERMANIC HISTORY; GREEK HISTORY; PERSIAN HISTORY; PHILOSOPHY OF WORLD HISTORY; STATE; WORLD HISTORY.

FREEMASONRY. Although there is no explicit evidence that Hegel was a freemason, a poem he dedicated to Friedrich Hölderlin from Bern (qq.v.), phrases in the funeral oration of Friedrich Förster (q.v.), and the contacts he made in Bern, Frankfurt am Main, Jena, and Berlin (qq.v.) suggest that he was familiar with the order and its principles. *See also* D'HONDT, JACQUES; SAXE-WEIMAR.

FRENCH REVOLUTION. Hegel was a student in Tübingen (q.v.) when the Bastille fell in Paris, and some of his fellow students came from across the Rhine, bringing with them the words of the *Marseillaise.* Later he anonymously translated into German *Lettres Confidentielles,* a revolutionary text by Jean-Jacques Cart. In his early years he maintained contact with Girondist publications and individuals and in 1822 visited the revolutionary General Carnot, imprisoned in the Magdeburg citadel. In that the revolution, for the first time, implemented the conviction that reason (q.v.) should govern social reality, Hegel says in the *Lectures on* *the Philosophy of World History* (q.v.) that "all thinking beings have joined together in celebrating this epoch." The French Revolution, however, appears in the *Phenomenology of Spirit* (q.v.) only in the guise of absolute freedom (q.v.) and the reign of terror. In France, the Enlightenment's (q.v.) commitment to the freedom of the will as the work of pure reason lacked the Protestant conscience (q.v.), with its certainty of what is universal (q.v.). What remained was simply the principle of universal utility (q.v.). When this was applied to people as well as to things, the singularity of their willed actions stood out as vicious because it distorted the good of all, and they were condemned to death (q.v.). *See also* BERN; CONSTITUTION; FRANKFURT AM MAIN; NAPOLEON; PROTESTANT REFORMATION.

FRIEDRICH II (THE GREAT) (1712–1786). In his *Lectures on the Philosophy of World History* (q.v.), Hegel describes Friedrich the Great as a world-historical person and philosopher king because even as he sat on the throne he was aware of, and acted on, universal (q.v.) principles rather than particular interests. This example of enlightened monarchy (q.v.) set Germany apart from the Roman Catholic countries of France, Spain, and Italy and prevented the emergence of revolutionary violence. *See also* ENLIGHTENMENT.

FRIES, JAKOB FRIEDRICH (1773–1843). Convinced of the importance of "pure feeling," Fries criticized the speculative philosophy of Karl Reinhold, Johann Fichte, and Friedrich Schelling (qq.v.) and argued for a descriptive philosophy based on knowing, faith (q.v.), and presentiment. Like Hegel, he returned to Jena (q.v.) in 1801 after a stint as private tutor in Switzerland. In 1805, both received promotions, but Fries went on to become professor of mathematics and philosophy in Heidelberg (q.v.). He returned to Jena in 1816, opening up the chair in Heidelberg for Hegel. In 1817, he participated in a festival organized by the Burschenschaft (q.v.) in the Wartburg which included a ceremonial burning of "reactionary books." Not only was the Duke Karl August of Saxe-Weimar (q.v.) forced to suspend him (though he was given a pension and later returned to his academic position), but his speech was subjected to ridicule in the preface to Hegel's *Philosophy of Right* (q.v.) because it based philosophy on immediate (q.v.) sense perception and the play of fancy. *See also* ROMANTICISM.

FUKUYAMA, FRANCIS. Influenced by Alexandre Kojève's (q.v.) view of the end of history (q.v.), Fukuyama argues that the fall of the Berlin Wall and the end of Soviet communism marked the apotheosis of liberal democracy, after which there will be no significant changes in the way human society functions. This is the result of the incremental advance of natural science (the work of reason [q.v.]), the development of capitalist economies (the achievement of desire [q.v.]), and the emergence of liberal democracies (as a result of the quest for recognition [q.v.]). The only threat to this new stability is that, while reason and desire are satisfied, the need for distinctive recognition is not met, leading to wars (q.v.) that could destroy the status quo. *See also* CAPITALISM.

– G –

GADAMER, HANS-GEORG. Gadamer discovers the power of Hegel's dialectic (q.v.) in its implicit reliance on natural language (q.v.), which finds expression in the spoken word. As a result, Hegel's attempt to move beyond language to thought must be countered with a move to the hermeneutical interpretation of the grammar and historical context of the language used.

GANS, EDUARD (1798–1839). The son of a Jewish merchant in Berlin (q.v.), Gans organized with others an academic discussion group that eventually became the Association for the Culture and Science of Judaism (q.v.). After studying with A. F. J. Thibault in Heidelberg (q.v.), a defender of Jewish emancipation, Gans returned to Berlin, where he came under the influence of Hegel. Although allowed to teach without stipend at the University of Berlin for a time, he was barred from any hope of advancement by a royal ordinance in 1822 that excluded Jews from academic and government positions. Following a sojourn in Paris that failed to open up prospects, he converted to Christianity (q.v.) and obtained an academic appointment, becoming full professor in 1829. A leading member of the Hegelian Society for Scientific Criticism, he took over Hegel's lectures on the philosophy of right (q.v.) until his enthusiastic suggestion that the state (q.v.) should introduce greater freedom (q.v.) for individuals to express their opposition to government led to censure from the Crown Prince. He edited the *Philosophy of Right* and the *Lectures on the Philosophy of World History* (qq.v.) for the first edition of Hegel's works, but, because of his continuing support for reform after the revolutions of 1830, his lectures were banned and he was dismissed. *See also JOURNAL FOR SCIENTIFIC CRITICISM.*

GENTILE, GIOVANNI (1875–1944). Influenced by Bertrando Spaventa and for a while associated with Benedetto Croce (q.v.), Gentile's "actual idealism" reflected the thought of Immanuel Kant and Johann Fichte (qq.v.). The true dialectic (q.v.) traces the act of thinking (q.v.) in which the transcendental ego constitutes itself by uniting theory and practice. Seeing the state (q.v.) as the embodiment of this fundamental logical category, Gentile became minister of education in Mussolini's first cabinet and continued to support the fascist state until his assassination in 1944. *See also* ITALY; TRANSCENDENTAL IDEALISM.

GEOGRAPHY. The role that states (q.v.) play in world history (q.v.) is conditioned by their geographic setting. A mountainous country supports herding; high plains encourage a nomadic existence; agriculture develops in wide river valleys; the sea coast promotes trade. As the continent most influenced by the sea, Europe provides an appropriate setting for the modern world. *See also* MONTESQUIEU, BARON CHARLES DE; PHILOSOPHY OF WORLD HISTORY.

GEOLOGY. Hegel incorporates geology into the section on Organics (q.v.) in his *Philosophy of Nature* (q.v.). The earth as a whole functions as a nonliving organism (q.v.), with the interaction of its various rock formations, the division between land and ocean, meteorological processes and incipient forms of life. He also took considerable interest in geological questions and while in Jena (q.v.) was named assessor of the Jena Mineralogical Society.

GERMANIC HISTORY. Hegel uses "German" to label all of the barbarian tribes that brought about the downfall of the Roman Empire, ranging from Scandinavia to Spain and Italy. They had a tradition of free association under a leader that, once united with the Christian conviction that all are free and equal in the sight of God, would establish the basis of the modern European state (q.v.). Christianity (q.v.) then overcame its reliance on external things as evidence of God's presence after the Germanic crusades successfully put Christ's tomb in Christian hands only to produce the realization that it was empty of substance and could provide no satisfaction. This set the stage for the Protestant Reformation (q.v.) through which the divine was brought into the conscience (q.v.) of believers, and individuals were made responsible for their own salvation. The modern Germanic states, with their conscientious middle class, their constitutional protections for individual rights, and their network of international relations, thereby realize spirit's (q.v.) quest for freedom (q.v.). *See also* CIVIL SOCIETY; CLASSES; CONSTITUTION; PHILOSOPHY OF WORLD HISTORY; WORLD HISTORY.

GERMANY. As Prussia (q.v.) moved further toward reaction after Hegel's death and competition for academic positions increased, his disciples divided into two camps. The "old Hegelians" (q.v.), who already had positions, tended to defend, or at least accommodate themselves to, the Prussian regime. The "young Hegelians" (q.v.), without hope of tenured appointments, explored the more radical implications of his philosophy: challenging Christian doctrine and espousing republican or democratic politics. With the failure of the Revolution of 1848, many of these abandoned their Hegelian roots. Then, in 1857, the liberal Rudolf Haym (q.v.) published *Hegel and His Time*, in which he charged Hegel with supporting the post-Napoleonic reaction. Karl Rosenkranz (q.v.) replied with his *Hegel als deutscher Nationalphilosoph*. In 1905, Wilhelm Dilthey's (q.v.) *Die Jugendgeschichte Hegels* initiated interest in the philosophical development that led to Hegel's final position. This inspired Richard Kroner's *Von Kant bis Hegel* and György Lukács's (q.v.) *The Young Hegel*, which draws parallels with the young Karl Marx (q.v.). While the Frankfurt school, including Theodor Adorno (q.v.) and Jürgen Habermas, continued to explore the close connections among Immanuel Kant (q.v.), Hegel, and Marx, Georg Lasson initiated an edition of Hegel's work that would make public previously unpublished manuscripts. When his collaborator and successor Johannes Hoffmeister died in 1955, the concern for scholarly documentation of Hegelian philosophy led Otto Pöggeler and Friedhelm Nicolin to found the Hegel Archiv (q.v.), the critical edition of Hegel's works, and the journal *Hegel-Studien*. More recently, Hans-Georg Gadamer (q.v.) and others were instrumental in establishing the Internationale Hegel Vereinigung (q.v.), while Wilhelm Beyer initiated the more left-wing Internationale Hegel Gesellschaft (q.v.), and Hans Heinz Holz and Manfred Buhr started the International Gesellschaft für dialektische Philosophie (q.v.) or Societas Hegeliana. *See also* HÄRING, THEODOR.

GOD (DER GOTT). God is the absolute essence (q.v.), or the underlying ground (q.v.) of all things. Although the arguments for God's existence (Dasein [qq.v.]) are inadequate when considered from the perspective of external reflection (q.v.), they nonetheless embody fundamental logical moves. When a complete concept (q.v.) fully determines itself, it must (as in the ontological proof) become objective. Although contingent conditions are continually passing out of existence, their totality (q.v.) is nonetheless grounded in a mediating dynamic that is to that extent necessary (the cosmological proof). The world of nature and spirit (qq.v.), organized so that each part is not independent but a member of a whole (q.v.), points to an integrating principle or concept that holds it all together (the physicoteleological proof). *See also* CHRISTIANITY; CONTINGENCY; LIFE; LOGIC; NECESSITY; OBJECTIVITY; PHILOSOPHY OF RELIGION; RELIGION.

GOETHE, JOHANN WOLFGANG von (1749–1832). As minister responsible for education and culture in the duchy of Saxe-Weimar (q.v.) and thus for the university at Jena (q.v.), the great German poet, novelist, and essayist Johann Wolfgang von Goethe interceded on occasion in support of Hegel, arranging for his appointment as an (unsalaried) extraordinary professor in 1805. They met often in the home of the publisher, Karl Fromann. Hegel was interested in Goethe's theory of colors and his mineralogy, and visited him when returning from Paris in 1827. *See also* ROMANTICISM.

GREEK HISTORY. In the Persian wars, the Greeks were able to resist the might of an Oriental power by relying on individual courage. Spirit (q.v.) thus became historically significant, although in the form of beauty (q.v.), it was still united with nature (q.v.). But particular (q.v.) interests led to continuing feuds among the various states (q.v.) and between the internal factions of a city. When Socrates (q.v.) raised subjectivity (q.v.) to a principle in refusing to acknowledge the prior interests of the community, a corrupting virus was introduced that led to the decline and fall of the Greek political order, even while the eastern Mediterranean was becoming infused with Greek culture through the conquests of Alexander. *See also* ANTIGONE; ARISTOTLE; CLASSICAL ART; COMEDY; DRAMA; EPIC; ETHICAL LIFE; GREEK RELIGION; HERACLITUS; LYRIC; PHILOSOPHY OF WORLD HISTORY; PLATO;

POETRY; RELIGION IN THE FORM OF ART; SCULPTURE; THALES; WORLD HISTORY.

GREEK RELIGION. In his *Lectures on the Philosophy of Religion* (q.v.), Hegel discusses Greek religion in tandem with Judaism (q.v.), distinguishing them by means of the aesthetic categories of the beautiful and the sublime (q.v.). In both traditions, the spiritual is no longer embedded in natural forces (as in the natural religions [q.v.]) but rather dominates them. This is represented in Greece by the victory of Zeus, the god of political life, over the Titans. The gods appear not only directly through oracles and dreams but indirectly through the self-conscious activity of inspired artists who mold natural objects and language to give deities beautiful form. Underlying the diversity of this tradition lies the abstract necessity of destiny, though individuals are free to determine how they will respond to this fate. In the *Phenomenology of Spirit* (q.v.), Hegel discusses Greek religion as religion in the form of art (q.v.). *See also* BEAUTY; CLASSICAL ART; COMEDY; DRAMA; EPIC; GREEK HISTORY; LYRIC; POETRY; RELIGION; SCULPTURE; TRAGEDY.

GREEN, THOMAS HILL (1836–1882). As a student and fellow of Balliol College, Oxford, Green was introduced to German philosophy by Benjamin Jowett (q.v.). Inspired by Immanuel Kant, Johann Fichte (qq.v.), and Hegel, he understood the world to be ultimately grounded in self-consciousness (q.v.), so that the consciousness of system (q.v.) or relationship—one (q.v.) in many, identity in difference (qq.v.)—is the condition of our having experience (q.v.). The state (q.v.) is the product of will (q.v.), insofar as the system of rights and duties rests on a moral as opposed to a merely natural foundation. Politically he was a strong supporter of John Bright against Lord Palmerston, and for a while he sat on the Oxford town council. *See also* BRITISH IDEALISM.

GROUND (DER GRUND). When a contradiction (q.v.) emerges, thought looks for its reason (q.v.) or ground. This can mean distinguishing between form and content, exploring conditions, or getting to the heart of the matter. *See also* ESSENCE; *SACHE SELBST; SCIENCE OF LOGIC.*

– H –

HÄRING, THEODOR L. (1884–1964). Häring's two-volume study, *Hegel: Sein Wollen und Sein Werk*, was the first to trace Hegel's development using the early manuscripts of theological writings and the Jena drafts for a system (qq.v.) as well as the *Phenomenology of Spirit* (q.v.). He concluded that Hegel attempted too much in striving for, and claiming to have reached, a whole (q.v.) that is beyond (q.v.) the grasp of any mortal. *See also* BERN; FRANKFURT AM MAIN; GERMANY; TÜBINGEN.

HARRIS, ERROL E. In his own writing, as well as in his articles and books on Hegel, Harris works from Hegel's thesis that the truth is the whole (qq.v.). Differences (q.v.) and distinctions are retained even as they are sublated (q.v.) into a more encompassing totality (q.v.). Hegel, he says, views nature (q.v.) as a world where the idea (q.v.) is immanent in every detail and out of which mind (q.v.) develops dialectically through a process of self-evolution. *See also* UNITED STATES.

HARRIS, HENRY STILTON. In two massive studies, *Hegel's Development* and *Hegel's Ladder*, both published in two volumes, Harris has examined every manuscript and text from the Stuttgart, Tübingen, Bern, Frankfurt am Main, and Jena (qq.v.) years and every paragraph on the *Phenomenology of Spirit* (q.v.). In each case, Hegel is shown to be commenting on, and developing insights of, the tradition. The absolute (q.v.) that knows its own history in this way becomes the universal brotherhood of man, where reason (q.v.) and sentiment are integrated and philosophy (q.v.) "speaks the vulgar tongue." *See also* CANADA.

HARRIS, WILLIAM TORREY (1835–1909). As a young schoolteacher in St. Louis, Harris was converted to Kantian and Hegelian philosophy by Henry Conrad Brokmeyer (q.v.) with whom he formed a Kant Club, which became the St. Louis Philosophical Society. His critical insight was that "all dependent being is a part of independent being; and all independent being is self-determined being." From studying Brokmeyer's translation of the *Science of Logic* (q.v.), he developed a familiarity with that work, which resulted in *Hegel's Doctrine of Reflection* (1881), supplementing J. H. Stirling's (q.v.) translation of the first book of the *Logic* with a translation and commentary of the second. Later, when he was U.S. commissioner of education, he published in the Griggs's Philosophical Classics *Hegel's Logic: A Book on the Genesis of the Categories of Mind* (1890). *See also* ESSENCE; REFLECTION; ST. LOUIS HEGELIANS; UNITED STATES.

HAYM, RUDOLF (1821–1901). In his lectures on *Hegel and His Time*, published in 1857, Haym presented Hegel's philosophy as an apology for the present and a justification for the "self-satisfied and anxiety-ridden" bureaucracy of the Prussian state (q.v.), defending it against the liberal quest for individual freedom (q.v.). This influential work determined the prevailing consensus concerning Hegel's philosophy during the 19th century in Europe and into the 20th. *See also* AVINIERI, SHLOMO; D'HONDT, JACQUES; GERMANY; POPPER, KARL; PRUSSIA; ROSENKRANZ, KARL; RUSSELL, BERTRAND; WEIL, ERIC.

HEART OF THE MATTER. *See SACHE SELBST.*

HEGEL ARCHIV. Founded in 1958 at Bonn, the Hegel Archiv, now at the University of Bochum in Germany, has collected not only the various editions of Hegel's works but also copies of works to which Hegel referred and a wide range of secondary sources. It is responsible for the critical edition of Hegel's *Collected Works* (*see* bibliography) and for editing *Hegel-Studien*. *See also* GERMANY.

HEGEL SOCIETY OF AMERICA. Founded in 1968, the Hegel Society of America holds biennial conferences on specified themes (many of whose proceedings have been published) and edits the *Owl of Minerva*, a twice yearly journal. *See also* CANADA; UNITED STATES.

HEGEL SOCIETY OF GREAT BRITAIN. Founded in 1979, the Hegel Society of Great Britain holds annual meetings at Oxford in September. Papers presented, as well as book reviews and other discussions, are published in the *Bulletin of the Hegel Society of Great Britain*. *See also* BRITISH IDEALISM.

HEIDEGGER, MARTIN (1889–1976). For Heidegger, Hegel's thought marks the culmination of Cartesian metaphysics, in that ultimate reality is found in the subjectivity (q.v.) of an absolute self and in the presence of a highest being (q.v.), both of which are beyond (q.v.) everything that is simply given to us. In this Hegel maintains the tradition of Western philosophy that forgets how we humans are thrown into existence (q.v.) and caught in the dispersed finitude of time (qq.v.).

HEIDELBERG. In 1816, Hegel accepted Karl Daub's (q.v.) warm invitation to assume the chair of philosophy at Heidelberg, vacated when Jakob Fries (q.v.) moved to Jena (q.v.). In consequence, he had to turn down advances from both Berlin (q.v.) and Erlangen. In addition to lectures on the history of philosophy and aesthetics (qq.v.), he began lecturing on his system (q.v.) and preparing the first edition of his *Encyclopedia of the Philosophical Sciences* (q.v.) as a manual for his students (who included Friedrich Carové [q.v.], Hermann Hinrichs, and an Estonian, Baron von Üxküll). He also became an editor of the *Heidelberg Yearbooks*, with responsibility for philosophy (q.v.), philology, and theology. In this journal, he wrote a sympathetic review of the third volume of Friedrich Heinrich Jacobi's (q.v.) works and a critique of the refusal of the Württemberg (q.v.) estates to accept a constitution (q.v.) proposed by the king. When Baron Karl von Altenstein, on assuming responsibility for education in Prussia (q.v.), reissued the invitation to take over Johann Gottlieb Fichte's (q.v.) chair in Berlin, Hegel accepted.

HENNING, LEOPOLD von (1791–1866). Like Friedrich Förster (q.v.) a veteran of the patriotic wars against Napoleon, von Henning became Hegel's assistant during the early years in Berlin (q.v.), introducing students to the Hegelian system (q.v.). He was imprisoned for 10 weeks, however, on suspicion of holding "Napoleonic opinions." A member of the editorial board of the *Journal for Scientific Criticism* (q.v.), he edited both the *Encyclopedia Logic* and the *Science of Logic* (qq.v.) for the first edition of Hegel's works. In the 1830s he became, with Karl Göschel, a leading spokesman for the Hegelian right. *See also* RIGHT-WING HEGELIANISM.

HERACLITUS OF EPHESUS. For Hegel, Heraclitus was the first speculative philosopher in that "becoming" turned both "being" and "nothing" (qq.v.) from absolutes into relatives. By applying this insight to time (q.v.) and fire he also became the first philosopher of nature. *See also* HISTORY OF PHILOSOPHY; *PHILOSOPHY OF NATURE;* SPECULATIVE REASON.

HERDER, JOHANN GOTTFRIED (1744–1803). Although a student of Immanuel Kant (q.v.) in Königsberg, Herder was subjected to Kant's critique when his *Ideas for a Philosophy of the History of Mankind* was published. In 1776, he became general superintendent of Lutheran clergy in Saxe-Weimar (q.v.) and so associated with Johann Goethe (q.v.). For him, art (q.v.) is the expression of the whole human personality and, along with language and culture (qq.v.) generally, has developed over time. So there is no universal human nature. Rather, each society develops in a distinctive manner and in response to the circumstances of its place and time. He thus anticipated themes in Hegel's philosophy of world history (q.v.). *See also* ROMANTICISM.

HESS, MOSES (1812–1877). Born in Bonn of Jewish parents, Hess called himself a Spinozist rather than a Hegelian. As an associate of Karl Marx and Friedrich Engels (qq.v.), he saw the inevitability of a society without class (q.v.) and wealth and stressed human creative power, which had previously been alienated into mythical transcendent powers: God, the state (qq.v.), and the laws of history or economics. In the 1860s, fearful for the future of Jews in Europe, he worked for a Jewish and socialist state in Palestine. *See also* ALIENATION; JUDAISM; SPINOZA, BARUCH.

HINDUISM. *See* **INDIAN RELIGION.**

HISTORY. *See* **WORLD HISTORY.**

HISTORY OF PHILOSOPHY (DIE GESCHICHTE DER PHILOSOPHIE). Hegel organizes the history of philosophy according to a conceptual schema. Greek and Roman philosophy explored the "idea" (q.v.): how concepts (q.v.) grasp and comprehend reality. This started with a focus on objectivity (q.v.) in the Pre-Socratics and then moved on to subjectivity (q.v.) in the Sophists, Socrates (q.v.), and the Socratics. These two moments were then integrated in the thought of Plato and Aristotle (qq.v.). Their philosophies, though comprehensive, lacked system (q.v.); this lack became explicit in the debates between the dogmatic philosophies of the Stoics (q.v.) and Epicureans, on the one hand, and Skepticism (q.v.), on the other, and was resolved in neo-Platonism, which provided the conceptual framework within which Christianity (q.v.) could find its place. Christianity introduced freedom (q.v.) as a property of all, a principle that was then worked out in medieval and modern philosophy as the "self-knowing idea." After an interim period that stretched from the church fathers to the Protestant reformation (qq.v.), modern philosophy began with Francis Bacon's appeal to experience (q.v.) and Jakob Boehme's speculative insight. It then separated into those who stressed the universal (q.v.) (Baruch Spinoza and René Descartes [qq.v.]) and those who stressed the particular (q.v.) (John Locke, Thomas Hobbes, Gottfried Leibniz, and David Hume [qq.v.]). Immanuel Kant and his successors, Johann Fichte, Friedrich Jacobi, and Friedrich Schelling (qq.v.), brought these two strands together into a single perspective. *See also* HERACLITUS; KANT'S CRITICAL PHILOSOPHY; KANT'S *CRITIQUE OF JUDGMENT*; KANT'S MORAL PHILOSOPHY; *LECTURES ON THE HISTORY OF PHILOSOPHY*; PROCLUS; THALES.

HOBBES, THOMAS (1588–1679). Hobbes saw that the natural state of desire (q.v.) produced a war (q.v.) of all against all. His solution, however, was not to move toward the rule of law (q.v.) as universal will (q.v.) but to promote the singular (q.v.) will of a sovereign. *See also* DEATH; HISTORY OF PHILOSOPHY; MONARCH.

HÖLDERLIN, JOHANN CHRISTIAN FRIEDRICH (1770–1843). Having relied on Hegel as a mentor during their shared years in Tübingen (q.v.), the poet Hölderlin maintained a correspondence with him during Hegel's time in Bern (q.v.) while he himself moved into the circles of Friedrich Schiller and Johann Fichte (qq.v.) at Jena (q.v.). Then Hölderlin took up a position as tutor in Frankfurt am Main (q.v.), where he was able to arrange a similar post for his friend. During Hegel's years in Frankfurt, Hölderlin had an unfortunate affair with the mistress of the household in which he was working and shortly began to show signs of the insanity (q.v.) that put him out of commission for the rest of his life. *See also* ROMANTICISM.

HOTHO, HEINRICH GUSTAV (1802–1873). Hotho attended Hegel's lectures on aesthetics (q.v.) twice, in 1823 and again in 1826, and prepared two editions of the lectures for the collected works. While he took over Hegel's lectures in the subject briefly after the philosopher's death, he soon became assistant in the picture gallery of the royal museums and later director of the copperplate engraving collection. While there he wrote reviews of musical performances in Berlin.

HOULGATE, STEPHEN. For Houlgate, freedom (q.v.) is fundamental to understanding how Hegel can integrate history with truth (q.v.). There are no external foundations for philosophy (q.v.). Rather, the indeterminate determines itself, so that the truth of development is its immanent, free process of self-determination. Philosophy thus understands what it means to be natural, historical or religious, while natural scientists, historians, and believers discover which processes are actually required to produce that truth. *See also* BRITISH IDEALISM.

HUME, DAVID (1711–1776). Hume quite rightly pointed out that perception (q.v.) could not provide any justification for universality or necessity (qq.v.), and so he set the stage for Immanuel Kant's (q.v.) critical philosophy (q.v.). To establish general principles in science and morals, then, Hume's empiricism (q.v.) could only rely on custom.

HYPPOLITE, JEAN (1907–1968). In 1941, Jean Hyppolite published the first translation of the *Phenomenology of Spirit* (q.v.) into French. In addition, he published *Genesis and Structure of Hegel's Phenomenology of Spirit* (1956), *Introduction to Hegel's Philosophy of History* (1948), *Logic and Existence* (1953), and *Studies on Marx and Hegel* (1955). As professor at the Collège de France, he inspired a generation of French thinkers, including Jacques Derrida, Jacques D'Hondt (qq.v.), Louis Althusser, Dominique Dubarle, Dominique Janicaud, and Marcel Régnier.

– I –

IDEA (DIE IDEE). Hegel uses this term for the intellectual operation that understands how thought's subjective concept (qq.v.) is integrated with objective actuality (qq.v.). Life (q.v.) captures this integration on a basic level, but its distinctive moments are developed in cognition (q.v.) (or the idea of the true), in principled action (q.v.) (or the idea of the good), and in the method (q.v.) of logical reason (q.v.) itself, which Hegel calls the absolute idea (q.v.). *See also* BEAUTY; *SCIENCE OF LOGIC.*

IDEALISM (DER IDEALISMUS). Idealism, as the certainty that all reality is thought, finds expression in René Descartes's (q.v.) conviction that clear and distinct ideas are true. Hegel explores the categories thought (q.v.) uses to do this in the chapter on reason (q.v.) in the *Phenomenology of Spirit* (q.v.). Because spirit overreaches (qq.v.) and incorporates nature (q.v.) into its life (q.v.), Hegel himself understands matter in terms of its meaning, rather than reducing meaning to matter, as does materialism. His philosophy has thus been called absolute idealism, and contrasted with the subjective idealism of Johann Fichte (q.v.) and the objective idealism of Friedrich Schelling (q.v.). These forms of idealism should not be confused with the idealism of Bishop George Berkeley, who claimed there is no matter at all, since everything is mind. *See also* TRANSCENDENTAL IDEALISM.

IDENTITY (DIE IDENTITÄT). For Hegel, identity is used by reflection (q.v.) to determine what is essential. However, because it presupposes difference (q.v.), it turns out to be a relational term. *See also* ESSENCE; LAWS OF THOUGHT; *SCIENCE OF LOGIC.*

IMAGINATION (DIE EINBILDUNG). Through the activity of imagination, intelligence (q.v.) relates something immediately intuited to images stored in its subconscious. On one level, this simply happens through association based on past experience (q.v.), but, as fantasy, intelligence takes the initiative to connect representations (q.v.), create signs, and then arbitrarily select some sound or image to represent a set of related images in speech. *See also* INTUITION; LANGUAGE; MEMORY; PSYCHOLOGY; RECOLLECTION; *PHILOSOPHY OF SPIRIT.*

IMMEDIATE (UNMITTELBAR). Any starting point will be immediate in that there has been no mediation (q.v.) to get to it. For Hegel, integrated results can be abstracted from their mediation by the understanding (q.v.) and considered as single, immediate starting points. At the same time, any immediate can be shown to be itself the result of mediation. *See also* METHOD.

IMMEDIATE KNOWING (DAS UNMITTELBARE WISSEN). Knowing directly without any intervening activity of reflection or thinking (qq.v.) is said to be immediate (q.v.). Hegel includes under this title the claims of common sense philosophy and of Friedrich Jacobi's romanticism (qq.v.) as well as the Cartesian identification of thinking and being (q.v.). Faith and intuition (qq.v.) are also said to have an unmediated idea of what is. By showing that immediate sense certainty (q.v.) cannot avoid the mediation (q.v.) that connects moments of time (q.v.) and points of space (q.v.), Hegel supports his claim that all immediates are in fact mediated, either by one's upbringing, or through being abstracted from their context. *See also* DESCARTES, RENÉ; KNOWLEDGE.

IN ITSELF (AN SICH). Immanuel Kant (q.v.) introduced the phrase *in itself* to distinguish what something is inherently from the way it appears. Hegel, unlike Kant, holds that what is in itself can become known through reflection (q.v.). In the *Phenomenology of Spirit* (q.v.), he identifies the "in itself" with what is "for us" (q.v.), the reflective philosophers, in contrast to what appears to someone unreflectively making a knowledge (q.v.) claim—that is, what is "for consciousness" (q.v.). *See also* APPEARANCE.

INDIAN HISTORY. In contrast to the patriarchal unity of Chinese history (q.v.), India represents difference and diversity (qq.v.), with its fixed caste system and local despots who maintain power only as long as they are strong and wealthy enough to command subservience. Despite its long existence, India never developed a tradition of historical literature since there was no conscious appropriation of the past when preparing for the future. *See also* INDIAN RELIGION; *LECTURES ON THE PHILOSOPHY OF WORLD HISTORY*; PHILOSOPHY OF WORLD HISTORY.

INDIAN RELIGION. In Hegel's *Lectures on the Philosophy of Religion* (q.v.), the religion of India is placed between Buddhism and the Parsee religion (qq.v). As a natural religion (q.v.), Hinduism worships the spiritual as the inherent power of the natural, but the nature (q.v.) to be spiritualized is no longer the inner realm of desire and will (qq.v.) found in Buddhism but the totality (q.v.) of concrete, external reality. Within the overarching unity of Brahman, the three central deities of Brahma, Vishnu, and Shiva represent creation, determinate actuality, and destruction. *See also* INDIAN HISTORY.

INDIVIDUAL (DAS INDIVIDUUM). Hegel uses two terms for individual. For the logical sense of the singular (q.v.) object of reference he uses *das Einzelne*. But when he wants to talk about a living individual that is centered by its basic principle or soul (q.v.), he uses the Latin term *das Individuum*.

INFERENCE. *See* SYLLOGISM.

INFINITE, INFINITY (UNENDLICH, DIE UNENDLICHKEIT). In the *Science of Logic* (q.v.), Hegel first uses *infinite* to name that which is beyond (q.v.) the qualitative limits of the finite (qq.v.). When any quality (q.v.) changes, the being (q.v.) it qualifies becomes something (q.v.) else. Since any such beyond becomes, in its turn, finite in quality and limited, one is led into an infinite regress where each new finite points to a succeeding one. This Hegel calls the "bad infinite." One can, however, look at the movement from a finite to an infinite beyond and back again as a pattern in which both the finite and the infinite are constituted within a single self-determining dynamic. Since that dynamic does not simply react to what is given but determines its own distinctive moments, it is a "true or valid infinite," self-contained on its own account. Life (q.v.) determines itself to be both finite yet also more than finite; so it, too, is genuinely infinite. Hegel distinguishes this qualitative infinite from a quantitative one, in which any definite quantum (q.v.) is part of a continuous sequence, ultimately defined by its relation to that infinite series. He also points out that the concept of something being either infinitely small or infinitely large really is contradictory, for it combines an indefinite quantitative series with a definite magnitude (q.v.) or size. Infinity appears a third time in the Doctrine of Being under the discussion of measure (q.v.). Here a gradual change of quantity (q.v.) along a series produces changes in quality. This combination of both the qualitative and the quantitative infinite leads to the thought of something underlying the transformations, which Hegel calls the "Sache selbst" (q.v.). *See also* ATOMISM; BEING FOR SELF; QUANTITY INTO QUALITY.

INNER/OUTER (DAS INNERE, DAS ÄUSSERE). The inner is a single immediate essence (qq.v.) while the outer is diverse mediated being (qq.v.). Yet considered in its totality (q.v.), the outer expresses the inner, and as ground (q.v.) the inner must externalize itself as outer. So the two moments imply each other and can be identified. *See also* EXTERNAL RELATIONS; INTERNAL RELATIONS; *SCIENCE OF LOGIC*.

INSANITY (DIE VERRÜCKTHEIT). Hegel explains madness or mental illness as the reemergence of some basic affectations of the soul out of more developed attitudes of consciousness and understanding (qq.v.) so that they become dominant. *See also* ANTHROPOLOGY; *PHILOSOPHY OF SPIRIT*.

INSIGHT, PURE (DIE REINE EINSICHT). While faith (q.v.) looks for the truth (q.v.) of the confusing world of culture (q.v.) in a pure beyond (q.v.), insight recognizes that the governing principle of this world is the self as rational, or the concept (q.v.). Although this principle cannot provide any determinate content, it does challenge the simple affirmations of faith, producing the struggle of the Enlightenment (q.v.) with superstition. *See also* CULTURE; *PHENOMENOLOGY OF SPIRIT*; SPIRIT.

INTELLIGENCE (DIE INTELLIGENZ). Hegel uses this term to represent the thinking (q.v.) side of spirit (q.v.) as distinct from the will (q.v.). The functions or activities of intelligence (previously called faculties)—intuition, imagination, representation (qq.v.), and thinking—are explored by psychology (q.v.). *See also PHILOSOPHY OF SPIRIT*.

INTERNAL RELATIONS. Francis Bradley, John M. E. McTaggart, and other British idealists (qq.v.) argue that all things are internally related through their meaning so that space and time (qq.v.) are ultimately not real. In contrast, Hegel distinguishes conceptual relations (which are internal) from the externality of natural space and time. *See also* EXTERNAL RELATIONS; INNER/OUTER.

INTERNATIONAL HEGEL ASSOCIATION (INTERNATIONALE HEGEL VEREINIGUNG). Founded in Heidelberg in 1962 by Hans-Georg Gadamer (q.v.), Alexandre Koyré, Joachim Ritter, and others, the

International Hegel Association has hosted conferences every six years in Stuttgart, as well as special colloquia on particular themes every two years. Their proceedings have been published as supplements to *Hegel-Studien*, the journal of the Hegel Archiv (q.v.). *See also* GERMANY.

INTERNATIONAL HEGEL SOCIETY (INTERNATIONALE HEGEL GESELLSCHAFT). Founded by Wilhelm Beyer in 1953 as the Deutsche Hegel-Gesellschaft (German Hegel Society) to bring together researchers from both sides of the Iron Curtain, the International Hegel Society acquired its current name at the second international congress of 1958. Since 1956, biennial congresses have brought together scholars from all over the world. Their proceedings have been published in the *Hegel Jahrbuch*. *See also* GERMANY.

INTERNATIONAL LAW (DAS ÄUSSERE STAATSRECHT). The state (q.v.) as singular (q.v.), centered in the actions of its monarch (q.v.), relates to other states in a pattern of mutual recognition (q.v.). The basic principle of international law is that treaties are to be kept, but unlike the contractual obligations between persons (q.v.), which can be enforced by the public authority or police (q.v.), the ultimate sanction for a breach of treaty is war (q.v.). *See also* CONTRACT; *PHILOSOPHY OF RIGHT*.

INTERNATIONAL SOCIETY FOR DIALECTICAL PHILOSOPHY (INTERNATIONALE GESELLSCHAFT FÜR DIALEKTISCHE PHILOSOPHIE or SOCIETAS HEGELIANA). The Societas Hegeliana was founded in Frankfurt am Main (q.v.) in 1981 by Hans-Heinz Holz, Manfred Buhr, and others to encourage the study of Hegelian philosophy and dialectical thinking and method, with particular attention to the development it has had in the context of the Marxist tradition. *See also* GERMANY; MARX, KARL.

INTUITION (DIE ANSCHAUUNG). While Immanuel Kant (q.v.) had limited human intuition to what appears as we sense and introspect, Johann Fichte and Friedrich Schelling (qq.v.) appealed to an intellectual intuition, in which an agent self is immediately aware of its real self as acting. In Hegel's psychology (q.v.), however, intuition is the most basic function of intelligence (q.v.). Attention is paid to the world's immediate (q.v.) impact on the soul (q.v.) and in so doing situates those feelings in time and space (qq.v.). The content intuited is then internalized as representations (q.v.). The truth (q.v.) of the world is discovered not through intuition but through conceptual thinking (q.v.). *See also* APPEARANCE; CONCEPT; JACOBI, FRIEDRICH; *PHILOSOPHY OF SPIRIT*; SCHLEIERMACHER, FRIEDRICH.

INVERTED WORLD (DIE VERKEHRTE WELT). In his discussion of understanding (q.v.) in the *Phenomenology of Spirit* (q.v.), Hegel describes a stage where understanding goes behind the surface of objects to get at their truth (q.v.), only to find that this is the opposite of what appears publicly. A similar analysis can be found in the discussion of appearance (q.v.) in the *Science of Logic* (q.v.). The end of the compass needle that points to the north, for example, is really the south pole of its magnet; and what first appears as ostracism and punishment is understood as a way of reintegrating the criminal into society.

INWOOD, MICHAEL. Published in a series called "Arguments of the Philosophers," Inwood's *Hegel* reconstructs a number of Hegel's arguments, particularly with regard to his logic and metaphysics (qq.v.), while offering Inwood's own counterarguments and assessments. Though he finds few, if any, of the arguments convincing, they nonetheless have an appeal because Hegel not only asks the right questions but assigns everything its place within a single, coherent whole (q.v.). *See also* BRITISH IDEALISM.

ISLAM. Although Hegel recognized that Mohammedanism (as he called it) was one of the most widespread religions (q.v.) in the world of his day, he does not discuss it as a separate tradition within his *Lectures on the Philosophy of Religion* (q.v.). It is mentioned as a universalized version of the religion of sublimity, or Judaism (q.v.), in which one god (q.v.) as absolute power creates the world of nature (q.v.) and is honored through submission and obedience. *See also* SUBLIME.

ITALY. While Italian students of Hegel began to translate abridgements of his work in the decades after his death, it was Francesco de Sanctis in the 1850s who saw that the humanism of Hegel's aesthetics (q.v.) could mediate between the formalism of the classics and the naturalism of the romantics (q.v.). About the same time Bertrando Spaventa read Hegel's *Logic* (q.v.) as the work of a transcendental subject. These thinkers inspired Benedetto Croce and Giovanni Gentile (qq.v.), who dominated Hegelian thought in Italy during the first half of the 20th century. In the years between the two world wars, Galvano della Volpe (who traced Hegel's thought back to both the Enlightenment [q.v.] and the mystic Meister Eckhart) and Enrico de Negri (who translated the *Phenomenology of Spirit*) developed new interpretations of Hegel's thought. More recently, the study of Hegel has been promoted through the lectures and publications of the Istituto Italiano per gli Studi Filosofici of Naples, and the work of Remo Bodei at Pisa, Franco Chiereghin at Padua, Domenico Losurdo at Urbino, and Valerio Verra at Rome, among others. *See also* TRANSCENDENTAL IDEALISM.

– J –

JACOBI, FRIEDRICH (1743–1819). Jacobi appealed to an immediate knowing or intuition (qq.v.) that works behind the conditioned knowledge (q.v.) of reason and the understanding (qq.v.), so that reason is basically conceived as instinct and feeling. By exalting the singular and particular above the concept (qq.v.), he gives expression to the subjective beauty (q.v.) of Protestantism. Hegel points out, however, that everything that is known immediately has been mediated by one's upbringing and that the being (q.v.) of what is known is mediated by its idea (q.v.) and vice versa, so that the "immediate" (q.v.) unity of being and idea is in principle mediated. In addition, without mediation (q.v.), there is no way of discriminating between good and bad, or between adequate and inadequate intuitions. *See also FAITH AND KNOWLEDGE*; HISTORY OF PHILOSOPHY; PROTESTANT REFORMATION; ROMANTICISM.

JAPAN. When Tokyo University was founded in 1877, the American Harvard graduate, E. F. Fenollosa, became the first lecturer on Western philosophy, focusing on German idealism and British 19th-century empiricism. He was followed by the Germans, L. Busse and R. Koeber. By the turn of the century Hegel's *Encyclopedia of the Philosophical Sciences* (q.v.) was being translated. After a period when Immanuel Kant (q.v.) drew the most attention, Hegel returned to prominence during the 1930s and into the postwar period. The most original and productive philosophers have been Nishida Kitaro and Tanabe Hajime (qq.v.), both of whom integrated Hegelian dialectic with Zen Buddhism (qq.v.).

JENA. An inheritance from his father enabled Hegel to leave his position at Frankfurt am Main (q.v.) at the end of 1800 and move to Jena, which, with Johann Wolfgang von Goethe (q.v.) the minister of education and culture in the duchy of Saxe-Weimar (q.v.), had become the center of German intellectual life. Both Karl L. Reinhold and Johann Fichte (qq.v.) had taught there, and in 1801, Johann Herder, Friedrich Schelling, Friedrich Schiller (qq.v.), and the brothers August Wilhelm and Friedrich Schlegel made a vital academic community. Hegel moved quickly to qualify as a private instructor, publishing a work on the *Difference between Fichte's and Schelling's System of Philosophy* (q.v.), defending a set of paradoxical theses, and writing a dissertation (q.v.), *On the Orbits of the Planets*. Until Schelling departed for Würzberg in 1803, the two collaborated in the *Critical Journal of Philosophy* (q.v.), although Hegel wrote the bulk of the material. He lectured on natural law, logic and metaphysics, philosophy of nature and spirit, mathematics, and the history of philosophy (qq.v.), while promising a textbook for student use. At the same time he explored physics, geology, chemistry (qq.v.), physiology, and medicine, becoming a member of several societies for the study of nature. The textbook he had promised for so long turned into the *Phenomenology of Spirit* (q.v.), which he completed just as Napoleon (q.v.) was defeating the Prussians and Austrians at the Battle of Jena and the presence of French troops was disrupting life in the city. Early in 1807, Johanna Burkhardt, the chambermaid in Hegel's residence, gave birth to his natural son, Ludwig. Without expectation of a salary from the university at Jena or of an academic appointment anywhere else, Hegel accepted a position as editor of a French-style newspaper in Bamberg (q.v.). *See also* FRIES, JAKOB; JENA DRAFTS FOR A SYSTEM; *LECTURES ON THE HISTORY OF PHILOSOPHY*; LECTURES ON THE PHILOSOPHY OF NATURE.

JENA DRAFTS FOR A SYSTEM (JENAER SYSTEMENTWÜRFE). In notes for his lectures (q.v.) and draft manuscripts intended for publication, Hegel, during the Jena (q.v.) years, worked on developing a systematic philosophy, starting with logic and metaphysics (qq.v.), then moving on to a philosophy of nature and a philosophy of spirit (qq.v.). He attempted various strategies for organizing the material. In the "System of Ethical Life," he counterposed the move from intuition to concept (qq.v.) against the move from concept to intuition. In the manuscript on logic and philosophy of nature of 1804–05 he adopted a method of construction (which would break up a topic into its parts) and proof (which would show how the parts were integrated through natural processes) that was derived from Immanuel Kant's (q.v.) *Metaphysical Foundations of Natural Science* and Friedrich Schelling's (q.v.) *Ideas for a Philosophy of Nature*. His dissatisfaction with these ventures meant that none were completed. He turned instead to writing the *Phenomenology of Spirit* (q.v.). Much of the content of this Jena material, though not its form, was later incorporated into the systematic structure of the *Science of Logic* and *Encyclopedia* (qq.v.), and some of the lecture material was used in preparing the additions (q.v.) to the early collected works. *See also* SYSTEM.

JESUS. While at Bern (q.v.) and as part of his plan for a religion (q.v.) of the people, Hegel wrote a life of Jesus that portrays him as a teacher and exemplar of human morality (q.v.), in accordance with reason (q.v.) itself as the Godhead. All mention of miracles (including the resurrection) is omitted. A second text showed how both the misunderstanding of his disciples and the context in which Jesus taught contributed to making Christianity (q.v.) a positive religion, based on authority. By the time of the Berlin *Lectures on the Philosophy of Religion* (q.v.), Jesus embodies uniquely the reconciliation of humanity with God (q.v.), a reconciliation that is achieved through renunciation and surrender. *See also* FRANKFURT AM MAIN; TÜBINGEN.

JOURNAL FOR SCIENTIFIC CRITICISM (*JAHRBUCH FÜR WISSENSCHAFTLICHE KRITIK*). Although Hegel was not elected to the Royal Prussian Academy of the Sciences, largely because of the opposition of Friedrich Schleiermacher (q.v.), his disciples and students worked with him to found in 1826 a Society for Scientific Criticism, with three divisions: philosophical, natural scientific, and philosophical-historical. Initially Eduard Gans (q.v.) took primary responsibility for editing the society's journal, the *Jahrbuch für Wissenschaftliche Kritik*. To this journal Hegel contributed essays on Karl Wilhelm von Humboldt, Karl Wilhelm Ferdinand Solger, Johann Georg Hamaan, and Karl Friedrich Göschel. It continued to be influential during the five years after Hegel's death but then entered into a period of decline, passing out of existence in the 1840s. In 1838, it was replaced as the active journal for discussion of Hegelianism by Arnold Ruge's (q.v.) and Theodor Echtermeyer's *Hallische Jahrbuch,* which, under attack from the reactionary right, soon became the organ of left-wing Hegelianism (q.v.). *See also* BERLIN; PRUSSIA.

JOWETT, BENJAMIN (1817–1893). In 1844, the 27-year-old tutor at Balliol College, Oxford, went to Germany to discuss with Johann Eduard Erdmann (q.v.) how best to approach Hegel's philosophy. On his return, he undertook with Frederick Temple a translation of the *Encyclopedia Logic* (q.v.), which was never completed. Although he later turned his attention to Greek philosophy, he introduced a generation of English philosophers to the study of Hegel, including Thomas Hill Green, Edward Caird, Bernard Bosanquet, and William Wallace (qq.v.).

JUDAISM. By citing the phrase "the fear of the Lord is the beginning of wisdom" in his discussion of master/slave (q.v.) in the *Phenomenology of Spirit* (q.v.), Hegel suggests that that analysis could be applied to the experience of the Jews. However, in the *Lectures on the Philosophy of Religion* (q.v.), Judaism, together with Greek religion (q.v.), is a development out of natural religion (q.v.) in that the spiritual now dominates the natural. God (q.v.) as absolute power and wisdom creates the natural order and is worshipped as the sublime (q.v.). In Judaism, he establishes a particular relationship with a particular people and a particular land. In Islam (q.v.), however, the divine authority is universalized to all people. Over the years, Hegel altered the location of his discussion of Judaism within his lectures. In 1821 and 1824, it precedes his discussion of the Greek religion of beauty (q.v.); in 1827, it comes after. However, in 1831, it is part of the transition from natural religion to the religion of freedom (Greek and Roman), following the discussion of Parsee religion (q.v.) and preceding Phoenician religion (which was a new addition) and Egyptian religion (q.v.). *See also* FACKENHEIM, EMIL; GANS, EDUARD; HESS, MOSES; ROSENZWEIG, FRANZ.

JUDGMENT (DAS URTEIL). The German term *Urteil* can be read etymologically as "primordial parts"; so Hegel reads judgment as dividing a concept (q.v.) into its universal and its singular (qq.v.) parts. Starting from the simple judgment in which a universal is predicated of some singular, Hegel in the *Science of Logic* (q.v.) shows how the inability of each judgment form to express its necessary conditions requires the introduction of more sophisticated forms. In this way he proceeds through the 12 types of judgment found in Immanuel Kant (q.v.) and traditional logic, concluding with necessary modal judgments. Since modal necessity (q.v.) must be mediated or justified, the discussion of judgment inevitably moves on to syllogism (q.v.) and proof.

– **K** –

KAINZ, HOWARD P. Working from the fundamental paradoxical unity of subject and object, Kainz argues that this and other paradoxes can be handled by a dialectic (q.v.) that is dynamic and demonstrable and involves the nonvicious circularity of mutual implication. Hegel's achievement lies in using this dialectic central to paradox to elaborate a detailed (though dated) system (q.v.). *See also* CIRCLE OF CIRCLES; UNITED STATES.

KANT, IMMANUEL (1724–1804). The philosophy of Immanuel Kant set the stage for the development of German idealism (q.v.). By placing the objectivity (q.v.) of our knowledge (q.v.) in the transcendental subject, rather than the givens of sense, and by moving metaphysics (q.v.) from the sphere of knowledge to the presuppositions of moral action (q.v.), he transposed the focus of philosophical reflection (q.v.) from the cosmos to the universal and necessary (qq.v.) conditions of human thinking and willing (qq.v.). His analyses of scientific knowledge and moral action offered a clear conceptual outline of their conditions. But he could not show the inherent rationality that integrated those various conditions into a coherent framework. To be sure, in his *Critique of Judgment* (q.v.), he discusses the kinds of integration found in art (q.v.) and biological organisms, but these remain subjective constructions rather than objective conditions. In the attempt to find a more systematic approach, Karl Reinhold and Johann Fichte (qq.v.) derived Kant's conclusions, first from consciousness (q.v.) and then from the fundamental "deed-act" of the subject. The subjectivity (q.v.) of this transcendental philosophy, as it was called, evoked in Friedrich Schelling (q.v.) and in the young Hegel the response that subjects are willy-nilly existing in an objective world and so already have immediate (q.v.) contact with it. The counterpart of transcendental idealism (q.v.), they claimed, was a philosophy of nature (q.v.), which shows the inherent rationality of natural phenomena; the two disciplines describe two sides of an indifferent and undifferentiated absolute (q.v.). Friedrich Jacobi and Friedrich Schleiermacher (qq.v.) looked for the ultimate that grounds both cognition (q.v.) and action in intuited faith (q.v.) or the feeling of absolute dependence. As Hegel matured, he took a more measured approach to Kant's critical philosophy, moral philosophy, and *Critique of Judgment* (qq.v.), balancing Kant's idealism (q.v.) with the empiricism (q.v.) of Aristotle (q.v.). *See also* ANTINOMIES; EPISTEMOLOGY; MORALITY; OBJECTIVITY.

KANT'S CRITICAL PHILOSOPHY. More radically than in the empiricism (q.v.) of David Hume (q.v.), Immanuel Kant (q.v.) separates the singulars of perception (qq.v.) from the universals of thinking (qq.v.). Human finitude (q.v.) is defined by the fact that thought and sensation, united in experience (q.v.), are separated into two fixed and contrary sides: the categories (q.v.) of the understanding (q.v.) are universal and possible, while the givens of sense are singular and actual. This separation reduces sensations to appearance (q.v.) and reality to the presuppositions required for moral action (q.v.). For Hegel, however, when we recognize limits (q.v.) in our experience, we have already moved beyond (q.v.) them; the task of philosophy lies in comprehending how the contrary moments of limit and beyond are both distinguished and united. He found his inspiration for this approach in the antinomies (q.v.) of the Transcendental Dialectic (q.v.) in which Kant argues that contradictions (q.v.) are inevitable whenever the understanding goes beyond experience to think metaphysical reality. In addition, Kant's theory of transcendental imagination (q.v.), which unites the universals of reason with the multiplicity of sensation, sets the stage for an Hegelian understanding of reason (q.v.) in which contradictions are both necessary and resolvable. *See also* ACTUALITY; *FAITH AND KNOWLEDGE*; FICHTE, JOHANN; HISTORY OF PHILOSOPHY; KANT'S *CRITIQUE OF JUDGMENT*; KANT'S MORAL PHILOSOPHY; MORALITY; POSSIBILITY.

KANT'S *CRITIQUE OF JUDGMENT.* For Hegel, this is the most speculative of Immanuel Kant's (q.v.) works. The intuitive understanding (q.v.) grasps the unity of both beauty and organic nature (qq.v.), in that contingent particulars are determined through the universal (q.v.). Unfortunately, Kant's critical philosophy (q.v.) prevents him from recognizing here the seeds of speculative reason (q.v.). Instead, his radical separation of thought and sense leaves art (q.v.) as just the expression of genius and imagination (q.v.), and the organic in nature as simply the subjective way we must think about its causal character. *See also* HISTORY OF PHILOSOPHY; KANT'S MORAL PHILOSOPHY; SCHELLING, FRIEDRICH.

KANT'S MORAL PHILOSOPHY. Immanuel Kant's (q.v.) thesis that freedom (q.v.) consists in the will (q.v.) determining its own laws makes an important contribution to philosophy. Hegel, however, criticizes the categorical imperative as too abstract. Unjust and immoral actions can equally satisfy the criterion of noncontradiction, since any application of the principle must presuppose some definite content or fixed standard that cannot itself be justified. *See also* CONSCIENCE*;* DUTY; HISTORY OF PHILOSOPHY; KANT'S CRITICAL PHILOSOPHY; KANT'S *CRITIQUE OF JUDGMENT*; MORALITY.

KAUFMANN, WALTER (1921–1980). Kaufmann's *Hegel: An Interpretation*, first published in 1965, challenged traditional interpretations of Hegel as a dry academic. Not only did he provide details of Hegel's turbulent early life, but he argued that the purported dialectical method (qq.v.) was really "a vision of the world, of man, and of history which emphasizes development through conflict, the moving power of human passions, which produce wholly unintended results, and the irony of sudden reversals." In his writing, however, Hegel sought to impose an alien and ineffective order on an exuberant range of topics and interests. *See also* UNITED STATES.

KIERKEGAARD, SØREN (1813–1855). Introduced to Hegel's thought by his tutor H. L. Martensen and the works of Philipp Marheineke and Johann Eduard Erdmann (qq.v.), Kierkegaard set the stance of the existential individual, confronted with ultimate decisions among radically different modes of life, over against Hegel's comprehensive understanding (q.v.) of the total history of spirit (q.v.). Free choice cannot build on past experience (q.v.) but rather faces an empty abyss with no appeal to absolutes (q.v.). And Christian faith (qq.v.) does not comprehend the essence of the perennial religious quest of humanity. Rather, an individual leaps in an instant to the universal truth (q.v.) of his or her singular existence (qq.v.). *See also* EXISTENCE; TOTALITY.

KNOWLEDGE (DAS WISSEN). Hegel distinguishes knowledge, which is the certainty of truth (q.v.), from cognition (q.v.), which involves subjective concepts (qq.v.) grasping objective actuality (qq.v.). The *Phenomenology of Spirit* (q.v.) explores the principles of various claims to knowledge, only to discover that in practice they fail to achieve what they anticipate. Absolute knowing (q.v.) has as its principle the claim that any self-certain knowledge, when put into practice, will find that it has to learn from the experience (q.v.) of its failures. The German word here is etymologically related to the English "wisdom." *See also* IMMEDIATE KNOWING.

KOJÈVE, ALEXANDRE (1902–1968). Kojève gave a series of lectures at the École Pratique des Hautes Études in Paris from 1933 to 1939. Among his students were Jean-Paul Sartre and Eric Weil (qq.v.), Raymond Aron, Georges Bataille, Georges Fessard, Jacques Lacan, Maurice Merleau-Ponty, and Raymond Queneau. Based on a reading of the master-slave (q.v.) and struggle to the death (q.v.) in the *Phenomenology of Spirit* (q.v.), his Hegel espouses a historical humanism, in which the human encounter with the negativity of death replaces the positivity of Christian theology and provides the foundation for human liberty. The Battle of Jena (q.v.) marked the fulfillment of this process and so, in writing the *Phenomenology of Spirit*, Hegel celebrated the end of history (q.v.). *See also* FRANCE; FREEDOM.

KOLB, DAVID. In Kolb's *The Critique of Pure Modernity*, Hegel, like Martin Heidegger (q.v.), analyzes the nature of modern society without identifying with it. When logical thought as the absolute idea (q.v.) comprehends its world, it does not move into some other world but rather grasps the way we are appropriated into any world. Nonetheless, Hegel fails because we live in a world that is multiform and lacks totality (q.v.), so that we have no foothold by which to reach a transcendental self-understanding. *See also* TRANSCENDENTAL IDEALISM; UNITED STATES.

KRUG, WILHELM TRAUGOTT (1770–1842). Although elected to Immanuel Kant's (q.v.) chair in Königsberg on Kant's death, Krug moved on to Leipzig in 1809. He attacked Friedrich Schelling's (q.v.) transcendental idealism (q.v.) because its systematic philosophy could not pretend to deduce everything, including Krug's own pen, from its first principles. Instead, Krug argued that consciousness had to take account of the unexplained given. This approach was subjected to Hegel's sarcasm in the first number of *Critical Journal of Philosophy* (q.v.).

– L –

LANGUAGE (DIE SPRACHE). In speaking, individuals objectify their inner selves in terms which can be heard and understood by others, so that what is most singular becomes universal (qq.v.). Language is thereby the medium or catalyst that integrates the social realm, or spirit (q.v.). In that the spoken word disappears and is reconstituted in the thinking (q.v.) of the listener, it embodies the dynamic of spirit, which lives by continually reconstituting itself out of the demise of its former states. Writing petrifies this dynamic into a fixed and permanent form, although alphabet scripts do retain some trace of the oral, in a way that hieroglyphs do not. *See also* IMAGINATION; *PHILOSOPHY OF SPIRIT*; PSYCHOLOGY; REPRESENTATION.

LAUER, QUENTIN. In Lauer's reading, what is most characteristically human for Hegel is rational thought. Indeed, reality is inconceivable except as the product of infinite (q.v.) thought. And while rational thinking (q.v.) does not guarantee rational living, one cannot live rationally without thinking rationally. So philosophy's task is to grasp in thought the structure of rationality. *See also* UNITED STATES.

LAW (DAS GESETZ). For justice to function in civil society (q.v.), it must be known by all and be applicable to all. This finds expression in law, which should have rational coherence and be applied to individual cases through the courts. Ultimately, law can only be effective if it enshrines the customs and mores of the ethical order (q.v.). In the Greek world, the law's authority was grounded in the divine order, even while it was being put into practice by the political authorities. Sophocles' *Antigone* (q.v.) traces the tragedy (q.v.) when the human and divine laws come in conflict. In the modern world, it is the constitution (q.v.) that establishes the authority of positive law. Law, however, functions in another sense as the way understanding and reason (qq.v.) categorize the universality of relationships. It therefore plays a role in observing reason, the laws of thought, the law of the heart, law-giving reason, and law-testing reason (qq.v.). *See also* CATEGORY; *PHILOSOPHY OF RIGHT*; RIGHT; UNIVERSAL.

LAW-GIVING REASON (DIE GESETZGEBENDE VERNUNFT). In the *Phenomenology of Spirit* (q.v.), once the claims of the spiritual animal kingdom (q.v.) break down, reason (q.v.) appeals to the category (q.v.) of universal law (qq.v.). The heart of the matter, or *Sache selbst* (q.v.), is what holds for all, not what is peculiar to individuals. However, to be genuinely applicable, universal laws must take account of contingent circumstances, so the universality of the category is lost. Reason can only test the laws for consistency. *See* LAW-TESTING REASON.

LAW OF THE HEART (DAS GESETZ DES HERZENS). Once reason (q.v.) in the *Phenomenology of Spirit* (q.v.) abandons the simple category of pleasure (qq.v.), it appeals to the law (q.v.) that everyone should follow the dictates of his own heart. When this is put into practice, however, the law takes on a life of its own and the heart finds itself at odds with the universal order. In recognizing that any simple affirmation of its own over against the universal is evil, the heart is led into seeing everyone else's actions as a similar sort of self-conceit. In consequence, the individual recognizes that he or she should become virtuous and that an action (q.v.) should express what is universally right, even though the world itself is perverted. *See also* VIRTUE.

LAWS OF THOUGHT. Hegel places his discussion of the traditional laws of thought—identity (q.v.), excluded middle, noncontradiction, sufficient reason—within the doctrine of essence (q.v.) of the *Science of Logic* (q.v.). He shows that identity presupposes difference (q.v.); that reflection (q.v.) on difference leads to diversity, opposition, and contradiction (qq.v.) (which is a form of the law [q.v.] of excluded middle). Since a contradiction cannot stand, it requires the search for a ground (q.v.) or sufficient reason. Identity and the various forms of difference Hegel calls "determinations of reflection." In the *Phenomenology of Spirit* (q.v.), the use of the laws of thought as categories (q.v.) that observing reason (q.v.) can use in its quest for knowledge (q.v.) fails to get at the truth (q.v.) of the integrated subject.

LAW-TESTING REASON (DIE GESETZPRÜFENDE VERNUNFT). In the *Phenomenology of Spirit* (q.v.), reason's (q.v.) use of categories (q.v.) to get at truth (q.v.) ends with it simply testing laws to ensure that they do not contradict themselves. However, any law (q.v.) on its own can be shown to be self-consistent, even though it could be incompatible with other laws. The result is an inversion: rather than reason determining what is right through its use of the category of consistency, it recognizes that the right (q.v.) is valid on its own, and reason simply uses its resources to gain an understanding of this substantial truth. What really holds for all, then, is the realm of spirit (q.v.), a deliberately ambiguous term: at this stage it can mean both what is divine, and what is the underlying ethical life (q.v.) of a community. *See also* INVERTED WORLD; LAW-GIVING REASON.

LECTURES. Once Hegel was established as full professor in Heidelberg and then Berlin (qq.v.), his attention turned from writing out his system (q.v.) in full to the lectures he gave to his students. Both the *Encyclopedia of the Philosophical Sciences* and the *Philosophy of Right* (qq.v.) were outlines in thesis form with the intention that they would be expanded and discussed orally in class. As time went on, he gave lectures on aesthetics, the philosophy of religion, the philosophy of world history, and the history of philosophy (qq.v.) even though these had no published manuals. The early editors of Hegel's works assembled Hegel's lecture manuscripts and student notes for these courses, as well as those on the science of logic, the philosophy of nature, the philosophy of spirit, and philosophy of right (qq.v.), in which the lecture material was added to the appropriate paragraph in the published outline. In each case, however, the editors took material from a variety of semesters and edited them into a single text. As a result, they were unable to maintain the specific systematic structure Hegel used, since he frequently rethought the framework each time he gave his lectures. Only in the last several decades have editions of single lecture series appeared, thanks to the leadership of Karl-Heinz Ilting, Walter Jaeschke, and others. *See also* ADDITIONS.

LECTURES ON AESTHETICS. Hegel began lecturing on aesthetics (q.v.) in Heidelberg (1818) (q.v.) and continued offering courses in Berlin (q.v.) on four occasions (1820–21, 1823, 1826, and 1828–29). In the final set of lectures (q.v.), Hegel revised his previous schema of universal (q.v.) themes and particular (q.v.) art forms to add a third part that discussed individual works of art (q.v.). Hegel's student, Heinrich G. Hotho (q.v.), who was himself interested in aesthetics, edited student notes from the various lecture series (and other material) into a single text, based on Hegel's final organizational structure—despite the fact that he found the 1828–29 lectures not as profound as the earlier ones. The first version of Hotho's text was translated by Francis P. B. Osmaston (1916–20); the second version by Thomas Malcolm Knox (1975). Georg Lasson died before completing an edition based on the 1826 lectures. In 1995, a student transcript from 1820 to 1821 was edited by Helmut Schneider, and in 1998, the notes taken by Hotho in 1823 were published separately by Annemarie Gethmann-Siefert as the "Philosophy of Art." *See also* ARCHITECTURE; BEAUTY; CLASSICAL ART; COMEDY; DRAMA; EPIC; LYRIC; MUSIC; PAINTING; POETRY; ROMANTIC ART; SCULPTURE; SYMBOLIC ART; TRAGEDY.

LECTURES ON LOGIC AND METAPHYSICS. Hegel announced lectures (q.v.) on logic and metaphysics (qq.v.) six times in Jena (q.v.) and for the summer semester of 1817 in Heidelberg (q.v.). Once he reached Berlin (q.v.), he lectured on logic every summer semester from 1819 to 1831. In both Heidelberg and Berlin he used the paragraphs from the *Encyclopedia* text as a base, shifting to the second edition in 1826 and the third edition in 1831. Leopold von Henning (q.v.), working from his own notes from 1819 and 1820, his memory, and notes from Heinrich Hotho, Karl Michelet (qq.v.), and others, edited this lecture material into the additions (q.v.) of the first and second edition of Hegel's works. Student transcripts from Jena in 1801–02 (edited by Klaus Düsing) and Heidelberg in 1817 (edited by Karen Gloy) have recently been published, and the transcript by Hegel's son, Karl, from the summer semester of 1831 is being prepared for publication. *See also ENCYCLOPEDIA LOGIC*; LECTURES ON THE *ENCYCLOPEDIA*; REMARKS.

LECTURES ON THE *ENCYCLOPEDIA*. Hegel gave lectures (q.v.) based on the full text of the *Encyclopedia of the Philosophical Sciences* (q.v.) in Heidelberg (q.v.) during the winter semester of 1816–17 and the summer semester of 1818, and again in Berlin during the winter semesters of 1818–19 and 1826–27.

LECTURES ON THE HISTORY OF PHILOSOPHY. Although the history of philosophy (q.v.) had not been part of the traditional curriculum, Hegel introduced lectures (q.v.) on the subject in Jena (q.v.) during the 1805–06 winter semester and offered the course twice in Heidelberg (q.v.) (1816–17, 1817–18). The lectures continued in Berlin (q.v.), five hours per week: in 1819, 1820–21, 1823–24, 1825–26, 1827–28, and 1829–30. He had just begun a seventh series when he died. Karl Michelet (q.v.) edited the student notes as well as manuscript material that reached back to the Jena years for the first and second edition of Hegel's works. The second edition was translated into English by Elizabeth S. Haldane and Frances H. Simson in 1895. Johannes Hoffmeister began a critical edition in 1940, but no more than the introduction appeared in print. From 1986 to 1996, Pierre Garniron and Walter Jaeschke edited the 1825–26 lectures from five transcripts, as well as versions of the introduction from all seven Berlin series. This is being translated into English by Robert Brown and others. *See also* ARISTOTLE; CHURCH FATHERS; DESCARTES, RENÉ; FICHTE, JOHANN; HERACLITUS; HISTORY OF PHILOSOPHY; HOBBES, THOMAS; HUME, DAVID; JACOBI, FRIEDRICH; KANT, IMMANUEL; KANT'S CRITICAL PHILOSOPHY; KANT'S *CRITIQUE OF JUDGMENT*; KANT'S MORAL PHILOSOPHY; LEIBNIZ, GOTTFRIED; LOCKE, JOHN; PHILOSOPHY; PLATO; PROCLUS; PROTESTANT REFORMATION; SCHELLING, FRIEDRICH; SOCRATES; SPINOZA, BARUCH; THALES.

LECTURES ON THE PHILOSOPHY OF NATURE. Although Hegel announced lectures on the philosophy of nature and spirit (qq.v.) four times in Jena (q.v.) from the winter semester of 1805–06 to the summer semester of 1807, only the summer 1806 course is known to have been given. Hegel's manuscript for this course has been published both by Johannes Hoffmeister (1931) and in the critical edition (1976). Apart from lectures on the *Encyclopedia* (q.v.) as a whole, he then lectured on the topic six times in Berlin (q.v.): 1819–20, 1821–22, 1823–24, 1825–26, 1828, and 1830. Karl Michelet (q.v.) collected material from all of these courses, including the manuscript from 1805–06, sometimes putting individual sentences from different years into a single paragraph, to produce the additions (q.v.) of the first and second editions of Hegel's works. Manfred Gies has published a transcript from the 1819–20 lectures. *See also* REMARKS.

LECTURES ON THE PHILOSOPHY OF RELIGION. In Berlin (q.v.) on four different occasions Hegel lectured on the philosophy of religion (q.v.), a subject that had not previously been part of the curriculum in German universities. In all cases, he started with a discussion of the concept of religion (q.v.), then turned to specific religions, providing a philosophical framework to justify the order of discussion, and concluded with what he called "The Consummate Religion," or Christianity (q.v.). Philipp Marheineke (q.v.) collated student notes from the 1824, 1827, and 1831 lectures (q.v.) with a manuscript from 1821 for the first edition of Hegel's works. A second edition, in which Bruno Bauer (q.v.) also participated, was translated by Ebenezer B. Spiers and J. Burdon Sanderson. However, the conceptual organization Hegel used altered considerably over the years (see in particular under JUDAISM). So the most recent editions, in both German (Walter Jaeschke) and English (Peter C. Hodgson et al.), reproduce the manuscript together with separate transcripts of the 1824 and 1827 lecture series. The lectures show Hegel's broad familiarity with literature on the religious practices of the Arctic, Africa, China, and India, as well as the ancient religions of Persia, Greece, Israel, and Rome. *See also* BUDDHISM; CHINESE RELIGION; EGYPTIAN RELIGION; GREEK RELIGION; INDIAN RELIGION; ISLAM; NATURAL RELIGION; PARSEE RELIGION; ROMAN RELIGION.

LECTURES ON THE PHILOSOPHY OF RIGHT. Shortly after the appearance of the *Encyclopedia of the Philosophical Sciences* (q.v.), Hegel began giving a separate course on "Natural Law (q.v.) and Political Science." In his lectures (q.v.) at Heidelberg (1817–18) and Berlin (qq.v.) (1818–19, 1819–20), he expanded and developed this material in preparation for the publication of his *Philosophy of Right* (q.v.). Thereafter, he used this larger text as a basis for courses in 1821–22, 1822–23, and 1824–25. He handed the course over to his assistants, Leopold von Henning, Eduard Gans, and Karl Michelet (qq.v.), until the crown prince expressed displeasure with Gans's lectures and Hegel had to reassume responsibility just before his death in 1831. In the first and second edition of Hegel's works, Gans relied on transcripts from 1822–23 and 1824–25 for his additions (q.v.). In 1972–74, Karl-Heinz Ilting published transcripts from 1818–19, 1822–23, and 1824–25. Then in 1983 transcripts from the Heidelberg lectures of 1817–18 were edited by both Ilting and a group from the Hegel Archiv (q.v.), and a manuscript from 1819–20 was edited by Karl Düsing. Michael Stewart and Peter Hodgson have translated the 1817–18 series into English. *See also* REMARKS.

LECTURES ON THE PHILOSOPHY OF SUBJECTIVE SPIRIT. Although Hegel announced lectures (q.v.) on the philosophy of nature and spirit (qq.v.) four times in Jena (q.v.) from the winter semester of 1805–06 to the summer semester of 1807, only the summer 1806 course is known to have been given. Hegel's manuscript for this course has been published both by Johannes Hoffmeister (1931) and in the critical edition (1976). Apart from lectures on the *Encyclopedia* (q.v.) as a whole, he then lectured on subjective spirit (q.v.) (which is to be distinguished from objective spirit [q.v.] or philosophy of right) five times in Berlin (q.v.): 1820, 1822, 1825, 1827–28, and 1829–30 and announced in the *Philosophy of Right* (q.v.) his intention of elaborating this part of the system (q.v.) further. Ludwig Boumann used manuscript material and student transcripts for his additions (q.v.) to the *Encyclopedia* paragraphs in the first and second editions of Hegel's works. In 1978, Michael Petry (q.v.) included excerpts from transcripts of the 1822 and 1825 lectures in his bilingual (German and English) edition of the *Philosophy of Subjective Spirit*. Then, in 1994, Franz Hespe and Burkhard Tuschling published an edition of the 1827–28 lectures, based on notes taken by Johann Eduard Erdmann (q.v.) and Ferdinand Walter. *See also* REMARKS.

LECTURES ON THE PHILOSOPHY OF WORLD HISTORY. Initially Hegel lectured on world history (q.v.) as the conclusion to his *Philosophy of Right* (q.v.). In the winter semester of 1822–23, however, for four lectures (q.v.) a week he expanded on the principles and the application of philosophical history, and he repeated the lecture course four more times: in 1824–25, 1826–27, 1828–29, and 1830–31. Manuscripts survive from his lectures for the introduction in 1828 and 1830, as well as student notes from all five lecture series. The early editions by Eduard Gans (1837) and (after Gans's death) Hegel's son, Karl (1840, translated by John Sibree in 1899, introduction translated by Robert Hartman in 1953, and Leo Rauch in 1988) sought to provide a single sequential text and so collated and abridged material from various lecture series and a few manuscripts. In 1917, Georg Lasson brought out an edition that contained much more detail on world history itself, and he supplemented this with new material in 1920 and 1930. In 1955, Johannes Hoffmeister prepared a new edition of the introductory lectures, organized around Hegel's own manuscripts, and this has been translated by Hugh Barr Nisbet (1975). Because all of these editions collated material from different lecture series, they omitted the organizing principles that structured each one, since Hegel rethought the systematic framework whenever he gave the course. Now, in the critical edition, we have the manuscripts from 1828 and 1830 (1995). In addition, Karl-Heinz Ilting, Karl Brehmer, and Hoo Nam Seelmann have edited the 1822–23 lectures, based on the student transcripts of Karl von Griesheim, Heinrich Hotho (q.v.), and Friedrich von Kehler (1996). *See also* BERLIN; CHINESE HISTORY; EGYPTIAN HISTORY; GEOGRAPHY; GERMANIC HISTORY; GREEK HISTORY; INDIAN HISTORY; PERSIAN HISTORY; PHILOSOPHY OF WORLD HISTORY; ROMAN HISTORY.

LEFT-WING HEGELIANS. As outsiders, Friedrich Carové, August Cieszkowski, and Moses Hess (qq.v.) in their different ways used Hegelian philosophy to advocate a change in practice. In seeing the goal to be attained as the reconciliation of religion and politics, however, they were left behind by those who saw Hegelianism as heralding a new humanistic age, in which the human present and future replaces a transcendent God (q.v.) as the focus of commitment. These latter—Arnold Ruge, David Strauss, Bruno Bauer, Ludwig Feuerbach, and Max Stirner, as well as the young Karl Marx and Friedrich Engels (qq.v.)—have traditionally been called the left-wing or young Hegelians (q.v.). *See also* RELIGION IN THE YOUNG HEGELIANS.

LEGAL STATUS (DER RECHTSZUSTAND). In the *Phenomenology of Spirit* (q.v.), when the ethical order (q.v.) of an integrated community breaks down, the universal structure of law (q.v.) is identified with the rights of individual persons (q.v.). The legal order with its multiplicity of persons is held together by a single person who functions both as lord of the world and as an existing god. The sanction of law is implicitly affirmed by the individuals, even as they explicitly assert their independence. Culture (q.v.) emerges when this tension between universal law and singular interests becomes explicit and individuals come to be aware of themselves as alienated from their true selves. *See also* ABSTRACT RIGHT; ALIENATION; ANTIGONE; ROMAN HISTORY; SINGULAR; STOICISM; UNIVERSAL.

LEGISLATURE (DIE GESETZGEBENDE GEWALT). Within the constitution (q.v.) described in Hegel's *Philosophy of Right* (q.v.) the legislature has responsibility for passing laws (q.v.) and approving taxes, on the advice of the executive (q.v.) and for final action (q.v.) by the monarch (q.v.). Because they mediate between the private interests of the individuals and the universal interests of society, the classes (q.v.) determine the legislative structure. The agricultural class, rooted in the family (q.v.) and holding property (q.v.) through inheritance, sits in one chamber; in the other, the middle class is represented by people appointed through the corporations (q.v.), associations, and communities found in civil society (q.v.). In this way the community at large participates in government not as isolated individuals in the mass but through the concrete interests and activities that have been formed out of their particular economic activities.

LEIBNIZ, GOTTFRIED WILHELM (1646–1716). In sharp contrast to the monism of Baruch Spinoza (q.v.), Leibniz (with John Locke [q.v.]) stressed the importance of multiplicity and particularity through his principle of the identity of indiscernibles, even though he then had to appeal to God's preestablished harmony to hold them together within an abstract unity. *See also* HISTORY OF PHILOSOPHY.

LIFE (DAS LEBEN). In Hegel's *Science of Logic* (q.v.), life describes a being whose subjective concept (q.v.) or principle overreaches (q.v.) and integrates objective reality to form a living individual. By uniting subjectivity with objectivity (qq.v.), it constitutes the basic form of the idea (q.v.). Organisms in nature (qq.v.), and particularly animals, offer instances of this logical structure. *See also* BODY (DER LEIB); BOTANY; ORGANICS; SOUL; ZOOLOGY.

LIMIT (DIE GRENZE). When something (q.v.) is qualitatively determined, it is defined by a limit. This means that it is finite (q.v.), for the limit becomes a barrier or limitation beyond (q.v.) which the thing becomes something else. *See also* DETERMINATION; INFINITE; QUALITY; *SCIENCE OF LOGIC*.

LOCKE, JOHN (1632–1704). Locke quite rightly saw that experience starts with particulars (q.v.), and that universals (q.v.) are the product of consciousness (q.v.). He failed, however, to establish the truth (q.v.) of universal representations (q.v.). *See also* EMPIRICISM; HISTORY OF PHILOSOPHY; LEIBNIZ, GOTTFRIED.

LOGIC (DIE LOGIK). In the *Phenomenology of Spirit* (q.v.), Hegel considers the claim that we can rationally know the human self by observing the laws of thought (q.v.), and he shows that these are both too formal and too diverse to capture the dynamic unity of the subject. In the *Science of Logic* (q.v.), however, he examines the most basic concepts (q.v.) that are fundamental to all thinking (q.v.). Each is first fixed and defined by the understanding (q.v.). Thought, however, dialectically (q.v.) moves over to other related concepts—contraries that are essential components of the original definition. Speculative reason (q.v.) then reflects on this network of meanings to determine how the two opposites require, yet are distinct from, each other. This new conceptual unity is in its turn fixed by the understanding. The concepts examined are not only those used in traditional logic—concept, judgment, and syllogism (qq.v.)—but also such basic categories (q.v.) as being, nothing, becoming, finite, quality, quantity, measure, essence, identity, difference, contradiction, ground, actuality, necessity, substantiality, causality, and reciprocity (qq.v.). The logic also considers concepts by which thought organizes its thinking of objects: mechanism, chemism, teleology, life, and cognition (qq.v.), and finally defines its own method (q.v.). *See also* ABSOLUTE IDEA; IDEA; METAPHYSICS; OBJECTIVITY; SUBJECTIVITY; TRANSITION.

LUKÁCS, GYÖRGY (1885–1971). From within the Marxist tradition, Lukács traces in *The Young Hegel* Hegel's intellectual development and finds that a crisis disrupted his ideals during the Frankfurt am Main (q.v.) years from which he recovered through an exploration of the political economy of Sir James D. Steuart (q.v.). As a result, he distanced himself from his predecessors by giving the dialectic (q.v.) a materialistic basis. Because he remained a philosopher within a capitalist society, however, the reconciliation he proposed could only be an expression of "false consciousness." *See also* CAPITALISM; MARX, KARL.

LYRIC (DAS LYRISCHE). In contrast to the objectivity of epic (qq.v.), lyric poetry (q.v.) is the self-expression of the poet's inner feelings. Through the use of appropriate images, meters, and such devices as alliteration, rhyme, and assonance, it gives a passion objective form, purifying it from accidental moods, while enriching it and making it fully self-conscious. *See also* AESTHETICS; ART; DRAMA; IMAGINATION.

– M –

MAGNITUDE (DIE GRÖSSE). This is Hegel's name for the second part of the first book (on being [q.v.]) of the *Science of Logic* (q.v.), although it is usually given its parenthetical name of "Quantity" (q.v.). The discussion emerges from the reciprocal relationship of attraction and repulsion (qq.v.) in that quantity in general is the combination of continuous and discrete magnitude. Discreteness requires a determinate quantity or quantum (q.v.), whereas continuity leads into an infinite (q.v.) series of quanta. Within the series, quanta are distinct from each other, and a particular relationship between two such quanta constitutes a ratio (q.v.) or proportion. The limit (q.v.) which defines both their difference and the nature of their relation to each other (called an "exponent" by the mathematicians) is really qualitative rather than quantitative. So while quality (q.v.) leads into quantity through the logic of being for self (q.v.), quantity leads into quality through the logic of ratio. Hegel notes that this necessity of a double transition (q.v.) is significant for understanding the scientific method (q.v.). *See also* CIRCLE OF CIRCLES; MATHEMATICS; SCIENCE.

MAN (DER MANN). In drawing a distinction between the genders, Hegel assigns to the masculine the self-consciousness (q.v.) of conceptual thought and responsibility for public order. In contrast to woman's (q.v.) commitment to the family and religion (qq.v.), man's life is centered on political, academic, and military matters. *See also* ANTIGONE; CONCEPT; THINKING.

MANIFEST RELIGION (DIE OFFENBARE RELIGION). *See* **CHRISTIANITY.**

MARCUSE, HERBERT (1898–1979). As a student of Martin Heidegger (q.v.), Marcuse found in Hegel's logic of life (qq.v.) the theoretical ground for understanding our human existence as historical. In light of the emergence of National Socialism in Germany, he then recognized that the key to Hegel's reason is the power of the negative, which (as Karl Marx [q.v.] saw) Hegel failed to follow through to its limits. "From this stage on, all thinking that does not testify to an awareness of the radical falsity of the established forms of life is faulty thinking." *See also* ADORNO, THEODOR; NEGATION OF NEGATION.

MARHEINEKE, PHILIPP (1780–1848). Along with his theological colleague, Karl Daub (q.v.), Marheineke, professor of theology in Berlin (q.v.), found the Hegelian philosophy better able to do justice to the speculative nature of Christianity (q.v.) than the theology of Friedrich Schleiermacher (q.v.). Actively associated with Eduard Gans (q.v.) and others in founding the *Journal for Scientific Criticism* (q.v.), he gave a eulogy at Hegel's funeral and edited Hegel's *Lectures on the Philosophy of Religion* (q.v.) for the collected works.

MARX, KARL (1818–1883). In his dissertation on Epicurus and Democritus (1841), Marx anticipated that Hegel's philosophy, like that of Aristotle (q.v.), would give way to materialism. Associated briefly with Arnold Ruge (q.v.), Marx turned against the young Hegelians (q.v.) because their challenge to Hegel remained at the level of theory. Practical action (q.v.), or praxis, both produces the alienated state of modern labor and provides the means for transforming society. Although Marx left philosophy behind to concentrate on economics, he nonetheless relied on an Hegelian understanding of the dialectic (q.v.) to explain the inherent dynamic of economic activity. *See also* ALIENATED LABOR; BLOCH, ERNST; CAPITALISM; ENGELS, FRIEDRICH; LUKÁCS, GYÖRGY.

MARX, WERNER. The idea of the *Phenomenology of Spirit* (q.v.), according to Marx, is the principle of self-consciousness (q.v.) which is able increasingly to overcome the opposition (q.v.) between knowledge (q.v.) and its object. Full liberation, however, requires the guidance and inspiration of the philosopher.

MASTER-SLAVE (HERRSCHAFT UND KNECHTSCHAFT). In the *Phenomenology of Spirit* (q.v.), Hegel suggests that one of the early moments in the process of self-knowledge occurs when the vanquished in battle submits completely to the victor rather than be put to death (q.v.). Masters gain self-awareness through being recognized by their slaves; they think of themselves as independent because dependent serfs both cater to their desires (q.v.) and protect them from the recalcitrance of natural things. Hegel describes how this initial assumption is turned upside down. Masters are really dependent on slaves to make explicit their sense of superiority. Slaves, on the other hand, first learn that life (q.v.) with its dynamic is more important than prestige; and then independently become aware of the living dynamic of their own life in the products of their labor. This section inspired Karl Marx's (q.v.) theory of alienated labor (q.v.), and has continued to play a major role in left-wing (q.v.) interpretations of Hegel. Alexandre Kojève's (q.v.) *Introduction to the Reading of Hegel* uses this discussion as the clue to Hegel's secret. *See also* INVERTED WORLD; KNOWLEDGE; RECOGNITION; SELF-CONSCIOUSNESS; STOICISM.

MATHEMATICS. Having taught mathematics in both Jena and Nürnberg (qq.v.), Hegel took the opportunity, in the *Science of Logic* (q.v.), to discuss the justification of the differential calculus, which uses infinitesimals. He points out that a proper justification would come from the concept of infinity (qq.v.) and distinguish between a determinate quantum (q.v.) and the alteration required as one moves from it towards the infinitely small or the infinite limit (q.v.). Since any alteration or becoming (q.v.) is not quantitative but rather qualitative, the concept of infinitesimals involves both quantity and quality (qq.v.).

McTAGGART, JOHN M. E. (1866–1925). A fellow of Trinity College, Cambridge, from 1891 to 1923, McTaggart wrote a commentary on the larger *Science of Logic* (q.v.) and developed a cosmology based on Hegelian methods of reasoning. For McTaggart, the dialectic (q.v.) is a process whereby one-sided abstractions need to be completed by their contrary complements and the two reconciled in a higher category. As a result, only the highest category—the Absolute Idea (q.v.)—has independent existence. *See also* BRITISH IDEALISM; INTERNAL RELATIONS.

MEASURE (DAS MASS). Hegel explores the logic of using quantities (q.v.) to measure things and their qualities (q.v.) in the *Science of Logic* (q.v.). Thought moves from measuring by means of some conventional ruler, to using ratios (q.v.) between features (as in measuring velocity and acceleration). Since those measurements reflect the external interests of the one measuring, thought then turns to measuring a real thing (q.v.) using a ratio between two of its qualities (as in specific weight, which is a proportion of weight to volume). Eventually Hegel discusses how gradual changes in quantitative ratios can transform the quality of a thing and so turn it into something (q.v.) else. (An example: by changing the ratio of nitrogen to hydrogen we can turn ammonia into hydrazine.) The reality or *Sache* (q.v.) that underlies these changes is, however, measureless; so thought moves on to exploring what this subsisting essence (q.v.) might be. *See also* ELECTIVE AFFINITY; NODAL LINE; QUANTITY INTO QUALITY.

MECHANICS (DIE MECHANIK). In the *Philosophy of Nature* (q.v.), Hegel develops the basic terms of mechanics out of the definitions of space and time (qq.v.). The combination of place and movement leads to the thought of inert matter, subject to thrust and free fall. The mechanical interaction of bodies then requires that each be its own center, even as all together move with reference to a more universal center. The conceptual framework for this understanding of natural phenomena was developed in the *Science of Logic* (q.v.) as mechanism (q.v.). *See also* BODY (DER KÖRPER); NEWTON, ISAAC.

MECHANISM (DER MECHANISMUS). A mechanical way of thinking (q.v.) about the objective world understands objects to be independent of, yet act and react on, each other. It expands into the thought of a mechanical system, whose independent parts are also mechanical systems, each unit both functioning independently on its own and, in consort with others, in relation to a more all-encompassing center. Natural mechanics (q.v.) instantiates this logical structure. *See also* CONCEPT; OBJECTIVITY; *SCIENCE OF LOGIC*.

MEDIATION (DIE VERMITTLUNG). Upon reflection (q.v.), any immediate transition (qq.v.) can be shown to be mediated, in that it is conditioned by its starting point and there will be a middle term that bridges the transition from the beginning (q.v.) to the result. Since the mediation that leads to a result may not necessarily be of the same order as the development that takes off from it, that new beginning can be considered as immediate with regard to the new context.

MEMORY (DIE GEDÄCHTNIS). As an activity of intelligence (q.v.), memory reproduces the dynamic of recollection (q.v.), but with respect to signs rather than to intuitions (q.v.) and images. A sign or word is connected to a meaning in the storehouse of the subconscious not only once, but consistently. In mechanical memory words can be rhymed off without thinking (q.v.), because meaning and word are united. The converse of this activity is the ability to think thoughts without consciously having to use words. *See also* IMAGINATION; LANGUAGE; PSYCHOLOGY; REPRESENTATION.

METAPHYSICS (DIE METAPHYSIK). In metaphysics, the philosopher uses thoughts to define what being (q.v.) in general, the soul (q.v.), the cosmos, and God (q.v.) really are. Traditional metaphysics took these subjects as given and ascribed predicates to them, relying on the law (q.v.) of noncontradiction. However, it left the predicates as simple, independent terms, collected together. For Hegel, the primary task is to explore the predicates themselves to determine how they are intrinsically related to each other. Since thinking (q.v.) grasps the universal (q.v.) significance of what is sensed and experienced, such an exploration investigates the ultimate principles of reality. So his logic (q.v.) fulfills the function of traditional metaphysics. *See also SCIENCE OF LOGIC.*

METHOD (DIE METHODE). Hegel discusses his philosophical method in the chapter on absolute idea (q.v.) in the *Science of Logic* (q.v.). Starting from an immediately (q.v.) given, universal concept (qq.v.), one thinks it through to its limits (q.v.) and thereby distinguishes it from its opposite (q.v.) as one particular (q.v.) over against another. Reflection (q.v.) on this second particular leads back to the first. The two are thus directly related to each other, making a union of opposites, or contradiction (q.v.), which leads into an infinite (q.v.) regress. The third move is to think of this cycle as a totality (q.v.) and discover there a new concept within which the earlier ones are simply transient moments. Determining the limits of a concept is called *understanding* (q.v.); the transition (q.v.) to an opposite is called *dialectic* (q.v.); reflection on the totality is the work of *speculative reason* (q.v.). Sometimes the beginning is called the *thesis* (q.v.), the opposite is called the *antithesis,* and their unity is called the *synthesis,* but this language misses the dynamic of conceptual thinking (q.v.). *See also* CIRCLE OF CIRCLES; MAGNITUDE; SUBLATE.

MICHELET, KARL LUDWIG (1801–1893). Forced to justify for his father his conversion to the Hegelian philosophy, Michelet claimed that philosophical comprehension "is elevated above the limitations of the world and lives eternally in the realm of truth" (q.v.). In the first edition of Hegel's *Works*, he edited the volumes on the philosophy of nature and the lectures on the history of philosophy (qq.v.). One of the center Hegelians (q.v.), he claimed that, while Hegel had already completed the theoretical comprehension of reality, reality had to be permeated with his principles. A friend of August von Cieszkowski (q.v.), he cooperated with Arnold Ruge (q.v.) in the *Hallische Jahrbuch für Deutsche Wissenschaft und Kunst* (*Halle Journal for German Science and Art*) until it took a more radical turn toward the left.

MILLER, ARNOLD V. (1899–1991). In a Cotswold commune during the 1920s, Miller met Francis Sedlák, Czech author of a creative restatement of Hegel's *Science of Logic* (q.v.). After his retirement from the British civil service, Miller prepared translations of Hegel's *Phenomenology of Spirit, Science of Logic, Philosophy of Nature* (qq.v.), and revisions to William Wallace's (q.v.) translations of the *Encyclopedia Logic* and *Philosophy of Mind (Spirit)* (qq.v.), all of which were published with the encouragement of John N. Findlay (q.v.).

MIND. English translators used this term to translate the German *Geist*. However, it tends to focus on the intellect, leaving aside the will (q.v.) and the objective embodiment of spirit (q.v.) in public institutions, and so "spirit" has come to be preferred. *See also* INTELLIGENCE; PSYCHOLOGY.

MONARCH (DIE FÜRSTLICHE GEWALT). In Hegel's constitution (q.v.), the state's singularity (qq.v.) finds expression in the monarch or prince, whose public decisions are the actions of the state. To avoid having this position the basis of partisan conflict, it should be hereditary and based on custom. At the same time, the crown acquires its authority because it is embedded in a constitution (q.v.) where the legislative and executive (qq.v.) functions are exercised by other institutions, so that the king does not play an independent role, but simply confirms the actions of his ministers and parliament Such a view of the monarchy was not taken kindly by Friedrich Wilhelm III, the king of Prussia (q.v.) at the time. *See also PHILOSOPHY OF RIGHT.*

MONTESQUIEU, BARON CHARLES de (1689–1755). Hegel adopted from Montesquieu the conviction that a political philosophy must take account of the national character and historical circumstances that concretely determine a state (q.v.). Nonetheless, it must also consider how these specifics are integrated into a conceptual whole. *See also* CONCEPT; GEOGRAPHY.

MORALITY (DIE MORALITÄT). In the *Philosophy of Right* (q.v.), the chapter on "Morality" discusses the status within political philosophy of subjective willing in contrast to the abstract objectivity (q.v.) of property and contract (qq.v.). At the most basic level, one is responsible for only those results that are immediately intended. However, one must also take into consideration the larger picture of one's overall welfare as well as the well-being of others. Even that is not enough, for one cannot justify doing something morally wrong (q.v.) simply on the basis that it promotes the well-being of self or others. Therefore, one has the duty (q.v.) to bring about the good. This general principle is given specific content through one's individual conscience (q.v.). Unfortunately, the dictates of conscience can lead to evil as well as to good. The concrete social world of ethical life (q.v.)—family, civil society, and the state (qq.v.)—provides a universal context that informs conscience and gives the good a more precise definition. In the *Phenomenology of Spirit* (q.v.), Hegel explores the experience (q.v.) of the individual who adopts moral rules as a way of life. The immediate sense of duty is defined over against both the external nature that is to become moral and the internal nature that too frequently motivates action (q.v.) simply on the basis of desire (q.v.) and feeling. So there are always unresolved tensions between the duty to do what is right and the achievement of happiness, between following what duty prescribes and the conflicting enticements of desires and pleasure, between the pure principle of duty and determinate duties as they arise in specific situations. The ultimate reconciliation of such conflicts is projected onto a postulated beyond (q.v.). Unfortunately, since moral action often does bring satisfaction, what actually happens does not fit the projected model, and the moral person hypocritically dissembles. The next stage, then, is to move away from being obliged by abstract duty to the realm of conscience and the beautiful soul (qq.v.). Hegel in this chapter is describing the experience (q.v.) of trying to live according to the principles of Immanuel Kant's moral philosophy (qq.v.). *See also* ABSTRACT RIGHT; WILL.

MURE, G. R. G. (1893–1979). A student of H. H. Joachim at Merton College, Oxford, and associate of Robin G. Collingwood (q.v.), Mure defended the British idealist (q.v.) tradition long after it had fallen out of fashion, writing primarily on Hegel's *Logic* (q.v.). He argues that Hegel cannot do justice to the eternal and the supraspatial, since they are antitheses to time and space (qq.v.) yet also ultimately syntheses. *See also* THESIS.

MUSIC (DIE MUSIK). As the art (q.v.) specifically related to sound, music expresses the inwardness of sentiment, each note passing away in time (q.v.) to be reconstituted in the soul (q.v.). It is structured around tempo, harmony, and melody but, lacking any determinate content on its own, requires words to give it meaning. Therefore, its highest expression is opera, where it is combined with the poetry of drama (q.v.). On a visit to Vienna in 1824, Hegel took great delight in the operas of Wolfgang Mozart and Gioacchino Rossini. *See also* AESTHETICS; ART.

– N –

NAPOLEON (1769–1821). In the aftermath of the Battle of Jena (q.v.), Hegel "saw the emperor—this world soul—ride through the city on reconnaissance. It is, in fact, a wonderful impression to see such an individual who, concentrated here in a single point and sitting on a horse, overreaches [q.v.] and rules the world." Because Napoleon brought the achievements of the French Revolution (q.v.) to the German states, Hegel shared his friend Friedrich Niethammer's (q.v.) concern about the reactionary implications of his downfall. *See also* BAMBERG; BAVARIA; BERLIN; NÜRNBERG.

NATURAL LAW (DAS NATURRECHT). In the final numbers of the *Critical Journal of Philosophy* (q.v.), Hegel wrote an essay "On the Scientific Ways of Treating Natural Law." He criticized both the deduction of political philosophy from a single principle and the appeal either to tradition or to empirical givens. Natural law is not a universal that remains the same in all circumstances. Instead, one starts from the particular geographic and historical circumstances of a people and shows how individuals both freely appropriate its customs and mores and at the same time act independently as distinctive members, contributing to the diversity of the whole and its ongoing development. So it is not surprising that in his lectures, as well as on the second title page of the *Philosophy of Right* (q.v.), he labels this part of his philosophy "Natural Law and Political Science." *See also* GEOGRAPHY; KANT'S MORAL PHILOSOPHY; LECTURES ON THE PHILOSOPHY OF RIGHT; MONTESQUIEU, BARON CHARLES DE; OBJECTIVE SPIRIT.

NATURAL RELIGION (DIE NATÜRLICHE RELIGION, NATURRELIGION). Hegel uses these terms to refer to those religious traditions where the spiritual is embedded within the natural realm, whether human or nonhuman. In the *Phenomenology of Spirit* (q.v.) of 1807, he refers to the religions (q.v.) where light, then plants and animals, and finally the artificer or master craftsman are worshipped. While the first refers to the Parsee religion (q.v.) and the third to ancient Egyptian religion (q.v.), the second appears to include aspects of a number of traditions: Apis, the bull, in Egypt; elephants, monkeys, and cattle in India; snakes in Greece. By the time of the *Lectures on the Philosophy of Religion* (q.v.) in the Berlin (q.v.) years, he shows greater familiarity with contemporary literature on the various traditions. Magic, as found in the Arctic and Africa, is the basic form of nature religion, but it acquires more organized expression in the traditional religion of imperial China. Buddhism (q.v.) (and in 1827 Taoism) internalizes the spiritual quest within human nature; Indian religion (q.v.) externalizes it into nature's totality (qq.v.); the Parsee or Zoroastrian religion abstractly focuses on light and the good as opposed to evil; while ancient Egypt incorporates the negativity of death (q.v.) into the riddles of the tombs, labyrinths, and sphinxes. *See also* CHINESE RELIGION; PHILOSOPHY OF RELIGION.

NATURE (DIE NATUR). Nature is what is other than pure thought (or the idea [q.v.]). So its determinations (q.v.) have the appearance (q.v.) of being indifferent and externally related to each other in space and time (qq.v.). Through the philosophy of nature (q.v.) thought discovers the increasingly complex stages of its inner rationality. Since nature does not freely determine itself, it is the sphere of necessity and contingency (qq.v.). *See also* EXTERNAL RELATIONS; FREEDOM.

NECESSITY (DIE NOTWENDIGKEIT). The *Science of Logic* (q.v.) presents at least three different senses of this modal term. In the first place, whatever actually is cannot now be otherwise and is to that extent necessary. In the second place, contingent conditions, when brought together, may be sufficient to require necessarily a consequent. In the third place, when one looks at the total picture, it is absolutely necessary that contingencies (q.v.) emerge to become the necessary conditions for other parts of the whole (q.v.). In the *Phenomenology of Spirit* (q.v.), necessity experienced as fate frustrates reason (q.v.) when it claims that the truth (q.v.) of human existence is the quest for pleasure (q.v.). *See also* AC-TUALITY; CATEGORY; POSSIBILITY.

NEGATION OF NEGATION (DIE NEGATION DER NEGATION). Hegel turns Baruch Spinoza's (q.v.) saying "All determination [q.v.] is negation" around and says, "All negation is determination." Dialectic (q.v.) is the process by which the understanding (q.v.) of specific determinations leads into the opposite (q.v.) or negation of what thought started with. But the exploration of that opposite leads back to its contrary, the original term, so the negation comes to be negated. The mutual negation (and implication) then becomes the focus of reflection or speculative reason (qq.v.) that discovers the positive that is contained within the two negatives. *See also* ABSOLUTE IDEA; CIRCLE OF CIRCLES; METHOD.

NEWTON, ISAAC (1642–1727). Hegel took issue with Newton's mechanics (q.v.), preferring the laws of Johannes Kepler. Newton abstracted from real bodies to create the mathematical fiction of a parallelogram of centripetal and centrifugal forces, whereas Kepler made detailed observations, and then looked for the rational principles underlying the way real matter moved through space and time (qq.v.). To this extent, Kepler was more empirical. *See also* DISSERTATION; EMPIRICISM; MATHEMATICS.

NIETHAMMER, FRIEDRICH IMMANUEL (1766–1848). An acquaintance of Hegel from his time in Tübingen (q.v.), Niethammer went on to teach philosophy and theology at Jena (q.v.), where he was associated with Johann Fichte (q.v.) in the publication of a philosophical journal. In 1803, he moved to Würzburg to teach theology and was able to negotiate Hegel's appointment as editor in Bamberg (q.v.). In 1806, he was made responsible for education and religion in the Bavarian (q.v.) government under Maximilian Josef von Montgelas. He then appointed Hegel rector of the reorganized secondary school in Nürnberg (q.v.) and continued to be a regular correspondent through Hegel's subsequent years in Heidelberg and Berlin (qq.v.).

NIGHT IN WHICH ALL COWS ARE BLACK. In the preface to the *Phenomenology of Spirit* (q.v.) Hegel characterized the indifferent and undifferentiated absolute (q.v.) espoused by Friedrich Schelling (q.v.) and his disciples as a dark night in which all cows are black. Lacking internal differentiation, it could not provide any insight into the nature of truth (q.v.). Schelling took umbrage at this comment and in effect broke off their partnership.

NISHIDA KITARO (1870–1945). In providing a framework, consistent with traditional Western philosophy, for his essentially Zen intuitions, Nishida developed a dialectic (q.v.) from the self-determination or self-consciousness of nothing (qq.v.). Hegel had failed to see that being (q.v.) is grounded in absolute nothingness. *See also* BUDDHISM; JAPAN.

NODAL LINE (DIE KNOTENLINIE). The use of elective affinity (q.v.) to measure (q.v.) real things has its limits. For two things can combine according to different ratios (q.v.), and thereby produce quite different compounds. (Thus, nitrogen and oxygen can form nitrous oxide, nitric oxide, nitrogen dioxide, nitrogen tetroxide, and nitrogen pentoxide, each with distinctive qualities [q.v.].) One can then think of any such combination as a continuous string interrupted by knots, or a nodal line. This image illustrates how a gradual change in quantitative ratios can lead to a transformation of quality. *See also* QUANTITY; QUANTITY INTO QUALITY; *SCIENCE OF LOGIC*.

NOTHING (DAS NICHTS). The second term in Hegel's *Science of Logic* (q.v.) is nothing. It captures the emptiness of being's (q.v.) indeterminacy. But nothing is nonetheless being thought, and so it *is* in an indeterminate way. In other words, this term turns out to involve the same definition as being has, even though it started out as its polar opposite (q.v.). The resolution of this paradox leads to the thought of becoming (q.v.).

NOTION (DER BEGRIFF). Many translators and interpreters have used "notion" rather than "concept" (q.v.) for the German *Begriff* because it evokes the Greek term *nous* or mind (q.v.). It is then contrasted with "picture thinking" and "conception," which have been used for *Vorstellung*. In this dictionary "concept" is preferred, because it has the verbal form *conceive* and retains some sense of the "grasping" expressed in the original. *See* REPRESENTATION.

NUMBER (DIE ZAHL). A determinate quantity or quantum (qq.v.) is indicated by a number, specifying either an amount or a degree. While the Pythagoreans recognized that numbers stood between the concrete givens of experience (q.v.) and the realm of pure concepts (q.v.), numbers as abstract quantities lack an internal principle or meaning that can lead on to other thoughts.

NÜRNBERG. In the fall of 1808, Hegel's friend, Friedrich Niethammer (q.v.), who was responsible for education in Bavaria (q.v.), arranged for his appointment as headmaster of a classical gymnasium in Nürnberg that was being reorganized in accordance with Niethammer's educational program. Not only did Hegel take responsibility for the school administration, but he taught courses in philosophy and mathematics (qq.v.) and had to worry about the physical plant. While teaching a version of his philosophical system (q.v.) to the students, Hegel finished the three books of his *Science of Logic* (q.v.). In late 1811, he married Marie von Tucher, who bore him a daughter who died in infancy and two sons. With the defeat of Napoleon (q.v.), the reform government in Bavaria lost its patron, and its educational program came under threat. At the same time, peace gave the universities in Germany a more stable footing, so Hegel entered into negotiations with Erlangen, Berlin, and Heidelberg (qq.v.). When the Prussian administration hesitated, Hegel accepted the offer of Karl Daub (q.v.) to become professor of philosophy at Heidelberg. *See also* BAMBERG; FAMILY.

– O –

OBJECTIVE SPIRIT (DER OBJEKTIVE GEIST). When people will (q.v.) to act, they translate their subjective worlds into an objective realm by overreaching (q.v.) and appropriating things around them. Through contracts (q.v.) and moral commitments they organize their lives into institutional structures, which range from the intimacy of the family to international relations and world history (q.v.). So the philosophy of objective spirit offers Hegel's discussion of natural law (q.v.) and political science. *See also* ABSTRACT RIGHT; ACTION; CIVIL SOCIETY; ETHICAL LIFE; MORALITY; OBJECTIVITY; *PHILOSOPHY OF RIGHT*; *PHILOSOPHY OF SPIRIT*; PROPERTY; STATE.

OBJECTIVITY (DIE OBJEKTIVITÄT). Hegel uses *objectivity* for the way thinking (q.v.) comprehends anything that is in and of itself. When logical thought fully defines its concepts, judgments, and inferences (qq.v.), it realizes that these are subjective and hence limited; to be complete it must come to terms with objectivity. Objects are organized conceptually in mechanical, chemical, and teleological ways. *See also* CHEMISM; COGNITION; CONCEPT; GOD; IDEA; LIFE; MECHANISM; *SCIENCE OF LOGIC*; SUBJECTIVITY; TELEOLOGY.

OBSERVING REASON (DIE BEOBACHTENDE VERNUNFT). In the *Phenomenology of Spirit* (q.v.), reason's (q.v.) claim to know by means of categories (q.v.) starts by exploring the categories or laws that classify what it observes. This fails as full knowledge (q.v.) because natural things continually change; in addition, organisms (q.v.) do not present to pure observation anything that can reveal what life (q.v.) really is. The observation of conscious selves starts with the laws of thought (q.v.) and the correlations of empirical psychology (q.v.), neither of which do justice to a person's (q.v.) individuality. While physiognomy and phrenology (qq.v.) use the observation of physical characteristics to identify the nature of the individual, both miss what is inner (q.v.) and essential. Reason then turns to the categorization of inner motivation as pleasure, the law of the heart, and finally virtue (qq.v.).

OHIO HEGELIANS. In 1848, John Bernard Stallo (1823–1900) of Cincinnati, Ohio, published *General Principles of the Philosophy of Nature*, which discusses the systems of Friedrich Schelling (q.v.), Lorenz Oken, and Hegel. Shortly thereafter, he brought to Cincinnati August Willich (1810–1878), who had been active in the revolution of 1848 as president of the Cologne Communist League and was later an associate of Karl Marx and Friedrich Engels (qq.v.) in London. Willich became editor of the *Cincinnati Republikaner*. The Congregationalist minister, Moncure D. Conway (1832–1907), a close friend of Stallo and Willich and influenced by David F. Strauss (q.v.), developed a naturalistic, socially liberal philosophy of religion (q.v.). The three were subject to the criticism of William Nast (d. 1899), a former roommate of Strauss and Christian apologist, who blamed godlessness, materialism, and communism for the failure of the German revolution. *See also PHILOSOPHY OF NATURE*; UNITED STATES.

OLD HEGELIANS. This term was used by Arnold Ruge (q.v.) to group the right-wing Hegelians and the center Hegelians (qq.v.) no matter what their age, who were primarily interested in the religious significance of Hegel's philosophy and in making society more equitable. In this they were contrasted with the "young" Hegelians (q.v.) of the revolutionary left wing (q.v.) who were interested in challenging traditional religion (q.v.) and political structures. More strictly, one could use this term for those students of Hegel who worked closely with him during the 1820s and cooperated in the preparation of the collected works: Johannes Schulze, Friedrich Förster, Leopold von Henning, Eduard Gans, Friedrich Carové, Philipp Marheineke, Karl Daub (qq.v.), George Gabler, Karl Hinrichs, and Julius Schaller. With them could be included students of the next generation: Karl Rosenkranz, Karl Michelet, and Heinrich Hotho (qq.v.).

ONE (DAS EINS). In the *Science of Logic* (q.v.), a being for self (q.v.) that is related simply to itself is a unit, or one. It differentiates itself from the void and in so doing repels other ones that are equally self-contained. Their similarity, however, involves an implicit relation, which is the basis for an attraction (q.v.) that draws them to each other. This set of logical terms underlies both the theory of atomism (q.v.) and Leibniz's (q.v.) monadology. *See also* REPULSION.

OPPOSITION (DER GEGENSATZ). Opposition is a form of difference (q.v.) in which the same content is treated both negatively and positively, though from different perspectives. The *Science of Logic* (q.v.) argues that it is a way reflection (q.v.) organizes diversity (q.v.). When the positive and negative mutually exclude each other, opposition turns into a full-blown contradiction (q.v.). *See also* IDENTITY; LAWS OF THOUGHT; NEGATION OF NEGATION.

ORGANICS (DIE ORGANIK). In the *Philosophy of Nature* (q.v.), Hegel uses this term to cover the phenomena explored by geology, botany, and zoology (qq.v.). All of them involve some sort of organic structure, although only animals incorporate differentiated organs as constitutive members of a living organism (q.v.). *See also* LIFE.

ORGANISM (DER ORGANISMUS). Immanuel Kant's *Critique of Judgment* (q.v.) noted that living organisms appear to escape the rigorous linear sequence of cause and effect. Each organ is simultaneously cause and effect of the other organs as well as of the whole organism. Friedrich Schelling (q.v.) used this model as the basis for his idealistic philosophy of nature (q.v.). While Hegel initially followed Schelling, he later saw that spirit (q.v.) as fully self-conscious (q.v.) is more than just an organism. As the culmination of his *Philosophy of Nature* (q.v.), his discussion of organics (q.v.) sets the stage for moving on to the discussion of spirit. *See also* CAUSALITY; IDEALISM; LIFE; RECIPROCITY.

OTHER (DAS ANDERE). In the *Science of Logic* (q.v.), Hegel recognizes that the thought of "something" (q.v.) inevitably leads to the thought of something else, or an other. To distinguish between them, we need to define their determinations (q.v.). *See also* DASEIN; QUALITY.

OVERREACH (ÜBERGREIFEN). Spirit (q.v.), for Hegel, can overreach both nature (q.v.) and its own past and incorporate them into its present life (q.v.). This term, then, serves as an analogue in the real world for the logical term *sublation* (q.v.).

OWL OF MINERVA. In the preface to the *Philosophy of Right* (q.v.), Hegel says that philosophy (q.v.) does not talk about what the world should be like but rather comes late on the scene and grasps the world only as it already is, both in its study of nature (q.v.) and in its study of politics and world history (q.v.). "When philosophy paints its grey on grey, then has a shape of life grown old. By philosophy's grey on grey it cannot be rejuvenated but only understood. The owl of Minerva [the goddess of wisdom] spreads its wings only with the falling of the dusk." Karl Marx (q.v.) took issue with this in the *Theses on Feuerbach*:

"Philosophers have only interpreted the world in various ways; the point is to change it." So he preferred the image of the French cock who heralds a new dawn. The Hegel Society of America (q.v.) adopted Hegel's image of the owl to name its journal.

– P –

PAINTING (DIE MALEREI). With its use of light and dark, color and perspective, painting can capture the inwardness of human subjectivity (q.v.). Working with the flat plane of a painted surface it may evoke a three-dimensional insight into religious suffering and love as well as the ordinary activities of every day. At the same time it reveals the subjective genius of the individual artist. So it is the plastic art form most typical of romantic art (q.v.). *See also* AESTHETICS; INNER/OUTER.

PARSEE RELIGION (ZOROASTRIANISM). In Hegel's *Lectures on the Philosophy of Religion* (q.v.), the traditional Persian religion represents the transition from natural religion (q.v.) to the religions of beauty and the sublime (qq.v.) or (in 1831) the religion of freedom (q.v.). The spiritual principle of the good (Ormazd) is raised above the natural, and identified with light in the abstract. Eternally confronted by evil or darkness (Ahriman), it nonetheless is destined to overcome it. Hegel refers to the religion of light as the basic form of natural religion in the *Phenomenology of Spirit* (q.v.). *See also* GREEK RELIGION; JUDAISM; PERSIAN HISTORY; PHILOSOPHY OF RELIGION.

PARTICULAR (BESONDER). A particular universal (q.v.) is a general term or concept (q.v.) that is nonetheless subsumed under a broader universal or genus that includes other particulars (or species) from which it is distinguished. *See also* CONCEPT; SINGULAR.

PASSIONS (DIE LEIDENSCHAFTEN). In his *Lectures on the Philosophy of World History* (q.v.), Hegel identifies the passions as the engine that effects the transformations of world history (q.v.). Far from being a sign of the irrationality of human affairs, the passions are used by the cunning of reason (q.v.) to generate the conditions for the modern constitutional state (q.v.) with its entrenched freedoms (q.v.).

PERCEPTION (DAS WAHRNEHMEN). In the *Phenomenology of Spirit* (q.v.), perception is a mode of knowledge (q.v.) in which consciousness (q.v.) organizes the givens of sense under universals (q.v.), assembling a set of diverse sensations into the thought of a "thing" (q.v.), and the features that many different things share into the thought of a "property." Consciousness finds itself unable to determine which of these two aspects is really known and which is the product of its own subjective limitations, so it turns to understanding (q.v.) the relationships between them. *See also* SENSE CERTAINTY.

PERSIAN HISTORY. By uniting into a single regime diverse cultures and peoples, each maintaining its own tradition, the Persian empire combined both the unity of Chinese and the diversity of Indian history (qq.v). The defeat of Persia by Greece marked the transition from the Oriental world, where only one is free, to the classical world, where some are free. *See also* FREEDOM; GREEK HISTORY; *LECTURES ON THE PHILOSOPHY OF WORLD HISTORY*; PARSEE RELIGION; PHILOSOPHY OF WORLD HISTORY; WORLD HISTORY.

PERSON (DIE PERSON). In contrast to immediate self-consciousness (qq.v.), the legal person is related to himself in his singularity, while knowing himself to be an infinite, universal (qq.v.) and free "I," abstracted from his environment. The term *person* thus marks the bearer of rights (q.v.), able to appropriate property (q.v.) and enter into contracts (q.v.), but it is not to be confused with an individual's arbitrary will (q.v.), with its drives, desires, and inclinations. The latter, however, introduces the possibility of doing wrong (q.v.), requiring that philosophy consider the individual as moral subject. *See also* ABSTRACT RIGHT; FREEDOM; LEGAL STATUS; MORALITY; *PHILOSOPHY OF RIGHT*; WILL.

PETRY, MICHAEL J. Petry not only translated into English Hegel's *Philosophy of Nature* (q.v.) and *Philosophy of Subjective Spirit,* but also incorporated into his notes detailed references to the scientific texts of the day, particularly those to which Hegel himself referred. These texts offer "a sensitively structured, deeply informed and infinitely rewarding assessment of the whole range of early 19th century science." *See also PHILOSOPHY OF SPIRIT.*

PHENOMENOLOGY (DIE PHÄNOMENOLOGIE). In the *Philosophy of Spirit* (q.v.), Hegel moves from the immediacy of the soul (q.v.) in "Anthropology" (q.v.) to the self-contained spirit (q.v.) in "Psychology" (q.v.) by way of a chapter on the "Phenomenology of Spirit." Spirit appears as consciousness and self-consciousness (qq.v.), in which one is aware of an object, whether that object be external or one's own self. Hegel here summarizes the discussion of sense certainty, perception, understanding, desire, recognition, death, and master-slave (qq.v.) already found in the *Phenomenology of Spirit* (q.v.). The main differences are two: he removes the dialectic of space and time (qq.v.) from sensible consciousness and places it later in the discussion of intuition (q.v.) in the psychology; and master-slave leads directly to mutual recognition and thereby to the integration of consciousness and self-consciousness in reason (qq.v.), without passing through the stages of stoicism, skepticism, and unhappy consciousness (qq.v.). In his remarks, Hegel notes that the philosophies of Immanuel Kant and Johann Fichte (qq.v.) both should be called *phenomenology*. *See also* APPEARANCE.

PHENOMENOLOGY OF SPIRIT (PHÄNOMENOLOGIE DES GEISTES). This was Hegel's first major work, written and published in 1807 while he was a junior member of faculty at the university of Jena (q.v.). It has been translated into English by John B. Baillie and Arnold V. Miller, into French by Jean Hyppolite, and into Italian by Enrico de Negri. The problem it sets for itself is epistemological: what constitutes genuine or absolute knowing (q.v.). Rather than assuming what knowledge (q.v.) should be, Hegel has different knowledge claims measure (q.v.) themselves against their own standards until he reaches a kind of knowing that is fully self-confirming. For Hegel, knowledge claims encompass not only what we know of objects and ourselves but also what we know of our society and of the very principles of the universe. So the work includes discussions of social, ethical, historical, and religious matters that stretch the limits of traditional epistemology (q.v.). Since self-conscious life, or spirit (q.v.), makes its appearance (q.v.) through these various modes of self-confident affirmation, he replaced his original title "Science of the Experience of Consciousness" (qq.v.) with *Phenomenology of Spirit* (in other words, the way spirit appears). In the *Philosophy of Spirit* of the *Encyclopedia of the Philosophical Sciences* (qq.v.), Hegel has a chapter called "Phenomenology" (q.v.) that contains a summary of the first two sections of the larger work (on our immediate consciousness [qq.v.] of objects and our immediate self-awareness). There has been considerable discussion on how the two texts are related. *See also* AB-SOLUTE FREEDOM; ALIENATION; ANTIGONE; BEAUTIFUL SOUL; CHRISTIANITY; CIRCLE OF CIRCLES; CONSCIENCE; CULTURE; DEATH; DESIRE; ENLIGHTENMENT; ETHICAL LIFE; FAITH; FOR CONSCIOUSNESS; FOR US; FRENCH REVOLUTION; INSIGHT; INVERTED WORLD; LAW-GIVING REASON; LAW OF THE HEART; LAW-TESTING REASON; LEGAL STATUS; MAS-TER-SLAVE; MORALITY; NATURAL RELIGION; OBSERVING REASON; PERCEPTION; PHRENOLOGY; PHYSIOGNOMY; PLEA-SURE; REASON; RECOGNITION; RELIGION IN THE FORM OF ART; *SACHE SELBST*; SELF-CONSCIOUSNESS; SENSE CER-TAINTY; SKEPTICISM; SPIRITUAL ANIMAL KINGDOM; STO-ICISM; UNDERSTANDING; UNHAPPY CONSCIOUSNESS; UTIL-ITY; VIRTUE.

PHILOSOPHY (DIE PHILOSOPHIE). Philosophy offers the culminat-ing mode by which humans comprehend absolute spirit (q.v.). Using the tools of logic (q.v.) to grasp conceptually how the universe is integrated within the life of spirit (q.v.), it distinguishes various moments into their discrete structures but also explores the inferences by which these are nonetheless interconnected into one totality (q.v.). Philosophy thus com-bines the intuitive insight of art (q.v.) with the discrete moments spelled out in religion (q.v.). The reality that is to be comprehended is spiritual and develops over time (q.v.) as more details become evident; so philos-ophy has a history. But at the same time, philosophers are simply think-ing through the concepts (q.v.) that determine the nature of truth (q.v.); so there is only one philosophy. The variety of philosophical systems is a result of finite (q.v.) perspectives that have not yet probed the limits (q.v.) of their partial understanding (q.v.). *See also* HISTORY OF PHI-LOSOPHY; *LECTURES ON THE HISTORY OF PHILOSOPHY*.

PHILOSOPHY OF ART. *See* AESTHETICS.

PHILOSOPHY OF NATURE. Hegel began lecturing on the philosophy of nature after Friedrich Schelling (q.v.) left Jena (q.v.), and he included it in an early systematic manuscript. It later became the second part of the *Encyclopedia of the Philosophical Sciences* (q.v.), translated into English (along with additions [q.v.] from the lectures assembled by Karl Michelet [q.v.]) by Arnold V. Miller and Michael J. Petry (qq.v.), the latter with extensive notes on the science of Hegel's day. Having articulated the fundamental ways in which thought thinks (*Science of Logic* [q.v.]), philosophical thought turns to the givens of nature (q.v.) that are quite other (q.v.) than thought, and organizes them into a systematic pattern by working from the simplest kinds of external relations (q.v.) toward phenomena that are progressively more complex: from space and time (qq.v.) through the mechanical, the physical, and the chemical to the biological. Once living organisms become self-conscious, Hegel moves to the philosophy of spirit (q.v.). *See also* BODY (DER KÖRPER); BOTANY; CHEMICAL PROCESS; GEOLOGY; JENA DRAFTS FOR A SYSTEM; LECTURES ON THE PHILOSOPHY OF NATURE; MECHANICS; ORGANICS; PHYSICS; REMARKS; ZOOLOGY.

PHILOSOPHY OF RELIGION. In introducing lectures on the philosophy of religion, Hegel distanced himself from the tradition, which simply included natural theology within metaphysics (q.v.). Religion (q.v.) considers not only God (q.v.) as the truth or absolute essence (qq.v.) of the cosmos, but also how this essence makes itself manifest, how humans respond to it, and how the divine and the human are integrated in cultic practice. By including human feelings, representations, concepts (qq.v), and practices, this discipline examines the concrete historical setting of religious traditions while organizing them philosophically from the most immediate to the most mediated (qq.v.). *See also LECTURES ON THE PHILOSOPHY OF RELIGION.*

PHILOSOPHY OF RIGHT. In 1821, to satisfy the need for fuller documentation in his lectures on natural law (q.v.) and political science, Hegel expanded the section on objective spirit (q.v.) from his *Philosophy of Spirit* (q.v.) into *Elements of the Philosophy of Right*, translated into English by Samuel W. Dyde (1896), Thomas Malcolm Knox (1942), and Hugh Barr Nisbet (1991). This work explores how the concept of justice or fairness (right [q.v.]) finds expression in human life. Starting from the abstract exercise of will (q.v.) in property, contracts, and wrong (qq.v.) or injustice, Hegel systematically moves on to morality (q.v.) and then to the integration of abstract right (q.v.) and subjective intention in the life of the family, civil society, state, and world history (qq.v). The early editions of the collected works contained an abstract of Hegel's lectures (q.v.) appended to the various paragraphs. *See also* ABSTRACT RIGHT; ADDITIONS; AVINIERI, SHLOMO; CLASSES; CONSCIENCE; CONSTITUTION; CORPORATIONS; DIVISION OF LABOR; DUTY; ETHICAL LIFE; EXECUTIVE; HAYM, RUDOLF; INTERNATIONAL LAW; LECTURES ON THE PHILOSOPHY OF RIGHT; LEGISLATURE; MONARCHY; PERSON; POLICE; POVERTY; REMARKS; WAR; WEIL, ERIC.

PHILOSOPHY OF SPIRIT. This is the third part of Hegel's *Encyclopedia of the Philosophical Sciences* (q.v.), translated into English by William Wallace and Arnold V. Miller (qq.v.); Michael Petry (q.v.) has translated the first part, the philosophy of subjective spirit (q.v.), and included student transcripts of several of the lecture series. *Spirit* (q.v.), or self-conscious life, is the term Hegel uses for both individuals and human societies, but it can also be extended to the realm of the divine. The *Philosophy of Spirit* organizes the various aspects of human existence into a systematic pattern, starting from the most basic ways humans respond to their natural environment through to political organizations, world history, art, religion, and philosophy (qq.v.). The section on objective spirit (q.v.) was expanded into the *Philosophy of Right* (q.v.), while the brief discussion of absolute spirit (q.v.) was elaborated in his lectures on world history, aesthetics, religion, and history of philosophy (qq.v.). *See also* ABSTRACT RIGHT; ADDITIONS; ANTHROPOLOGY; ETHICAL LIFE; LECTURES ON THE PHILOSOPHY OF RIGHT; LECTURES ON THE PHILOSOPHY OF SUBJECTIVE SPIRIT; MORALITY; PHENOMENOLOGY; PSYCHOLOGY; REMARKS; RIGHT.

PHILOSOPHY OF WORLD HISTORY. The events of world history (q.v.) can be understood philosophically because they are inherently rational. Spirit's (q.v.) destiny is to realize freedom (q.v.), but it does so by means of the passions (q.v.) that drive individuals to act. Through the cunning of reason (q.v.), these passions and their consequences rub against each other and wear each other down, producing a structure of custom and law (q.v.) that becomes the state (q.v.). It is within states, and more widely through international law (q.v.), that the goal of free self-determination is fully realized. This rational framework enables the philosopher to grasp how a nation's political, social, religious, scientific, and economic life are integrated around a single principle, which in turn contributes to the development of spirit's freedom. In the Oriental world only one was free, in the Greek and Roman world some were free, but in the modern world all are free. *See also* CHINESE HISTORY; CIESZKOWSKI, AUGUST; EGYPTIAN HISTORY; GERMANIC HISTORY; GREEK HISTORY; INDIAN HISTORY; *LECTURES ON THE PHILOSOPHY OF WORLD HISTORY*; PERSIAN HISTORY; *PHILOSOPHY OF RIGHT*; ROMAN HISTORY.

PHRENOLOGY (DIE SCHÄDELLEHRE). Taking the nodes on the skull as the truth (q.v.) of a person's character is reason's (q.v.) ultimate strategy in using observation to gain knowledge (q.v.). This reliance on dead bones to tell the truth of what is living reduces to absurdity the whole approach of observing reason (q.v.) and shows that reason must take account of the inner considerations that motivate people: pleasure, the law of the heart, and virtue (qq.v.). *See also* CATEGORY; INNER/OUTER; *PHENOMENOLOGY OF SPIRIT*; PHYSIOGNOMY.

PHYSICS (DIE PHYSIK). In Hegel's *Philosophy of Nature* (q.v.), physics stands between the discussion of mechanics (q.v.), or matter in motion, and organics (q.v.), or organized and living bodies. It explores the way matter is qualitatively differentiated. In general, physics individuates through light; the classical elements of air, fire, water, and earth; and the interaction of all these in the meteorological process. Specific weight, cohesion, sound, and conductibility of heat provide a more particular (q.v.) way of physically distinguishing bodies. Finally, a body considered in its totality (q.v.) is qualified through its magnetism; its color, smell, and taste; its electrical polarization; and its susceptibility to chemical transformation. In 1807, Hegel was named an honorary member of the Physics Society of Heidelberg (q.v.). *See also* BODY (DER KÖRPER); CHEMICAL PROCESS; MEASURE; QUALITY.

PHYSIOGNOMY (DIE PHYSIOGNOMIE). The quest of observing reason (q.v.) to find true categories (q.v.) through simple observation leads to reading facial structure (physiognomy), handwriting, and the features of speech as evidence of a person's individuality. Because people can deliberately dissemble, this approach fails and leads on to phrenology (q.v.), where it is claimed that the skull immediately reveals the truth (q.v.) of a person's character. *See also PHENOMENOLOGY OF SPIRIT*; REASON.

PICTURE THINKING. *See* **REPRESENTATION.**

PINKARD, TERRY. For Pinkard, Hegel's *Phenomenology of Spirit* (q.v.) shows how the modern world has achieved freedom (q.v.): those who are reflecting on ethical ends are continuous with those who make up the institutions of contemporary society. Their rational comprehension involves understanding how modern structures have successfully made up for the insufficiencies of what preceded historically. The future is not closed, however, for Hegel allows for an ongoing series of dialectical reflections (qq.v.) on the possibilities open to us as humans, and what happens when they are put into practice. *See also* END OF HISTORY; UNITED STATES.

PIPPIN, ROBERT B. In *Hegel's Idealism: The Satisfactions of Self-Consciousness*, Pippin argues that Hegel's project can be understood as an extension of Immanuel Kant's (q.v.) critical idealism (q.v.): what for Kant is the *spontaneity* of apperception becomes the self-determining nature of pure thought; and Kant's *necessary unity* of apperception becomes the systematic, dialectical (q.v.) interrelatedness of any possible concept or notion (qq.v.). This idealism can be separated from the consequences Hegel draws in the rest of his system (q.v.) about nature, spirit, art, religion and philosophy (qq.v.). *See also* THINKING; UNITED STATES.

PLANT, RAYMOND. In *Hegel: An Introduction*, Plant argues that Hegel's system (q.v.) is designed to resolve the challenges he set himself in the early Tübingen (q.v.) essay on religion (q.v.): to restore the harmony of personal experience (q.v.) and to re-create a closely knit community. His reflections in Frankfurt am Main (q.v.) led him to turn from a religion of the people to philosophy (q.v.), since the conflicts inherent in the modern world can only be resolved through a comprehensive grasp of experience. Once we gain a firm insight into the nature of the world confronting us, it will no longer appear as a source of alienation (q.v.). While Hegel claimed too much in saying this had been achieved with the modern state (q.v.), a more skeptical use of his approach may well succeed. *See also* BRITISH IDEALISM; THEOLOGICAL WRITINGS.

PLATO. While Plato recognized that the ethical nature of humans was to be integrated into the life of the state (q.v.), his republic, by excluding both private property (q.v.) and marriage, wanted to isolate the rulers from any trace of particular interests and individualism, both of which would lead to the demise of the Greek city-state. For Hegel, the modern state (q.v.), in recognizing the role of individualism in civil society (q.v.), represents a more developed political form. In this, and in other ways, Plato's idea (q.v.) showed itself to be simply a universal (q.v.) thought, lacking the potential to actualize itself. *See also* ARISTOTLE; ETHI-CAL LIFE; FAMILY; GREEK HISTORY; SOCRATES.

PLEASURE (DIE LUST). In the *Phenomenology of Spirit* (q.v.), having abandoned simple observation as the way to get at true categories (q.v.), reason (q.v.) turns to immediate (q.v.) feeling, or pleasure, as the key to the truth (q.v.) of the self. Taking this as the goal of action (q.v.), how-ever, inevitably leads to an encounter with fate, an unarticulated neces-sity (q.v.) that frustrates pleasure's simple quest. The need for a more universal (q.v.) category leads to the law of the heart (q.v.). *See also* OB-SERVING REASON.

POETRY (DIE POESIE). Poetry unites the subjectivity of music (qq.v.) with the structure of the plastic arts; drama (q.v.), and in particular Greek drama, with its staging, the actors as living sculptures (q.v.), and the mu-sicality of its language, integrates all the arts. The material of poetry is representations (q.v.)—concrete thoughts that are communicated through words as signs; but it structures its various moments around an individ-ual purpose so that they become members of an organic whole. Epic (q.v.) has a sculptural quality in developing the totality (q.v.) of an event; lyric (q.v.) explores the inner movement of subjectivity; drama centers on willed action (q.v.) that turns out to be one sided. In tragedy (q.v.) the individual comes to grief at the hand of the substantial ground of spiri-tual existence; in comedy (q.v.) the individual subjects destroy their own partiality. *See also* AESTHETICS; ART; CLASSICAL ART; ORGAN-ISM; RELIGION IN THE FORM OF ART; ROMANTIC ART.

POLICE (DIE POLIZEI). Although the German term now has the same sense as the English one, a better counterpart for Hegel's use of it in the *Philosophy of Right* (q.v.) can be found in the French *police,* meaning all the organs and institutions that assure the maintenance of public order. Civil society, with its division of labor (qq.v.), develops a network of mutual interdependence even though it is based on the satisfaction of individual needs. This network then has to be reinforced and maintained by public structures: security of person and property (qq.v.), institutions for exchange, trade and education, programs to prevent extreme inequalities in wealth producing social disruption (such as care for wastrels and the poor), and colonization to absorb excess population not needed for the efficient production of goods. These functions can be distinguished from those of the state (q.v.) as such, whose specific role is to integrate the diversity of civil society into a single, coherent nation, inspired by patriotism and structured by the constitution (q.v.). *See also* CAPITALISM.

POPPER, KARL R. (1902–1994). In what he admits is a playful attack on a philosopher he could not take seriously, Popper argues in *The Open Society and Its Enemies* that Hegel's dialectical logic (q.v.), by claiming that contradictions (q.v.) are desirable, stops rational argument; that his identification of fact with value legitimizes the Prussian state of Friedrich Wilhelm III; and that his philosophy (q.v.) encourages totalitarian modes of thought. *See also* ACTUALITY OF THE RATIONAL; PRUSSIA.

POSSIBILITY (DIE MÖGLICHKEIT). The third of the modal categories (q.v.), along with actuality and necessity (qq.v.), possibility can have at least three different meanings. The first is something that is not itself contradictory and so logically possible; the second refers to the conditions that make something really possible, though when all such conditions are present, that possibility necessarily becomes actual; the third is the absolute possibility involved in the question "Why is there something rather than nothing?"—a question for which there is no answer. Unlike Aristotle and Friedrich Schelling (qq.v.) for whom possibility precedes actuality, Hegel moves to the concept of possibility from the concept of actuality. Since actualities for which there are no fully explanatory possibilities are contingent, Hegel is one of the few philosophers who argues for the necessity of contingency (q.v.). *See also* SCIENCE OF LOGIC.

POVERTY (DIE ARMUT). The individualism of civil society (q.v.), based on the satisfaction of needs and division of labor (q.v.), produces wealth but lacks controls to distribute it equitably. Extremes of wealth and poverty emerge, and the unskilled poor become a rabble that threatens to destablize the community. The public authority (police [q.v.]), to ensure the functioning of civil society, undertakes initiatives to reduce this threat by providing institutions for the poor and developing colonies to absorb the excess population, but Hegel confesses that neither can be ultimately successful. *See also* AVINIERI, SHLOMO; CAPITALISM; *PHILOSOPHY OF RIGHT*; WEIL, ERIC.

PROCLUS. Proclus gave neo-Platonic philosophy its most developed logical form. The triad of One (q.v.), Unlimited, and Limit (q.v.) is broken up into three triads, each one of which is self-determined, even as it is incorporated into the all-encompassing totality (q.v.). His thought thus contains a genuine trinity, and to that extent it marked a significant advance in the history of philosophy (q.v.), setting the stage for the appearance of Christianity (q.v.). *See also* CHURCH FATHERS.

PROPERTY (DIE EIGENSCHAFT). *See* THING (DAS DING).

PROPERTY (DAS EIGENTUM). The will (q.v.) takes possession of a thing (*eine Sache* [q.v.]) either directly or by some kind of sign and makes it into a person's (q.v.) private property. Property, both physical and spiritual, can be relinquished and so becomes the matter for contracts (q.v.). Since this is the systematic foundation of civil law (q.v.), property is the first topic handled in Hegel's *Philosophy of Right* (q.v.), although it only gets legal recognition and authority in civil society (q.v.). For Karl Marx (q.v.), property can be commonly held, and private property is the result of labor, which produces more than it directly needs and as a result alienates the laborer from himself, his product, and his fellows. *See also* ABSTRACT RIGHT; ALIENATED LABOR; CAPITALISM.

PROTESTANT REFORMATION. By placing the substantial presence of absolute spirit or God (qq.v.) within the conscience (q.v.) of individuals rather than in external authority and miracles, the Lutheran reformation transformed Christianity (q.v.) so that it could become the foundation of the modern constitutional state (q.v.). However, the content believed in was left in the form of dogmas to be accepted simply on faith (q.v.). Theological representations (q.v.) needed to be transformed into philosophical concepts (q.v.) before the modern world could fully emerge. The lack of a religious reformation was a contributing cause to the political revolutions that occurred in France, Spain, and elsewhere. *See also* ENLIGHTENMENT; FRENCH REVOLUTION; GERMANIC HISTORY; HISTORY OF PHILOSOPHY.

PRUSSIA. Under the weak leadership of Friedrich Wilhem III, Prussia collapsed after its defeat at the Battle of Jena (q.v.) in 1806, and the king was forced to appoint Freiherr Karl von Stein as minister of state. Von Stein abolished serfdom, reintroduced municipal self-government, and replaced cabinet government with a forward-looking bureaucracy, before he was forced to resign in 1808. When Karl August von Hardenberg became head of government in 1810, he continued with Stein's reforms, reorganizing the financial and administrative system as well as the army, freeing industry from bureaucratic restrictions, and appointing his friend Karl von Altenstein as minister of education. The indecisive and pedantic king, however, did not follow through with the promise, made during the patriotic wars against France, to introduce some form of parliamentary government; and his more conservative councillors worked to frustrate the liberal tendencies of Hardenberg. Thus, although Hegel enjoyed the patronage of von Altenstein, he also came under the suspicion of the chief of political police. A decade after his death, the more conservative crown prince assumed the throne as Friedrich Wilhelm IV and appointed Friedrich Schelling (q.v.) to the university of Berlin (q.v.) to combat Hegelianism. *See also* CONSTITUTION.

PSYCHOLOGY (DIE PSYCHOLOGIE). In the *Philosophy of Spirit* (q.v.), psychology moves beyond the simple immediacy of anthropology (q.v.) and the division between consciousness and its object in phenomenology (q.v.) to the integrated activity of subjective spirit (q.v.), which culminates in human freedom (q.v.). Although Hegel distinguishes a number of activities—intuition, recollection, imagination, memory, thinking, will (qq.v.)—he resists dividing them into separate faculties. Rather, they function as one activity of a single finite spirit. Hegel began making notes about the psychological faculties while he was a tutor in Bern (q.v.); in the *Phenomenology of Spirit* (q.v.), he shows that the attempt to develop psychological laws from simple observation is bound to fail because it cannot do justice to the integrated subject. *See also* INTELLIGENCE; LANGUAGE; OBSERVING REASON; REPRESENTATION.

– Q –

QUALITY (DIE QUALITÄT). Quality is the way a being (Dasein [q.v.]) is determined in general, whether it is simply determinate or constituted by something else. The logic of this term is explored in the first section of the first book in the *Science of Logic* (q.v.), extending to the way a finite (q.v.) being is limited by its quality and the way a being for self (q.v.) becomes a self-contained one (q.v.). The abstract relationship of one and many leads into the discussion of quantity (q.v.). *See also* BEING; DETERMINATION; INFINITE; LIMIT; MEASURE; QUANTITY INTO QUALITY, SOMETHING.

QUANTITY (DIE QUANTITÄT). Self-contained beings for self (q.v.), abstracted from their quality (q.v.), can be considered simply in terms of their attraction to, and repulsion (q.v.) from, each other. As thus abstracted, attraction becomes continuous magnitude (q.v.) and repulsion discrete magnitude. Quantity in general is simply this union of continuity and discreteness. Determinate quantity or quantum (q.v.) translates these two aspects into an intensity of degree or a magnitude of number (q.v.). The logic of magnitude or quantity is considered in the second section of the first book in the *Science of Logic* (q.v.). Since nature (q.v.) is defined by the externality of space and time (qq.v.), it is particularly susceptible to abstract quantitative analysis. *See also* ABSTRACT/CONCRETE; ANTINOMIES; MATHEMATICS; MEASURE; NODAL LINE; QUANTITY INTO QUALITY; RATIO.

QUANTITY INTO QUALITY. In his discussion of measure (q.v.), Hegel shows how, by gradually altering quantities and ratios (qq.v.), one may produce a transformation in quality (q.v.), so that the thing we start with becomes something (q.v.) quite different. Friedrich Engels (q.v.) used this as one of the defining marks of the dialectic (q.v.). *See also* NODAL LINE.

QUANTUM (DAS QUANTUM). In the *Science of Logic* (q.v.), Hegel distinguishes a quantum, or determinate quantity (q.v.), from quantity in general. Using numbers (q.v.), a quantum can be determined either extensively, by counting out a definite amount, or intensively, in terms of degrees. Since any such quantum is a discrete part of a continuum, thought always moves beyond the limits (qq.v.) of its determinate number to another one, leading into an infinite (q.v.) regress. The full sense of quantum, then, involves this quantitative infinity, since any number is defined by its role within an unending succession. *See also* MAGNITUDE; MATHEMATICS; RATIO.

– R –

RAMEAU'S NEPHEW. See **DIDEROT, DENIS.**

RATIO (DAS QUANTITATIVE VERHÄLTNIS). Quantitative infinity (q.v.) involves a quantum (q.v.) or determinate quantity being related to other quanta in a series. Ratio focuses on the relationship between two quanta: first as a direct proportion, then as an inverse ratio, and finally as a ratio of powers. As one proceeds, the limits (q.v.) that define the proportion become more important, but since limits are qualitative, rather than a function of the continuous and discrete character of simple quantity (q.v.), the next stage is to look at how quantities are related to qualities (q.v.) through the act of measuring. *See also* MAGNITUDE; MEASURE.

RATIONALITY OF THE ACTUAL. *See* ACTUALITY OF THE RATIONAL.

REASON (DIE VERNUNFT). In the *Phenomenology of Spirit* (q.v.), reason names a mode of knowledge (q.v.) in which the self looks for a shared set of principles (or categories [q.v.]) that apply both to itself and to what is known. Reason then uses these categories to observe the sensible, assess human actions, and determine the essential structures of a world that incorporates both. Within Hegel's logical method (q.v.), reason, as distinct from the understanding (q.v.), is of two sorts. Dialectical reason (q.v.) passes over from the limits (q.v.) of an understood concept (q.v.) to those contrary terms that are needed to define its boundary. Speculative reason (q.v.) grasps the opposing terms thus defined in a unified perspective and articulates both the positive and the negative features of their relationship. *See also* LAW-GIVING REASON; LAW OF THE HEART; LAWS OF THOUGHT; LAW-TESTING REASON;

LOGIC; OBSERVING REASON; PHRENOLOGY; PHYSIOGNOMY; PLEASURE; PSYCHOLOGY; REFLECTION; SPIRITUAL ANIMAL KINGDOM; TRANSITION; VIRTUE.

RECIPROCITY (DIE WECHSELWIRKING). The relationship in which the causal working of a substance is itself stimulated by the passivity of the substance it works upon produces the concept (q.v.) of mutual interaction. On reflection (q.v.), this reciprocity of action (q.v.) sets out the details of absolute necessity (q.v.). The total structure, though internally mediated, is itself immediate (q.v.), a simple being (q.v.). So this final concept in the doctrine of essence (q.v.) leads back to the beginning (q.v.) of the doctrine of being (q.v.). Considered as a totality (q.v.), the mediated immediacy of integrated reciprocity is a universal (q.v.) pattern that, though singular (q.v.), particularizes itself by giving itself a determination (q.v.). Thus, the ingredients are in place for a shift to the doctrine of concept. *See also* CATEGORY; CAUSALITY; CIRCLE OF CIRCLES; MEDIATION; PARTICULAR; *SCIENCE OF LOGIC*; SUBSTANTIALITY.

RECOGNITION (DIE ANERKENNUNG). The process whereby people recognize or acknowledge each other is fundamental to Hegel's treatment of spirit (q.v.), since it shows how individuals become part of a community. Each self-consciousness (q.v.) first discovers an other (q.v.) to be the same as it is, then affirms its uniqueness over against that other, and finally acknowledges that both identity and difference (qq.v.) are in play, since the other reacts in the same way. The reciprocity (q.v.) of that dynamic creates an interpersonal reality that is social in character. Recognition first appears in the struggle to the death (q.v.) and then acquires an unequal form in the master–slave (q.v.) relationship. It also functions in international law (q.v.) to define the relationship among states (q.v.). *See also* FUKUYAMA, FRANCIS; *PHENOMENOLOGY OF SPIRIT*; WILLIAMS, ROBERT.

RECOLLECTION (DIE ERINNERUNG). Hegel plays on both senses of the German word, in that the intellectual action of *recalling internalizes* the content of intuition (q.v.) by transferring the immediate (q.v.) image into the self's own space and time (q.v.). When the image passes out of our attention, it disappears into the storehouse of the subconscious, from which it can be recalled on the stimulus of another intuition. What is recalled now becomes the possession of intelligence (q.v.) as a representation (q.v.). *See also* IMAGINATION; PSYCHOLOGY.

REFLECTION (DIE REFLEXION). Reflection is a way of thinking (q.v.) that takes its distance from the object thought about in order to distinguish what immediately shows from what is essential and uses the laws of thought (q.v.)—identity (q.v.), noncontradiction, excluded middle, and sufficient reason—to do so. This makes it the appropriate kind of reasoning for the logic of essence (qq.v.), the second book of the *Science of Logic* (q.v.). *See also* CONTRADICTION; DIFFERENCE; GROUND.

REFORMATION. *See* PROTESTANT REFORMATION.

REIGN OF TERROR. *See* FRENCH REVOLUTION.

REINHOLD, KARL LEONHARD (1758–1823). In 1786–87, Reinhold published his "Letters on the Kantian Philosophy," which both served to popularize Immanuel Kant's (q.v.) *Critique of Pure Reason* and established his own reputation as an exponent of that philosophy. He was offered the chair in philosophy at Jena (q.v.) but moved on to Kiel (then in Denmark) in 1794 because he feared that the German reaction to the French Revolution (q.v.) would stifle any recognition of its merits. His own philosophy argued that the study of cognition (q.v.) must begin from consciousness (q.v.), which finds expression in ideas or representations (q.v.) (*Vorstellungen*): consciousness is passive in intuition (q.v.), active yet constrained in understanding (q.v.), and actively free in reason (q.v.). In his *Difference between Fichte's and Schelling's System of Philosophy* (q.v.), Hegel not only challenges Reinhold's assumption that the speculative philosophies of Johann Fichte and Friedrich Schelling (qq.v.) were identical, but also argues that Reinhold's analytical method, working from its absolute presupposition of the "arch-true," was internally inconsistent. *See also* KANT'S CRITICAL PHILOSOPHY.

RELIGION (DIE RELIGION). While a student in the seminary at Tübingen (q.v.), Hegel developed a plan for a religion that would do justice to reason (q.v.) while satisfying the hearts and imagination (q.v.) of the people. This led to several manuscripts written in Bern and Frankfurt am Main (qq.v.) on Jesus and Christianity (qq.v.). Religion, for the mature Hegel, is that sphere of human experience (q.v.) where the absolute essence (q.v.) of the world makes itself manifest and is consciously encountered, not simply in concepts (q.v.) but also in feelings, representations (q.v.), and cultic practices. The task of philosophy is to explain how these various moments fit together, how different manifestations of religion understand the way the world is in itself, and how all of them together provide a developmental pattern toward the consummate religion, or Christianity. *See also* BUDDHISM; CHINESE RELIGION; EGYPTIAN RELIGION; FAITH; *FAITH AND KNOWLEDGE;* GOD; GREEK RELIGION; INDIAN RELIGION; ISLAM; JUDAISM; *LECTURES ON THE PHILOSOPHY OF RELIGION*; PARSEE RELIGION; PHILOSOPHY OF RELIGION; RELIGION AND THE STATE; RELIGION IN THE YOUNG HEGELIANS; ROMAN RELIGION; THEOLOGICAL WRITINGS; UNHAPPY CONSCIOUSNESS.

RELIGION AND THE STATE. For Hegel, Christianity (q.v.) makes manifest the ultimate nature of the universe, though in feeling and representations (q.v.); the state (q.v.) embodies the public structure of the world for a particular people and presupposes citizens who are educated in disciplined thought. Since both articulate universal truth (q.v.) in a particular form, there is in principle no conflict. Indeed, both ultimately appeal to the authority of conscience (q.v.). However, the freedom, rights, and duties (qq.v.) enshrined in the modern state are not always reinforced by the doctrines of particular churches. Quakers and Mennonites, who refuse to commit themselves by oath or to military action, can be tolerated, because they nonetheless accept general responsibility for the well-being of the state. The Roman Catholic Church, in grounding faith (q.v.) on external authority rather than on the authority of conscience, fails to establish in its adherents that acceptance of personal responsibility that is fundamental to the modern liberal state. Hegel also defended the right of Jews to be accepted as full citizens. *See also PHILOSOPHY OF RIGHT*; PROTESTANT REFORMATION.

RELIGION IN THE FORM OF ART (DIE KUNST-RELIGION). In the *Phenomenology of Spirit* (q.v.), Hegel turns from natural religion (q.v.), in which the spiritual is embedded in the natural, to Greek religion (q.v.), in which the spiritual achieves dominance over the natural and finds expression in beautiful art (q.v.). Sacrifices before temples embellished with sculptures (q.v.), hymns, and oracles give way to the celebrations of the mysteries of Ceres and Bacchus (bread and wine). But the full artistic expression of this religion is found in epic, tragedy, and comedy (qq.v.), for language (q.v.) is the medium through which the spirit (q.v.) finds complete articulation. *See also* AESTHETICS; ARCHITECTURE; BEAUTY; DRAMA; *LECTURES ON AESTHETICS;* POETRY; SCULPTURE.

RELIGION IN THE YOUNG HEGELIANS. After his death, some of those inspired by Hegel took his philosophy of religion (q.v.) as the foundation for a move into humanism and atheism. For David Friedrich Strauss (q.v.), Hegel's translations of Christian doctrine from representations (q.v.) to thoughts and concepts (q.v.) showed it to be unreliable myth. Ludwig Feuerbach (q.v.) used motifs from Hegel's discussion of unhappy consciousness (q.v.) to show that God (q.v.) is but a projection of the human essence (q.v.) into an alien beyond (q.v.). The critique of religion thus becomes the basis for establishing human freedom (q.v.). Karl Marx (q.v.) saw the alienation (q.v.) of religion as rooted in alienated labor (q.v.) in which humans become estranged from their own labor, its products, and themselves and seek completeness and oblivion in faith (q.v.). *See also* BAUER, BRUNO; RELIGION; YOUNG HEGELIANS.

REMARKS (DIE ANMERKUNGEN). In writing the *Science of Logic* (q.v.), Hegel would frequently interrupt the flow of the logical analysis and introduce remarks that related the concepts (q.v.) and terms to the history of philosophy (q.v.), contemporary work in other disciplines, or common linguistic usage. These offer concrete illustrations of what is going on in the abstract logical discourse. He followed the same practice in both the *Encyclopedia of the Philosophical Sciences* and the *Philosophy of Right* (qq.v.), putting the remarks after the numbered, summary paragraphs that were to provide the basic structure for his lectures (q.v.). Unfortunately, in many English translations of the *Encyclopedia Logic, Philosophy of Nature,* and *Philosophy of Spirit* (qq.v.) these are not separated off typographically from the basic paragraphs. These remarks that Hegel himself added are to be distinguished from the additions (q.v.) that contain digests of his lecture material, taken from student transcripts, and were inserted into the text by the early editors of Hegel's works (and are usually indicated by the use of smaller type). *See also* ABSTRACT/CONCRETE.

REPRESENTATION (DIE VORSTELLUNG). This is the most commonly used translation for the German *Vorstellung*, although some people use "picture thinking" and others prefer "conception." Hegel distinguishes it from concepts or notions (qq.v.) in that representational thought does not understand the relationships and connections between its ideas but simply thinks of them as given. In his psychology (q.v.), he details the various intellectual activities involved in representation: recollection, imagination, and memory (qq.v.). The task of philosophy is to turn the representations of religion (q.v.) into concepts by showing how the various moments conceptually require, and lead into, each other. *See also* PHILOSOPHY OF RELIGION.

REPULSION (REPULSION). In the *Science of Logic* (q.v.), when beings are thought of as self-contained units or ones (q.v.), they must be distinguished from what they are not. At first, this contrary is the empty void, but the void is also thought of as populated by other ones, repelled by the first and repelling each other. Such mutual repulsion requires, however, that they be also drawn towards each other, as part of a single set of similar beings. *See also* ATOMISM; ATTRACTION; BEING FOR SELF.

REVEALED RELIGION (DIE GEOFFENBARTE RELIGION). *See* CHRISTIANITY.

RIGHT (DAS RECHT). In Hegel's usage, the term *right* names the basic human interest in justice and fairness, with regard to both public structures (property, civil society, the state [qq.v.]) and personal morality (q.v.). *See also PHILOSOPHY OF RIGHT*.

RIGHT-WING HEGELIANS. This term has been used to label all those who rejected the revolutionary application of Hegelianism to the transformation of society, whether they espoused the post-1830 reaction or advocated liberal, progressive reform. The genuine right wing supported the Prussian regime (Johannes Schulze, Friedrich Förster, Philipp

Marheineke, Leopold von Henning [qq.v.], Georg Gabler, Karl Göschel, Hermann Hinrichs, and Julius Schaller) and went along with its move into reaction either reluctantly or enthusiastically. While Karl Rosenkranz (q.v.) was closer to the Hegelians of the center, some, like Heinrich Leo, saw the main body of Hegelians as subversives. Johann Erdmann (q.v.) was the one who introduced Benjamin Jowett (q.v.) to Hegelian thought. Bruno Bauer (q.v.) belonged to this tendency before 1838. *See also* CENTER HEGELIANS; LEFT-WING HEGELIANS; OLD HEGELIANS; PRUSSIA; YOUNG HEGELIANS.

ROCKMORE, TOM. Rockmore sets Hegel within the history of philosophy (q.v.), struggling to overcome the arbitrary beginnings (q.v.) of first premises. Unfortunately, Hegel's use of circularity, by which beginnings are corrected in light of the experience (q.v.) of their results, cannot establish the unity of thought and being (q.v.), which is the necessary condition for absolute knowing (q.v.). *See also* CIRCLE OF CIRCLES; UNITED STATES.

ROMAN HISTORY. In Rome, the beautiful integration with nature that characterized Greek history (q.v.) is lost and everything is simply exploited by the human spirit (q.v.) in its quest for expediency. Thus, the political expands beyond particular city-states to a universal (q.v.) world order, and subjectivity (q.v.) is reduced to the legal person (q.v.). Within this desiccated existence, the seed of a richer, more dynamic spiritual life is sown with the birth of Christianity (q.v.). *See also* BEAUTY; LEGAL STATUS; PHILOSOPHY OF WORLD HISTORY; ROMAN RELIGION; STOICISM; UNHAPPY CONSCIOUSNESS; WORLD HISTORY.

ROMAN RELIGION. In *Lectures on the Philosophy of Religion* (q.v.), Hegel discusses Roman religion as a religion of expediency, which serves as the transition from Judaism and Greek religion to Christianity (qq.v). The divine lordship of the world, central to Judaism and Islam (q.v.), is invested in the emperor, and the gods of the empire are appropriated to meet the goals of the community. *See also* ROMAN HISTORY.

ROMANTIC ART (DIE ROMANTISCHE KUNSTFORM). The full integration of the ideal and the real in classical beauty (q.v.) breaks down when the ideal becomes focused on subjectivity (q.v.) and the internal life of spirit (q.v.). While the ultimate may now appear in the sensible, it can no longer be identified with it. Hegel discusses three forms of the romantic ideal: the stories of Christianity (q.v.); the honor, love, and faithfulness of chivalry; and the characters in Shakespearean drama. Once art (q.v.) has exhausted its religious foundation, there remains only the demonstration of the artist's skill and (in humor) his particular subjectivity. Painting, music, and poetry (qq.v.) are the distinctive forms of romantic art because they can suggest what is not immediately present. *See also* AESTHETICS; *LECTURES ON AESTHETICS*.

ROMANTICISM (DIE ROMANTIK). Romanticism developed as a reaction to the Enlightenment (q.v.) commitment to reason (q.v.) and ordered development, appearing in Germany as a movement called *Sturm und Drang* (Storm and Stress). Inspired by Jean-Jacques Rousseau (q.v.) and championed by Johann von Goethe (q.v.), it also drew on Immanuel Kant's (q.v.) relegation of reality (or the thing in itself) to a realm beyond (q.v.) the grasp of reason. In general, romantics argued that analytical reason was destructive of life (q.v.) and that one could attain truth (q.v.) only by going beyond reason: through intuition (Friedrich Schelling), faith (Friedrich Jacobi), the feeling of absolute dependence (Friedrich Schleiermacher), or art (Friedrich Schiller) (qq.v.). In his early theological writings (q.v.), Hegel expresses similar ideas, but in his developed system (q.v.), he uses the comprehensive dynamic of dialectical and speculative reason (qq.v.) to complement the abstracting and analytic work of understanding (q.v.). Life and love can be grasped within the rhythms of such pure thought. It was the romantic poets in England, and in particular Samuel Taylor Coleridge, who first became interested in the philosophies of Johann Fichte (q.v.) and Schelling. *See also* BEAUTIFUL SOUL; CONCEPT; FRIES, JAKOB; HERDER, JOHANN; HÖLDERLIN, FRIEDRICH.

ROSEN, STANLEY. In *G. W. F. Hegel: An Introduction to the Science of Wisdom*, Rosen shows how Hegel's self of pure negative activity both posits and absorbs the forms of normal mathematical cognition (q.v.) into a discursive whole. Dialectic and speculative reason (qq.v.) are the means by which this wisdom becomes scientific. However, Rosen argues, if form is produced by negative activity, then negative activity cannot be analyzed into formal constituents. Required is an intellectual intuition (q.v.) that sees both the forms and their oscillations. *See also* MATHEMATICS; NEGATION OF NEGATION; UNITED STATES.

ROSENKRANZ, KARL (1805–1879). Influenced by his pietist mother, Rosenkranz was first attracted to the theology of Friedrich Schleiermacher (q.v.) but began reading Hegel and, after studying with Karl Daub (q.v.) in Heidelberg, joined the Hegelian circle in Berlin, editing the *Philosophical Propaedeutic* in the first edition of Hegel's works and writing an important biography of Hegel (1844) to accompany the second edition. He continued to be a key defender of Hegelian philosophy throughout his life, arguing that the ideal was always in tension with existing conditions and rejecting Rudolf Haym's (q.v.) characterization of Hegel as antiliberal. Although he vigorously opposed revolutionary change in the Prussian form of government, he just as vigorously, and at personal risk, attacked the repressive policies of its administration. *See also* OLD HEGELIANS; PRUSSIA; RIGHT-WING HEGELIANS.

ROSENZWEIG, FRANZ (1886–1929). After *Hegel und der Staat*, which analyzed the development of Hegel's concept of the state (q.v.), Rosenzweig turned to Jewish philosophy. Hegel's philosophy attempted to reduce to one basic essence the three elements of reality—God, the world, and man—which, according to biblical religion, distinctly interact by way of creation, revelation, and redemption. *See also* EARLIEST SYSTEM-PROGRAM; JUDAISM.

ROUSSEAU, JEAN-JACQUES (1712–1778). In Hegel's view, Rousseau made a significant contribution to political philosophy when he grounded the state (q.v.) in the general will (q.v.). However, by considering will only in the form of contract (q.v.), consciously undertaken by persons (q.v.), he weakened the authority of the state, leaving it prey to the arbitrary will of individuals. He also explicitly excluded from the state any intermediate structures between the individuals and the government. For Hegel, the general will is implicitly present in the customs of the people and explicitly articulated through the intermediate organizations of family and corporation (qq.v.) as well as through the overall constitution (q.v.). *See also* HISTORY OF PHILOSOPHY; ROMANTICISM.

ROYCE, JOSIAH (1855–1916). Professor of philosophy at Harvard, Royce took issue with Francis Bradley (q.v.), arguing that the absolute (q.v.) was characterized not only as being (q.v.), but also as will (q.v.) and feeling and that individuality is the result of conscious purpose. This voluntaristic idealism (q.v.) developed into a theory of community, in which individuals who are loyal to loyalty itself can together represent their integrated reality. *See also* UNITED STATES.

RUGE, ARNOLD (1802–1880). As the *Journal for Scientific Criticism* (q.v.) (*Jahrbuch für wissenschaftliche Kritik*) became more conservative, Ruge saw the need for a more representative Hegelian journal and founded the *Hallische Jahrbuch für deutsche Wissenschaft und Kunst* (*Halle Journal for German Science and Art*). His conviction that "everything depends on history" led him to identify with the work of David Strauss, Bruno Bauer, and Ludwig Feuerbach (qq.v.), since the spirit of the times had changed from the days of the *Philosophy of Right* (q.v.), and the new age called for democracy and social progress. When, under Friedrich Wilhelm IV, the journal was suppressed in Halle, it moved to Dresden, changed its name to *Deutsche Jahrbuch,* and left behind the Hegelian center (q.v.). Later, in Paris with Karl Marx's (q.v.) collaboration, it became the *Deutsche-Französische Jahrbuch*. In German history no journal has been its equal in critical forcefulness, effectiveness, and influence on political theory. *See also* LEFT-WING HEGELIANS; YOUNG HEGELIANS.

RUSSELL, BERTRAND (1872–1970). In his *History of Western Philosophy*, Russell argues that Hegel's political theory is inconsistent with his logic and metaphysics (qq.v.). The logic argues that the true (q.v.) is a closely knit whole (q.v.) without independent constituents but united into an organism (q.v.) whose parts are interdependent and work toward a single end. At the same time, he makes the individual state (q.v.) (which is only a part) more important than the world community, while subordinating individuals completely to the law of the monarch (q.v.). Rather than a holistic logic such as Hegel espoused, one must begin by referring to singular (q.v.) things with discrete qualities (q.v.).

RUSSIA. Although Nicholas I banned philosophy from the universities, Hegelian thought was brought to Russian circles and salons by people who had studied under Hegel. Michael Bakunin (1814–1876) and Vissarion Belinski (1811–1848) were introduced to Hegel in the circle of N. V. Stankevich (1813–1840), though Bakunin, influenced by Arnold Ruge (q.v.), soon moved away from Hegel to anarchism. In exile, the "Westernizer," Alexander Herzen (1812–1870), spoke of Hegelianism as an "algebra of revolution." The Marxists Georgii Plekhanov (1856–1918) and Vladimir I. Lenin (1870–1924) integrated Hegelian motifs into their philosophies. Indeed, Lenin claimed that those who had not understood Hegel's *Science of Logic* (q.v.) could not hope to comprehend Karl Marx's (q.v.) *Capital*. Under Stalin, Hegelian philosophy was proscribed, and only began to reemerge after his death, when G. A. Bagaturiia and E. Ilienkov returned to the *Science of Logic* to explain dialectical logic and political economy.

– S –

***SACHE SELBST, DIE* (HEART OF THE MATTER, THING, FACT).** This is a difficult term to translate, and it appears as a variety of English words in different contexts. In the *Phenomenology of Spirit* (q.v.), it surfaces in the spiritual animal kingdom (q.v.) as "the heart of the matter" or "real fact," the essential category (q.v.) that integrates the diversity of intention, act, and result within sincere action (q.v.). In the 1813 *Science of Logic* (q.v.) discussion of ground (q.v.), it is used for the network of conditions or "fact" that emerges into existence (q.v.). When Hegel revised the first book of the *Science of Logic* in 1831, he introduced the term into the logic of the measureless as the "thing" that underlies those changes in quality (q.v.) that follow from altering quantities (q.v.), so that it anticipates the concept of essence (q.v.). The 1830 *Encyclopedia Logic* (q.v.) considers it as "the fact," "matter," or "thing in question" that is presupposed when analyzing necessity (q.v.) into its conditions and active implementation. In the *Philosophy of Right* (q.v.), Hegel uses *die Sache* to denote whatever is appropriated by the will (q.v.) that, as property (q.v.), becomes the subject of contracts (q.v.). *See also* MEASURE; NODAL LINE; QUANTITY INTO QUALITY.

SAINT LOUIS HEGELIANS. In 1858, Henry Conrad Brokmeyer converted William Torrey Harris (qq.v) to Hegelian philosophy and they soon formed a Kant Club which, after the Civil War, became the St.

Louis Philosophical Society, where they were joined by the historian of the movement, Denton J. Snider (1841–1925). The society published the *Journal of Speculative Philosophy*, in which appeared translations of a number of texts from Johann Fichte, Friedrich Schelling (qq.v.), and Hegel, as well as original pieces by leading American thinkers, from aging transcendentalists to the new wave of pragmatists. *See also* UNITED STATES.

SARTRE, JEAN-PAUL (1905–1980). A student of Alexandre Kojève (q.v.), Sartre was profoundly influenced by Hegelian themes. However, he challenged Hegel's assumption that the self-knowledge of consciousness (q.v.) is the same as its being (q.v.). In part, this view stems from the fact that the French *pour soi* is more closely related to Hegel's "for consciousness" than it is to the German "for itself" (qq.v.). But it also is grounded in Sartre's conviction that the self as consciousness is always confronted by an abyss of nothingness, which is not just the contrary of being but its contradiction (q.v.). *See also* NOTHING.

SAXE-WEIMAR. The university of Jena (q.v.) was situated within the duchy of Saxe-Weimar, whose duke, Karl August, invited his fellow freemason (q.v.) Johann von Goethe (q.v.) to become minister of culture. Under Goethe's tutelage, Weimar became the center of German cultural life, attracting Friedrich Schiller, Friedrich Hölderlin, Johann Herder (qq.v.), and many others. The university appointed first Karl Reinhold and later Johann Fichte (qq.v.) to the chair of philosophy and introduced empirical sciences for the first time into German academic life. Karl August resisted the repressive measures imposed by other German principalities in the aftermath of the French Revolution (q.v.) and either protected or intervened on behalf of those who were persecuted by reactionary governments (such as Jakob Fries [q.v.]) or (as in the case of Fichte) by enraged public opinion.

SCHELLING, FRIEDRICH WILHELM JOSEPH (1775–1854). A fellow student of Hegel and Friedrich Hölderlin (q.v.) in the theological seminary at Tübingen (q.v.), the precocious Schelling quickly obtained a university position at Jena (q.v.). When Hegel came into his father's inheritance, he joined Schelling in 1800 and collaborated with him in the *Critical Journal of Philosophy* (q.v.), taking over lectures on the philosophy of nature (q.v.) after Schelling departed for Würzburg in 1803. In his *Difference between Fichte's and Schelling's System of Philosophy* and *Lectures on the History of Philosophy* (qq.v.), Hegel credits Schelling with the speculative insight that one needs to think the unity of what has been distinguished, so that the absolute (q.v.) becomes the undifferentiated union of subjective and objective. The transcendental idealism of Johann Fichte (qq.v.) needed to be balanced by a speculative philosophy of nature, each of which leads into the other. Schelling, however, lacked a logic (q.v.) that would show the internal necessity (q.v.) of this union, and in the preface to the *Phenomenology of Spirit* (q.v.), Hegel characterized his absolute as a night in which all cows are black (q.v.). In 1841, Schelling was invited to the University of Berlin by King Friedrich Wilhelm IV to counterbalance the influence of the Hegelians, both Young and Old (qq.v.). Søren Kierkegaard, Friedrich Engels (qq.v.), and Michael Bakunin all sat in those lectures. For the elder Schelling, Hegel's move from the logic to the philosophy of nature was a philosophically unjustified leap from thought to reality. *See also* ABSOLUTE, THE (SCHELLING); HISTORY OF PHILOSOPHY; ROMANTICISM; RUSSIA; SPECULATIVE REASON.

SCHILLER, FRIEDRICH (1759–1805). Poet, playwright, and philosopher, Schiller was (like Hegel) born in Württemberg (q.v.); in due course he became professor of history at the university of Jena (q.v.) and member of the court of Duke Karl August of Saxe-Weimar (q.v.). His *Letters on the Aesthetic Education of Man*, which Hegel called a masterpiece on first reading, argued that the moral disposition of man (which seeks for rational unity) and human nature (which is immersed in a diversity of details) need to be integrated through art (q.v.), which is grounded in sentiment and free play, yet involves discipline and form. Schiller's play *The Robbers* probably was in Hegel's mind as he discussed virtue (q.v.) in the *Phenomenology of Spirit* (q.v.). Hegel also concluded that work with an excerpt from Schiller's poem *Friendship. See also* ROMANTICISM.

SCHLEIERMACHER, FRIEDRICH (1768–1834). In *On Religion* (1799), Schleiermacher defended religion (q.v.) by appealing to the feeling of absolute dependence that is the ground (q.v.) of both action and cognition (qq.v.), of both practical and theoretical reason. In 1810, he became professor of theology in Berlin, espousing liberal causes. Hegel took issue with Schleiermacher's first principles, saying that feeling could not distinguish humans from animals and that religion could only be defended by recognizing through disciplined thought that it was the expression of reason (q.v.). Schleiermacher, in turn, blocked Hegel's membership in the Prussian Academy of Sciences. Many of Hegel's early disciples, such as Karl Daub, Philipp Marheineke, and Karl Rosenkranz (qq.v.), came from theological faculties where they had become dissatisfied with Schleiermacher's approach. *See also* ROMANTICISM.

SCHULZE, GOTTLOB ERNST (1761–1833). In his anonymously published *Aenesidemus*, Schulze, then professor of philosophy at Helmstedt, attacked the critical philosophy of Immanuel Kant and Karl Reinhold (qq.v.) by showing that philosophy can establish neither the existence (q.v.) nor the nonexistence of things in themselves, nor can it set limits to our cognitive capacity. Johann Fichte (q.v.) began to develop the principles of his own *Science of Knowledge* in a review of this skeptical work. And Hegel's review of Schulze's later *Critique of Theoretical Philosophy* in the *Critical Journal of Philosophy* (q.v.) set this skepticism (q.v.), which did not doubt the reality of our representations (q.v.), against the ancient skepticism that challenged the givens of sense. He also contrasted Schulze's use of the disagreements among philosophers as reason to discredit them with Gottfried Leibniz's and Friedrich Jacobi's (qq.v.) suggestion that philosophers are in fact justified in the fundamentals that they affirm, though not in the theses they deny. In 1810, Schulze moved to Göttingen, where he had Arthur Schopenhauer as a student.

SCHULZE, JOHANNES (1786–1869). Invited by Prince Karl August von Hardenberg and Karl von Altenstein to be director of higher education in the Prussian Ministry of Education, Schulze, disillusioned by the post-Napoleonic reaction in the state of Hessen-Kassel, moved to Berlin (q.v.) in the hope that progress would be made toward constitutional government. He retained his position even though he came under suspicion as favorable to the "demagogic" student movement. Schulze attended all of Hegel's lectures over several years and worked with Hegel in placing Hegelian disciples (e.g., Friedrich Förster and Eduard Gans [qq.v.]) in teaching and administrative posts. After Hegel's death, he was one of those who collaborated in the first edition of the complete works, editing the *Phenomenology of Spirit* (q.v.). With von Altenstein, he began to lose influence after 1835. *See also* CONSTITUTION; PRUSSIA.

SCIENCE (DIE WISSENSCHAFT). Unlike English, in which the word *science* is frequently used only for the natural and social sciences, the German term applies to any disciplined body of knowledge (q.v.) that is developed according to rigorous systematic principles. So not only does Hegel have a science of logic (q.v.), but his first title for the *Phenomenology of Spirit* (q.v.) was "Science of the Experience of Consciousness" (qq.v.), and he frequently uses the term for his systematic philosophy as a whole. *See also* SYSTEM.

SCIENCE OF LOGIC (WISSENSCHAFT DER LOGIK). During the years (1808–16) while Hegel was headmaster of the secondary school in Nürnberg (q.v.), he wrote the first part of his system (q.v.). The *Science of Logic* examines the way thought functions when it is not thinking (q.v.) about things in the world but rather formulating and clarifying its own basic concepts (q.v.). Starting with "being" (q.v.), the most indeterminate of concepts, it explores the simple transitions (q.v.) of thought (sometimes called *implications*), the way thought reflects on content already present to determine what is essential, and the careful understanding (q.v.) of concepts, ending with a discussion of logical method (q.v.) in the absolute idea (q.v.). When Hegel died in 1831, he had just finished revising the first book of the *Science of Logic* on the doctrine of being. Most editions and translations (Walter H. Johnston and Leslie G. Struthers, or Arnold V. Miller into English) use the revision for this section, though Pierre-Jean Labarrière and Gwendolyn Jarczyk translated the first edition into French. In 1817, Hegel wrote the *Encyclopedia of the Philosophical Sciences* (q.v.) as a textbook for his lectures (q.v.). The first part provides a summary of the larger *Science of Logic*. This has been published separately, often with the same title as the larger work, and includes additions (q.v.) taken from lecture notes made by Hegel's students over the years. The abridgement did not always follow the same order as the full text and was revised twice, complicating later readings of this part of his system (q.v.). *See also* ABSOLUTE, THE; ACTUALITY; APPEARANCE; ATTRACTION; BECOMING; BEING FOR SELF; CAUSALITY; CHEMISM; COGNITION; CONTRADICTION; DASEIN; DETERMINATION; DIALECTIC; DIFFERENCE; DIVERSITY; ELECTIVE AFFINITY; *ENCYCLOPEDIA LOGIC*; ESSENCE; EXISTENCE; FINITE; FORCE; GROUND; IDEA; IDENTITY; INFINITE; INNER/OUTER; JUDGMENT; LAWS OF THOUGHT; LIFE; LIMIT; LOGIC; MAGNITUDE; MEASURE; MECHANISM;

METHOD; NECESSITY; NODAL LINE; NOTHING; OBJECTIVITY; ONE; OPPOSITION; OTHER; PARTICULAR; QUALITY; QUANTITY; QUANTITY INTO QUALITY; QUANTUM; RATIO; REASON; RECIPROCITY; REFLECTION; REMARKS; REPULSION; *SACHE SELBST*; SCIENCE; SOMETHING; SPECULATIVE REASON; SUBJECTIVITY; SUBLATE; SUBSTANTIALITY; SYLLOGISM; TELEOLOGY; THESIS; THING; UNIVERSAL; WHOLE/PART.

SCULPTURE (DIE SKULPTUR). Sculpture presents human spirituality in three-dimensional reality but in an idealized form, since any dynamic has been reduced to rest. The classical art (q.v.) of the Greeks brought this to the point of perfection, in that artists in their freedom incorporated a strict sense of proportion. Earlier Egyptian art was more static, lacking grace, as the craftsmen followed standard types. *See also* AESTHETICS; ART; EGYPTIAN RELIGION; GREEK RELIGION; RELIGION IN THE FORM OF ART; SYMBOLIC ART.

SELF-CONSCIOUSNESS (DAS SELBSTBEWUSSTSEIN). In the *Phenomenology of Spirit* (q.v.), Hegel turns from claims to know the objects of consciousness (q.v.) to types of self-knowledge. The immediate (q.v.), natural form of such self-awareness is found in desire (q.v.), which then seeks permanence through the struggle to the death, mastery, stoicism, skepticism, and the unhappy consciousness (qq.v). In the *Philosophy of Right* (q.v.), Hegel points out that self-consciousness of this sort does not yet know itself as a person (q.v.), as infinite, universal, and free (qq.v.). That will require legal status (q.v.). Because it incorporates our awareness of objects into our self-awareness, self-consciousness is the consummate example of being for self (q.v.). *See also* PHENOMENOLOGY.

SENSE CERTAINTY (DIE SINNLICHE GEWISSHEIT). In the *Phenomenology of Spirit* (q.v.), sense certainty is a mode of knowing in which we simply affirm what we *immediately* (q.v.) receive through the senses. It fails as knowledge (q.v.) because movement through space and time (qq.v.) continually *mediates* what is given. The self must intervene to connect past to present and here to there so immediacy is lost, leading to the knowledge claim of perception (q.v.). *See also* MEDIATION.

SINGULAR (DAS EINZELNE). This term has two complementary senses in Hegel's thought. On the one hand, it is an individual (q.v.) object of reference. On the other hand, where a number of diverse particulars are integrated into a totality (q.v.), a unique singular results. In this sense a singular is comparable to a concrete universal (q.v).

SKEPTICISM (DER SKEPTIZISMUS). Hegel's review of Gottlob Ernst Schulze's (q.v.) *Critique of Theoretical Philosophy* in the *Critical Journal of Philosophy* (q.v.) explored the relationship of skepticism to philosophy (q.v.), comparing the ancient skepticism that questioned the validity of the senses with the modern type that challenged the reliability of our thinking (q.v.) based on a dogmatic acceptance of the truth (q.v.) of the senses. The method of the *Phenomenology of Spirit* (q.v.) is described as a path of skepticism and despair, because each claim to firm knowledge (q.v.), when assessed against its own standards, proves to be inconsistent and false. Whenever skepticism shows the contradictions (q.v.) within everything finite (q.v.) and distinct, it is bringing to bear the implicit truth of the dialectic (q.v.) but fails to push this analysis to its limits, where its negating would itself be negated. Within the internal sequence of the *Phenomenology*, skeptics are described as people who, emerging from stoicism (q.v.), deny whatever "truth" is set forth to be believed. As this denial is implicitly maintained to be the truth, a tension is introduced between the changeless truth and changing untruths. Unhappy consciousness (q.v.) struggles to come to terms with this contradiction. *See also* HISTORY OF PHILOSOPHY; NEGATION OF NEGATION.

SOCRATES. In that Socrates appealed to his own immediate subjectivity (qq.v.) as the guarantee of truth (q.v.), he threatened the religious customs and political consensus that were the foundation of Athenian democracy. He was thus quite legitimately found guilty of both atheism and misleading the young. Nonetheless, the principle of subjectivity so infected Athenian society that it was unable to defend itself against the Spartans. This principle had to be woven into the whole fabric of ethical life (q.v.) in the Roman Empire before it could become the basis of a stable society. *See also* GREEK HISTORY; LEGAL STATUS; PERSON; ROMAN HISTORY.

SOLOMON, ROBERT. The title of Solomon's book, *In the Spirit of Hegel*, expresses its focus. While wanting to introduce Hegel to his contemporaries, Solomon also endeavors to maintain the spirit of his philosophy (q.v.) by reworking its details, arguing that there are two different phenomenologies within the *Phenomenology of Spirit* (q.v.), a phenomenology of theory (the work of the philosopher of the absolute [q.v.]) and a phenomenology of practice (the work of an historicist). The secret of Hegel is that, for all his explicit references to religion (q.v.), he was a humanistic atheist and pantheist. *See also* UNITED STATES.

SOMETHING (ETWAS). In the *Science of Logic* (q.v.), the concept of "something" is the simple way of thinking a qualified being (or Dasein [q.v.]). It inevitably leads on to the thought of an "other" (q.v.) and to the determinations (q.v.) that distinguish them from each other. *See also* QUALITY.

SOUL (DIE SEELE). Hegel uses this term for the most basic aspects of the human spirit (q.v.), those that are not mediated by consciousness or intelligence (qq.v.): natural genetic attributes and alterations, feelings, and unconscious habits. *See also* ANTHROPOLOGY; BODY (DER LEIB); IMMEDIATE; LIFE; MEDIATION; *PHILOSOPHY OF SPIRIT*.

SPACE (DER RAUM). Space is the most basic external relation (q.v.) to be incorporated into a *Philosophy of Nature* (q.v.). In Hegel's *Phenomenology of Spirit* (q.v.), it is discovered to be fundamental to all experience (q.v.). Because, as knowing subjects, we are always changing our spatial relationships to the objects we are sensing, we find it impossible to fix the content of pure unmediated sensation. *See also* IMMEDIATE; SENSE CERTAINTY; TIME.

SPECULATIVE PROPOSITION (DER SPEKULATIVE SATZ). In the preface to the *Phenomenology of Spirit* (q.v.), Hegel suggests that a philosophical sentence must be read speculatively. That is, the subject must not be taken as fixed and the predicate just added on, but the meaning of the subject must be used to interpret the predicate and vice versa, so the whole sentence both distinguishes its various moments yet shows how they are intrinsically integrated. *See also* SPECULATIVE REASON.

SPECULATIVE REASON (DIE SPEKULATIVE VERNUNFT). When dialectic (q.v.) shows the contradictions (q.v.) that result when understanding (q.v.) fixes its categories (q.v.), the result is not an abstract skepticism (q.v.) but a recognition that the contradiction has a determinate ground (q.v.). Each side of the opposition (q.v.) leads into the other in a circle of circles (q.v.) that becomes an infinite (q.v.) regress. Speculative reason then grasps the inherent unity that underlies dialectical opposition. This comprehension of differentiated determinations in a single thought produces a universal (q.v.) that is not abstract, like the universals of understanding, but concrete. This pattern can be seen in the organization of Hegel's works. In the *Phenomenology of Spirit* (q.v.), consciousness (q.v.) leads into self-consciousness (q.v.), whereas self-consciousness leads back to simple consciousness. Reason (q.v.) adopts categories as the expression of the speculative unity of the two sides. In the *Science of Logic* (q.v.), quality (q.v.) leads into quantity (q.v.) and quantity goes back to quality. Their speculative interrelation involves measure (q.v.). In the *Philosophy of Right* (q.v.), abstract right (q.v.) leads into reflection on subjective morality (q.v.), whereas morality needs the objectivity of right. The speculative integration of these two is the sphere of ethical life (q.v.). *See also* ABSTRACT/CONCRETE; ANTINOMIES; CONCEPT; LOGIC; METHOD; REASON; SINGULAR; SUBLATE; TOTALITY.

SPINOZA, BARUCH (1632–1677). While Spinoza's system (q.v.) resembles that of Hegel in arguing for the necessary interconnection of all parts within a totality (q.v.), Hegel finds it deficient. For the attributes and modes are not derived from substance (q.v.) through its own self-determination but are added by external reflection (q.v.) as further independent definitions. Thus, Spinza's absolute (q.v.) lacks personality, and the idea (q.v.) remains abstract and lifeless. *See also* ABSTRACT/CONCRETE; HESS, MOSES; HISTORY OF PHILOSOPHY; NEGATION OF NEGATION.

SPIRIT (DER GEIST). Spirit, for Hegel, means self-conscious life (qq.v.), and it applies to the divine as well as the human. The term *finite* (q.v.) *spirit* can be used for individuals, but it can also refer to a community in which the customs that govern social interaction create a field of forces with its own distinctive and unique character, such as a family, a civil society, a religion, and a state (qq.v.). In the *Phenomenology of Spirit* (q.v.), the chapter on spirit describes a kind of knowledge (q.v.) in which members of a community understand and grasp the complexity of their own interaction. Thus, Sophocles' *Antigone* (q.v.) captures the truth (q.v.) of ancient Greek culture; Denis Diderot's (q.v.) *Rameau's Nephew* does the same for the Enlightenment (q.v.). Some translators have used *mind* (q.v.) for the German word, but this approach misses both the divine and the communal aspects of its meaning.

SPIRITUAL ANIMAL KINGDOM (DAS GEISTIGE TIERREICH). In the *Phenomenology of Spirit* (q.v.), reason (q.v.) recognizes that efforts to get at the truth (q.v.) of *objects* through the categories of observing reason (qq.v.) and of *subjects* through the categories of pleasure, law of the heart, and virtue (qq.v.) are all one sided. Its first attempt to overcome this partiality is to see the actions of individuals as simply actualizing in complete sincerity their own capacities without any regard to external criteria or standards. This is the heart of the matter or *Sache selbst* (q.v.). But when any individual acts, she or he finds that what was to be simply the heart of the matter as such becomes distorted through the concern of others (*ihre Sache*), and these others see her or his action (q.v.) equally as that person's own peculiar, manipulative concern. The universal category is thus lost in a network of deceit, and has to be set out as law (q.v.). *See also* LAW-GIVING REASON; LAW-TESTING REASON.

STACE, WALTER TERENCE (1886–1967). Although Stace's own philosophy combined empiricism (q.v.) with mysticism, his *Philosophy of Hegel*, written while he was an imperial civil servant in Ceylon (Sri Lanka), provides a sympathetic and readable exposition of Hegel's system (q.v.) as found in the *Encyclopedia of the Philosophical Sciences* (q.v.) and the lectures on aesthetics and philosophy of religion (qq.v.). Hegel's method of deduction first shows there to be a contradiction (q.v.) in a concept (q.v.) or stage being analyzed, and then demonstrates the next stage to be the necessary resolution of that contradiction. Unfortunately, this ideal is not always achieved. In the logic (q.v.), metaphors with their illegitimate appeal to experience (q.v.) are on occasion required to effect transitions (q.v.); while in the philosophy of spirit (q.v.), even though the contradictions are evident, Hegel cannot always justify the specific solutions that he in fact advances. *See also* UNITED STATES.

STATE (DER STAAT). Rejecting the liberal view of the state that regards public administration (police [q.v.]) as merely moderating the free activities of civil society (q.v.), Hegel argues that the modern state is the realized goal of world history (q.v.), in that it not only integrates a people into a unified political order, mobilizing their patriotism and expecting their allegiance, but also provides a secure constitutional framework within which individuals are free to follow their interests and develop their abilities. The state's authority stems from its rational character as a cohesive universal (q.v.). At the same time, it necessarily distinguishes within itself particular functions so that contingencies (q.v.) can occur. Free citizens not only know and will (q.v.) their own actions (q.v.), but also, both implicitly and explicitly, know and will the actions of the state. The state becomes distinctive in its relations with other states, in which it acts as an individual (q.v.) through the decisions of the monarch (q.v.). In extreme cases, it calls on its citizens to risk their lives in war (q.v.), evidence that it is a more ultimate expression of free spiritual life than is any individual person (q.v.). *See also* CONSTITUTION; EXECUTIVE; FREEDOM; INTERNATIONAL LAW; LEGISLATURE; PHILOSOPHY OF WORLD HISTORY; REASON; RELIGION AND THE STATE; WORLD HISTORY.

STEUART, SIR JAMES D. (1712–1780). During his years in Frankfurt am Main (q.v.), Hegel not only read Steuart's *Inquiry Concerning the Principles of Political Economy* but also wrote out a detailed commentary. Steuart expounded an evolutionary theory of society, explaining it on the basis of two postulates: that humans are dominated by sexual desire, thus increasing the population; and that they are motivated by self-interest. Because of these forces, pastoral cultures give way to agricultural ones, and the latter to the exchange economy of commercial societies. *See also* LUKÁCS, GYÖRGY.

STIRLING, JAMES HUTCHISON (1820–1909). In 1856, the 36-year-old medically trained Scot went to Heidelberg, where he was introduced to Hegel's thought. After a long "struggle," he published in 1865 the first major book on Hegel in English: *The Secret of Hegel: Being the Hegelian System in Origin, Principle, Form, and Matter.* Whereas Immanuel Kant (q.v.) had assigned the role of thought in constituting the known world to subjective consciousness (q.v.), Hegel conceived it objectively as the absolute universal (qq.v.) principle on which the whole (q.v.) is founded. The book was hailed as a major achievement by Benjamin Jowett, Thomas Hill Green, Karl Rosenkranz, Johann Erdmann (qq.v.), Thomas Carlyle, and Ralph Waldo Emerson. *See also* TRANSCENDENTAL IDEALISM.

STIRNER, MAX (1806–1856). Johann Kaspar Schmidt adopted this pseudonym for his book *The Ego and His Own* (1845). A student of Hegel's in Berlin (q.v.), Stirner held that even the left-wing Hegelians (q.v.) were conditioned by the dominance of a universal spirit (qq.v.). The full transformation of the modern world would come not by displacing the transcendent into the human species-being, as Ludwig Feuerbach and Karl Marx (qq.v.) proposed, but by challenging all essences (q.v.) in the name of the will (q.v.) and instincts of the individual (q.v.), who, in rebelling against the state (q.v.), does not propose a new social order but simply affirms his or her own independence. *See also* YOUNG HEGELIANS.

STOICISM (DER STOIZISMUS). In the *Phenomenology of Spirit* (q.v.), stoics are those, whether slaves or emperors, who know themselves as essentially thinking (q.v.) beings. Since this self-definition offers no way of determining what is in fact to be thought, it easily converts into skepticism (q.v.), which simply questions whatever is proposed. The social context within which stoicism finds its place is discussed under legal status (q.v.). *See also* HISTORY OF PHILOSOPHY; ROMAN HISTORY.

STRAUSS, DAVID FRIEDRICH (1808–1874). The young theological student from Württemberg (q.v.) arrived in Berlin (q.v.) just a week before Hegel's death. He continued his studies with Philipp Marheineke and Leopold von Henning (qq.v.) but then returned to Tübingen to write his *Life of Jesus* as a negative critique of both traditional religious representation (q.v.) and theological rationalism. The gospel stories were myths, formed by religious consciousness to express spiritual truth. Only by abandoning belief in their historicity could philosophic comprehension become the basis of modern society. This work was the first shot in the Young Hegelians' (q.v.) attack on Christian transcendence, but Strauss was soon left behind by the more radical critique of Bruno Bauer and Ludwig Feuerbach (qq.v.). The only source we have for Hegel's lectures on the philosophy of religion in 1831 is an edited version Strauss made from the notes of an unknown student who was there. *See also* LEFT-WING HEGELIANS; RELIGION IN THE YOUNG HEGELIANS; YOUNG HEGELIANS.

STUTTGART. Hegel was born in Stuttgart on August 27, 1770, the son of an administrative official under the Duke of Württemberg (q.v.). He attended the local gymnasium (or secondary school) where he was introduced to the classics, philosophy (q.v.), and history, before proceeding in 1788 to the theological seminary in Tübingen (q.v.) on a government bursary. *See also* FAMILY.

SUBJECT. *See* **TRUTH AS SUBJECT.**

SUBJECTIVE SPIRIT (DER SUBJEKTIVE GEIST). While this term applies to individual human subjects who feel, think, and will, Hegel recognizes that developed human subjectivity (q.v.) is always the product of interpersonal relations, by which spirit (q.v.) becomes objective. Anthropology, phenomenology, and psychology (qq.v.) explore how, as soul, consciousness, intelligence, and will (qq.v.), the complex integrated self develops. *See also* LECTURES ON THE PHILOSOPHY OF SUBJECTIVE SPIRIT; OBJECTIVE SPIRIT; *PHILOSOPHY OF SPIRIT*; RECOGNITION.

SUBJECTIVITY (DIE SUBJEKTIVITÄT). In the *Science of Logic* (q.v.), subjectivity names a way of thinking (q.v.) about the processes of thinking itself. These include conceiving (or defining the particular determinations of a concept [q.v.]), judging (or connecting two or more concepts), and inferring (or showing the ground [q.v.] for the connection in a judgment [q.v.]). Because the transcendental idealism (q.v.) of Immanuel Kant and Johann Fichte (qq.v.) simply explored the way the self applies such categories (q.v.) and inferences, Hegel and Friedrich Schelling (q.v.) looked for a balancing objectivity (q.v.) in a philosophy of nature (q.v.) and in the actions (q.v.) and institutions of public life. *See also* OBJECTIVE SPIRIT; SUBJECTIVE SPIRIT; SYLLOGISM.

SUBLATE, SUPERSEDE (AUFHEBEN). This is a key weapon in Hegel's arsenal. The German word translated by these terms has three distinct meanings: to preserve, to cancel, and to raise to a higher level.

For Hegel, all three can function simultaneously. He discusses the term in connection with the move in the *Science of Logic* (q.v.) from becoming (q.v.) to determinate being (Dasein [q.v.]). Becoming is both a passing away (from being to nothing [qq.v.]) and a coming to be (from nothing to being). Taken together these two make a circle: from being to nothing to being to nothing to . . . . A being that comes from nothing and goes back to nothing is a determinate being. Sublate describes this kind of move in which pairs of moments, succeeding each other in an endless cycle, collapse into a new single thought. *See also* CIRCLE OF CIRCLES; OVERREACH; SPECULATIVE REASON.

SUBLIME (DAS ERHABENE). While beauty (q.v.) is the complete expression of the ideal in an art object, the sublime communicates a sense of the measureless by using symbols to negate their own immediate significance. Although there is some sense of this sublimity in Indian pantheism and the mysticism of Islam (q.v.), its finest expression can be found in Hebrew poetry, for the concept of creation out of nothing (q.v.) expresses the incomprehensible nature of God (q.v.), while affirming the capacity of created things to talk about his nature. *See also* AESTHETICS; INDIAN RELIGION; JUDAISM; MEASURE; *SACHE SELBST*.

SUBSTANTIALITY (DIE SUBSTANTIALITÄT). The relation between substance and its accidents is a way in which a whole (q.v.) necessarily determines its constituent moments. While accidents interact, they have no independent power. In contrast, substance is that which mediates itself and is thus a creative and destructive power. So the concept (q.v.) of substance leads over to the concept of causality (q.v.). *See also* NECESSITY; *SCIENCE OF LOGIC*; TRUTH AS SUBJECT.

SUPERSEDE. *See* SUBLATE.

SYLLOGISM, INFERENCE (DER SCHLUSS). Hegel explores the logic (q.v.) of mediated reasoning or inference in the third book of the *Science of Logic* (q.v.). Mediation (q.v.) can be a particular transition (qq.v.) from a universal to a singular (qq.v.) (as in the barbara syllogism), a singular reflection (q.v.) on a set of particulars to determine what is universal (as in induction), or a universal determining its particular moments to be contrary singulars (as in the disjunctive syllogism). Mediation, however, is a feature of the natural and social world as well. In addition, those real mediations turn out to have the same structure as the various syllogistic forms, depending on whether the mediating or middle term is singular, particular, or universal. *See also* CONCEPT; JUDGMENT; SUBJECTIVITY.

SYMBOLIC ART (DIE SYMBOLISCHE KUNSTFORM). In the Eastern traditions of India, Egypt, and Palestine, the ideal struggles to find appropriate expression in reality. The result is not beauty but the sublime (qq.v.). Works of art (q.v.), and particularly architecture (q.v.), suggest an incomprehensible beyond (q.v.). *See also* EGYPTIAN RELIGION; INDIAN RELIGION; JUDAISM; *LECTURES ON AESTHETICS*.

SYSTEM (DAS SYSTEM). In the preface to the *Phenomenology of Spirit* (q.v.), Hegel points out that, since truth is subject (qq.v.) as well as substance, knowing the truth involves grasping the way its various components contribute toward constituting not only the whole (q.v.), but each other as well. They are thus organically and systematically interrelated. In the *Phenomenology*, the *Science of Logic*, the *Encyclopedia of the Philosophical Sciences,* and the *Philosophy of Right* (qq.v.), then, the analysis of each stage shows not only how one moment leads on to the next, but also how that whole stage, once it reaches its complete analysis, is transformed into the nucleus for the following stage. *See also* JENA DRAFTS FOR A SYSTEM; ORGANISM; SUBSTANTIALITY.

– T –

TANABE HAJIME (1885–1962). After studying in Berlin and Freiburg, Tanabe made his name with work on Immanuel Kant (q.v.) and the philosophy of mathematics (q.v.). In the 1930s, he turned to Hegel's dialectic (q.v.) and developed a logic (q.v.) of absolute mediation (q.v.), with species mediating between genus and individual. If everything should be thoroughly mediated, and if nothing (q.v.) should be left immediate (q.v.), he claimed, only nothingness would remain. So Tanabe's philosophy ended where Nishida Kitaro's (q.v.) began. *See also* JAPAN.

TAYLOR, CHARLES. In Taylor's *Hegel*, he traces Hegel's roots to the writings of Johann Gottfried von Herder (q.v.), in which human activity and human life are seen as expressions of an ideal. So Hegel sees nature (q.v.) as an expression of spirit (q.v.), and humans are to recover an expressive unity with nature while aspiring towards a rational autonomy. Unfortunately, the Enlightenment's (q.v.) preoccupation with utility (q.v.) and the domination of nature has prevailed in modern culture. While Hegel's synthesis no longer has compelling power, it nonetheless is often appropriated by protest movements that challenge the present without any clear vision of the future. *See also* CANADA; HEGEL SOCIETY OF GREAT BRITAIN.

TELEOLOGY (DIE TELEOLOGIE). For Hegel, teleology describes the way thought cunningly organizes mechanical and chemical processes (q.v.) to achieve some conceptual end. He discusses Immanuel Kant's concept (qq.v.) of an organic teleology of whole and part (q.v.) under the concept of life (q.v.). *See also* CHEMISM; CUNNING OF REASON; KANT'S *CRITIQUE OF JUDGMENT*; MECHANISM; OBJECTIVITY; ORGANISM; *SCIENCE OF LOGIC*.

THALES OF MILETUS. Hegel calls Thales the first philosopher in that he looked for some one reality that is the essence (q.v.) of all and thus claimed that particulars (q.v.) have no independence. Nonetheless, his thesis that everything is water remains a one-sided materialism, lacking the dynamic of subjectivity (q.v.). *See also* HISTORY OF PHILOSOPHY.

THEOLOGICAL WRITINGS. While a student in the seminary at Tübingen (q.v.), the young Hegel developed a plan for a religion (q.v.) of the people that would exemplify the standards of reason (q.v.), satisfy the heart and imagination (q.v.), and incorporate the political and social structures that meet the needs of life. He worked this out in a number of drafts written during his time in Bern and Frankfurt am Main (qq.v.). The major texts are a life of Jesus (q.v.), which describes him as a moral teacher; an essay on how the moral initiative of Jesus was transformed into a positive religion relying on authority; and a study of Judaism and Christianity (qq.v.), showing how the spirit (q.v.) that animated them determined their destiny. Although some excerpts were reproduced in Karl Rosenkranz's (q.v.) biography, they were first published in their entirety by Hermann Nohl in 1907. They have been translated into English by

Thomas M. Knox (*On Christianity: Early Theological Writings*) and Peter Fuss and John Dobbins (*Three Essays 1793–1795*). *See also* DILTHEY, WILHELM; HÄRING, THEODOR; HARRIS, HENRY STILTON; PLANT, RAYMOND.

THESIS, ANTITHESIS, SYNTHESIS. The British idealists (q.v.) derived from Immanuel Kant's (q.v.) discussion of the categories (q.v.) the triad of thesis, antithesis, and synthesis to explain Hegel's philosophical method (q.v.). Each thesis generates its antithesis, and the contradiction that results requires a synthesis. Gustav E. Mueller showed that this vocabulary was never adopted by Hegel himself but had been used by a popular lecturer in Kiel to introduce students to Hegel's use of reason (q.v.). It should, therefore, be handled with a healthy grain of salt. *See also* METHOD.

THING (DAS DING). Things immediately exist. But when, in the *Science of Logic* (q.v.), reflection (q.v.) analyzes what things are, it comes upon properties (q.v.), at first distinguished from the thing in itself, but then recognized as essential to it. These properties develop an independent existence (q.v.) as materials that interpenetrate each other within the thing. The thing that started out simply as existing thus comes to be thought of as appearance (q.v.). *See also* PERCEPTION.

THING (DIE SACHE). *See SACHE SELBST.*

THINKING (DAS DENKEN). In Hegel's psychology (q.v.), the activity of thinking involves substantive thoughts that have moved beyond the distinction of word and meaning. In this way, intelligence (q.v.) is able to explain and grasp why singulars fall under universal categories (qq.v.); how different thoughts are related as complements, contraries, and conditions; and how thoughts can be integrated into an inferential totality (q.v.). *See also* CONCEPT; CONTRADICTION; DIALECTIC; MEMORY; JUDGMENT; REASON; SPECULATIVE REASON; SYLLOGISM; UNDERSTANDING.

TIME (DIE ZEIT). Time is one of the basic external relations (q.v.) that have to be incorporated into a *Philosophy of Nature* (q.v.). It adds the dynamic of becoming (q.v.) to the spatial relation of side by side. In Hegel's *Phenomenology of Spirit* (q.v.), it emerges as fundamental to all experience (q.v.). Because the passage of time changes our relationship to the objects we know through our senses, we find it impossible to fix a definite content for unmediated sensation. Instead, we know things that endure through a mediated series of temporal moments. *See also* IMMEDIATE; MEDIATION; SENSE CERTAINTY; SPACE.

TOTALITY (DIE TOTALITÄT). Speculative reason (q.v.) looks at the reciprocal implication of particulars (q.v.) as a totality, which is then integrated into a single concept. So totality frequently takes the place of singular (q.v.) as the third in a Hegelian triad.

TRAGEDY (DIE TRAGÖDIE). Underlying tragic drama (q.v.) are the substantive powers that work out the destiny of eternal justice. In specific and particular actions (q.v.), self-conscious knowledge (qq.v.) is pitted against an unknown reality, or two characters embody in their deeds eternal principles that are nonetheless partial and opposed to each other. Only the chorus reacts to the action as a whole, but the chorus remains a passive spectator. The ultimate demands of justice are achieved in a final resolution that brings to naught those individuals who have violated its principles. While classical drama works within the world of the Olympian gods, modern drama explores the tragic implications of great human commitments: love of parent, child, sister, or beloved, patriotism, and the passionate actions of religious faith (q.v.). *See also* AESTHETICS; *ANTIGONE*; ART; COMEDY; POETRY; RELIGION IN THE FORM OF ART; SCHILLER, FRIEDRICH.

TRANSCENDENTAL IDEALISM (DER TRANSCENDENTALE IDEALISMUS). Immanuel Kant (q.v.) in his *Critique of Pure Reason* showed that empiricism (q.v.) could be justified only through an analysis of the subjective conditions that are required to have any knowledge (q.v.) at all. Because these conditions are not present to observation, he called them transcendental in that they applied to all experience (q.v.) whatever. (This is to be distinguished from "transcendent," which talks about God and the beyond [qq.v.].) Johann Fichte (q.v.) then derived the Kantian categories (q.v.) from the transcendental subject; Friedrich Schelling (q.v.) balanced the resulting system (q.v.) of transcendental idealism with its contrary, a philosophy of nature (q.v.). Some have read Hegel's *Science of Logic* (q.v.) as an extension of this process of deriving the subjective categories that condition all experience whatsoever. Hegel himself does not use this language, suggesting rather that the dynamic of rational thinking (q.v.) unfolds the inherent structure of reality itself. *See also* KANT'S CRITICAL PHILOSOPHY; METAPHYSICS; PIPPIN, ROBERT.

TRANSITION OR PASSING OVER (DAS ÜBERGEHEN). The most basic mode of thinking (q.v.) that characterizes the logic of Being (qq.v.) is the simple transition or immediate (q.v.) shift in thought that leads from one concept (q.v.) to another. Thought passes over, for example, from being to nothing, from something to other, or from quality to quantity (qq.v.). *See also* BECOMING.

TRUTH (DIE WAHRHEIT). In the *Phenomenology of Spirit* (q.v.), Hegel contrasts the certainty with which someone holds a knowledge (q.v.) claim with the truth that is to be known. Truth confounds certainty when experience (q.v.) shows that things do not turn out as expected. The aim of the work is to find a kind of knowing where certainty fully corresponds with the truth. British idealism (q.v.) took seriously Hegel's claim that truth is fully systematic and argued that truth is coherence (q.v.). Not only is the coherence of our descriptions evidence of their truth, but reality itself is essentially interrelated in a coherent network. *See also* SYSTEM; TRUTH AS SUBJECT.

TRUTH AS SUBJECT (DAS WAHRE ALS SUBJEKT). In the preface to the *Phenomenology of Spirit* (q.v.), Hegel points out that the truth (q.v.) is not only substance, but also subject. By this he means that the truth constitutes itself by first becoming different from what it starts out to be, and then reincorporating this difference into itself as a reconstituted whole (q.v.). The absolute (q.v.), then, is spirit (q.v.). *See also* ABSOLUTE SPIRIT; BACCHANALIAN REVEL; SPINOZA, BARUCH; SUBSTANTIALITY; SYSTEM.

TÜBINGEN. In the fall of 1788, Hegel, along with the future poet, Friedrich Hölderlin (q.v.), matriculated in the Theological Seminary at Tübingen, where they studied philosophy (q.v.) for two years and theology for three. (During one extended stay in Stuttgart [q.v.] because of illness, Hegel turned his attention to biology as well.) Friedrich Schelling (q.v.) joined them in 1790. Some of the students at the seminary came from across the Rhine, sharing with their German compatriots an enthusiasm for the French Revolution (q.v.). Shortly before completing his studies in 1793, and while spending some time at home in Stuttgart, Hegel drafted a proposal for a religion (q.v.) of the people: whose doctrines would be grounded on universal reason (qq.v.); where fancy, heart, and sensibility would not be sent empty away; and into which all the needs of life including the public affairs of the state (q.v.) would be incorporated. Rather than proceeding with ordination on the completion of his studies, he obtained permission to accept a position as tutor for a family in Bern (q.v.). *See also* CHRISTIANITY; THEOLOGICAL WRITINGS.

– U –

UNDERSTANDING (DER VERSTAND). This term plays a number of roles within Hegel's system (q.v.). At times he contrasts the sterility of understanding's abstractions with the fruitfulness of dialectical and speculative reason (qq.v.). At other times he argues that the dead abstractions of understanding are necessary conditions for a full philosophical comprehension. Three different texts play a role in the discussion of this term. First, the *Phenomenology of Spirit* (q.v.) discusses understanding as the way a knowing consciousness (q.v.) endeavors to get at the universal truths (qq.v.) of the sensed and perceived world. Using laws (q.v.) and explanations, it discriminates between what appears and what is real. Second, the *Encyclopedia of the Philosophical Sciences* (q.v.) introduces its *Science of Logic* (q.v.) by listing the three moments or stages of logical thought. Understanding determines the exact meaning of concepts (q.v.) only to discover that those meanings imply contrary terms—a shift that is the work of dialectical reason. Speculative reason then puts the whole business into perspective. Third, the *Science of Logic* places its discussion of understanding in the section on the particular (q.v.) concept. The conceptual act of particularizing—of spelling out all the features that distinguish one concept from other similar ones—is the way understanding abstracts. *See also* ABSTRACT/CONCRETE; APPEARANCE; INVERTED WORLD; KNOWLEDGE; METHOD.

UNHAPPY CONSCIOUSNESS (DAS UNGLÜCKLICHE BEWUSST-SEIN). In the *Phenomenology of Spirit* (q.v.), unhappy consciousness is a mode of knowing in which the self seeks the truth (q.v.) about itself not within its own changing nature, but in an alien, unchanging reality. The self thus discounts and cancels itself to the point of self-mortification, striving to achieve an immediate, conscious (qq.v.) relationship with its other (q.v.). This process of self-externalization is a condition for a reasoned approach to knowledge (q.v.). *See also* ALIENATION; CHRISTIANITY; FAITH; FEUERBACH, LUDWIG; REASON; SKEPTICISM.

UNITED STATES. Hegel was introduced to the United States by German immigrants after the revolutions of 1848, and his thought soon became the focus of study and discussion for a wider circle in Cincinnati (John B. Stallo and August Willich) and St. Louis (Henry Brokmeyer and William T. Harris [qq.v]). Josiah Royce (q.v.) espoused a form of voluntaristic idealism, and John Dewey (q.v.) adapted Hegelian concepts (q.v.) to pragmatic purposes. In the early part of the 20th century, Hegelian studies were maintained by Walter Stace (q.v.), Gustav E. Mueller, and Jacob Loewenberg and later by John Findlay and Walter Kaufmann (qq.v.). In 1968, under the leadership of Darrel Christensen, the Hegel Society of America (q.v.) was formed to hold regular conferences and publish the *Owl of Minerva* (q.v.). In the latter part of the 20th century, Hegelian scholarship has flourished, with important works by Clark Butler, William Desmond, Joseph Flay, Errol E. Harris, Howard Kainz, David Kolb, Quentin Lauer, Terry Pinkard, Robert Pippin, Tom Rockmore, Stanley Rosen, Robert Solomon, Kenneth Westphal, Merold Westphal, Robert Williams, and Richard Winfield (qq.v.), among others. *See also* OHIO HEGELIANS; ST. LOUIS HEGELIANS.

UNIVERSAL (ALLGEMEIN). Hegel distinguishes between an abstract (q.v.) universal, which is something common, found in a number of different things (such as the red of an apple, a fire truck, a flag, and a rose) and a concrete universal, in which a number of particular (q.v.) features are integrated into a singular totality (qq.v.) (such as India, which integrates all the distinctive traditions, political and social structures, nationalities, religions, economic styles, and regions that make up a single country). A universal only becomes determinate by being particularized. *See also* CONCEPT; SINGULAR.

UTILITY (DIE NÜTZLICHKEIT). The French Enlightenment (q.v.) lacked the Protestant principle of conscience (q.v.) instructed inwardly by the spirit (q.v.). Therefore, once it had conquered the otherworldliness of faith (q.v.), it could appeal only to utility as a standard. Put into practice as the standard of government, pure utility led into the reign of terror, during which all willed actions, because they were singular (q.v.) acts and worked against the interests of all, were condemned, and their perpetrators put to death (q.v.) as traitors. *See also* ABSOLUTE FREEDOM; ACTION; FRENCH REVOLUTION; PROTESTANT REFORMATION; WILL.

– V –

VALUE (DER WERT). For Hegel in the *Philosophy of Right* (q.v.), economic value is determined by the usefulness of a thing in satisfying needs. For Karl Marx (q.v.), in contrast, the value of a thing is the amount of labor that went into its production. *See also* ALIENATED LABOR; CIVIL SOCIETY; UTILITY.

VIRTUE (DIE TUGEND). In the *Phenomenology of Spirit* (q.v.), the virtuous individual rationally categorizes the world as a struggle between the universal (q.v.) good and the evil of singularity. The good is understood to be implicit in the way of the world, even though blind fate overwhelms pleasure (q.v.) and self-conceit perverts well-intentioned hearts. By surrendering his own individuality, the virtuous person wields a weapon through which this implicit universal good is to be actualized. However, when acts become actual, they turn out to be singular (q.v.). So the beliefs of the virtuous are shown to be nothing but overblown rhetoric. Hegel applies this analysis only to the modern world, drawing a distinction from the classical understanding of virtue as found in Aristotle (q.v.). *See also* ACTUALITY; CATEGORY; LAW OF THE HEART; REASON; SCHILLER, FRIEDRICH.

– W –

WAHL, JEAN (1888–1974). In *The Unhappiness of Consciousness in the Philosophy of Hegel*, Wahl argues that a romantic theologian is to be found within the rationalist philosopher. Underlying Hegel's concepts of separation and unity is to be found a sensitivity to, and feeling for, agony and evil on the one hand and love on the other. Unfortunately, his final system (q.v.) is not rich enough to retain the full range of thought, imagination, hope, and despair of his early years. *See also* FRANCE; ROMANTICISM; UNHAPPY CONSCIOUSNESS.

WALLACE, WILLIAM (1844–1897). A student under Benjamin Jowett and successor of Thomas H. Green (qq.v.) in the chair of moral philosophy at Oxford, Wallace published translations of the *Encyclopedia Logic* (1874) and *Philosophy of Mind (Spirit)* (qq.v.) as well as his own *Prolegomena to the Study of Hegel's Philosophy* (1894), and he began a Hegelian tradition at Merton College, Oxford, that included Francis H. Bradley (q.v.), H. H. Joachim, and G. R. G. Mure (q.v.). *See also* BRITISH IDEALISM; MILLER, ARNOLD V.

WALSH, WILLIAM H. For Walsh, Hegel's philosophical history stands or falls with his ethics. While Hegel's morality takes seriously human satisfactions and human achievements in all their diversity, it is also primarily a social phenomenon, because the individual is a part of a series of wider wholes. Hegel's concern to present historical facts as a coherent and intelligible whole contributed substantially to the development of historiography as a complex and critical subject during the 19th century. *See also* BRITISH IDEALISM.

WAR (DER KRIEG). When international disputes move beyond particular issues and concern the well-being of the state (q.v.), they can erupt into war. War thus is an extreme form of the differentiation among states by which each one becomes an individual (q.v.). The risk of death (q.v.) to which the state calls its courageous citizens reinforces their commitment to its integrity and unity. Hegel notes that, with gunpowder, courage has moved from being a concrete struggle of individual with individual, to being an abstract virtue, affecting people simply as anonymous members of the army. Because war is a transient phenomenon, certain conventions of international law (q.v.) are to be respected even while it is being waged, such as the safety of ambassadors and the freedom of civilians from attack. *See also* ABSTRACT/CONCRETE; RECOGNITION.

WATSON, JOHN (1847–1939). A student of Edward Caird (q.v.) in Glasgow, Watson taught for 50 years at Queen's University, Canada (q.v.), and wrote studies of Immanuel Kant, Friedrich Schelling, and the philosophy of religion (qq.v.). For him, philosophy is the systematic formulation of the single self-differentiating or rational principle that underlies all human experience (q.v.).

WEIL, ERIC (1904–1977). Weil shows that Hegel, far from glorifying the status quo in Prussia (q.v.) in the *Philosophy of Right* (q.v.), was making a proposal for the constitution (q.v.) that Friedrich Wilhelm III had promised. Further, the state (q.v.) that he describes is not ideal, since it offers no satisfactory means of resolving the disparity between rich and poor in a capitalist economy; and in international relations the ultimate sanction the state could use to promote its interests is war (q.v.). International law (q.v.) is little more than a moral obligation. *See also* CAPITALISM; FRANCE; HAYM, RUDOLF; POVERTY.

WESTPHAL, KENNETH R. In *Hegel's Epistemological Realism*, Westphal shows from the introduction to the *Phenomenology of Spirit* (q.v.) that Hegel argues for a world independent of knowing subjects which can nevertheless be adequately known. Such knowledge (q.v.) is a social phenomenon, since it involves becoming actively engaged with a naturally structured world. *See also* UNITED STATES.

WESTPHAL, MEROLD. In Westphal's reading of the *Phenomenology of Spirit* (q.v.), once the representations of religion (qq.v.) are converted into concepts (q.v.), the divine is nothing more than the social whole (q.v.) of which we are parts through our mutual interaction. Thus, the wholly other of Protestant Christianity is domesticated, the individualism of bourgeois culture is transcended, and the instrumental knowledge (q.v.) of modern science becomes absolute knowing (q.v.). Hegel fails to take genuine reciprocal love seriously, because his theory of recognition (q.v.) involves an erotic quest for what the self lacks. *See also* GOD; UNITED STATES.

WHOLE/PART (DAS GANZE UND DIE TEILE). In the *Science of Logic* (q.v.) Hegel discusses the relation between whole and part as one way of showing how appearance (q.v.) is related to its essence (q.v.). The whole requires the part for its proper definition just as much as the part requires the whole. So when, in the preface to the *Phenomenology of Spirit* (q.v.), Hegel says that the true is the whole, he adds that the whole is the essence that completes itself through its development or parts. *See also* CIRCLE OF CIRCLES.

WILL (DER WILLE). In Hegel's psychology (q.v.), will is the activity of spirit (q.v.) that is urged by passions (q.v.), inclinations, and drives to transform a general, indeterminate practical feeling into a particular action (q.v.), which can then be evaluated and affirmed rationally in light of the original range of possibilities. At the subjective level, will functions arbitrarily (*die Willkur*), but once the self takes as its purpose bliss or happiness, it must use intelligence (q.v.) to consider the total picture and thus may become genuinely free. The total picture, however, includes the objective social and political world in which one acts, so that freedom (q.v.) only becomes fully possible within a framework of law (q.v.) and custom. Hegel explores this realm of objective spirit (q.v.) in his *Philosophy of Right* (q.v.). *See also* ABSTRACT RIGHT; ETHICAL LIFE; *PHILOSOPHY OF SPIRIT*; SUBJECTIVE SPIRIT; TOTALITY.

WILLIAMS, ROBERT R. Williams points to the importance of otherness in Hegel's philosophy, since spirit (q.v.) is constituted through mutual recognition (q.v.) in which the integrity of the other (q.v.) must be respected and enhanced. *See also* UNITED STATES.

WINFIELD, RICHARD DIEN. For Winfield, Hegel offers a way of developing a systematic philosophy that is not based on external foundations. Pure thought, by showing that alternative options involve contradictions (q.v.), can demonstrate not only the way determinations of logic (q.v.) develop, but also the essential features of nature (q.v.) and public social life. *See also* SYSTEM; UNITED STATES.

WOMAN (DAS WEIB). In drawing a distinction between the genders, Hegel assigns to the feminine the virtue of piety—that is, the intuitive sense for what is substantial and fundamental to the life of the family (q.v.). This finds its purest expression in the role of the sister, who is free both from the natural bonding of husband and wife and from the deference that a daughter owes to her parents. *See also* ANTIGONE; MAN.

WORLD HISTORY (DIE WELTGESCHICHTE). The universal spirit (qq.v.) becomes actual in the lived history of the world. As a result, history is not just a series of contingent events. Rather, each nation benefits from the demise of its predecessor, inaugurating a new integrating principle. This principle becomes enriched as over time it is put into practice in the constitution (q.v.) of a state (q.v.). Within the cultural life of the state, individuals come to grasp its principle intellectually and react to it, initiating the nation's decline and fall and opening the way for another people to take up the torch at a more complex level. This process by which the universal spirit determines itself embodies the structure of reason (q.v.) and moves toward freedom (q.v.) or full self-determination. *See also* ACTION; CHINESE HISTORY; CONTINGENCY; CUNNING OF REASON; EGYPTIAN HISTORY; GERMANIC HISTORY; GREEK HISTORY; INDIAN HISTORY; *LECTURES ON THE PHILOSOPHY OF WORLD HISTORY*; PERSIAN HISTORY; *PHILOSOPHY OF RIGHT*; PHILOSOPHY OF WORLD HISTORY; ROMAN HISTORY.

WRONG (DAS UNRECHT). Abstract injustice emerges in the *Philosophy of Right* (q.v.) when an individual's arbitrary will (q.v.) contravenes the just exchange willed in common through a contract (q.v.). This can happen at three levels: nonmaliciously, when an individual wills an action (q.v.) that does not in fact conform to the intended principle of fair exchange; fraudulently, when an individual deliberately deceives; and criminally, when an unfair exchange is coerced. Wrong done to an individual becomes more serious when set in the context of civil society (q.v.), for it there breaks the law (q.v.) that is binding on all; at the same time, the strength of a secure society reduces the threat any individual action (q.v.) poses to social stability. *See also* ABSTRACT RIGHT.

WÜRTTEMBERG. As the son of a civil servant in the duchy of Württemberg, Hegel continued to take an interest in its political affairs. In the immediate aftermath of the French Revolution (q.v.), he helped found a political club advocating constitutional government; and in Frankfurt am Main (q.v.) at a time of transfer of power, he wrote a tract proposing constitutional changes. When, after the restoration, the estates rejected the newly appointed King Wilhelm I's offer of a constitution (q.v.) in favor of the traditional arrangement in which they had substantial independence, Hegel wrote an essay in the *Heidelberg Yearbook* defending the action of the king. This brought him into conflict with his fellow Swabians, Heinrich Paulus and Friedrich Niethammer (q.v.), who sided with the estates. *See also* HEIDELBERG; STUTTGART; TÜBINGEN.

– Y –

YOUNG HEGELIANS. This term was used by Arnold Ruge (q.v.) for the humanistic left-wing Hegelians (q.v.) of the 1830s and 1840s, even though anticipations of their approach can be found in the writings of Friedrich Carové and Eduard Gans (qq.v.) from the 1820s. The key names associated with this movement are Ruge, David Strauss, Bruno Bauer, Ludwig Feuerbach, and Max Stirner, as well as the young Karl Marx and Friedrich Engels (qq.v.). *See also* RELIGION IN THE YOUNG HEGELIANS.

– Z –

ZIZEK, SLAVOJ. Inspired by the French structuralist, Jacques Lacan, Zizek and his colleague, Mladen Dolar, have established in Ljubljana, Slovenia, a school of Hegelian interpretation where the subject is understood to be a void. The experience of the nothing (q.v.) behind appearances (q.v.) is the real appearance of the subject, and dialectic (q.v.) is a kind of retroactive "unmaking."

ZOOLOGY (DER TIERISCHE ORGANISMUS). The study of the animal organism (q.v.) marks the culmination of Hegel's *Philosophy of Nature* (q.v.). Animals embody in some detail the structure of the concept of life (qq.v.), for they are integrated, centered bodies, made up of organs that for their part function as centered members of the whole. An animal's inability to transcend disease and death (q.v.), however, marks it as still affected by nature's contingency (qq.v.) and powerlessness. *See also* ORGANICS.

ZOROASTRIANISM. *See* **PARSEE RELIGION.**

Glossary of German Terms

A definition for each word may be found under the entry for its English counterpart.

Absolute, das: Absolute, the
Absolute Freiheit, die: Absolute freedom
Absolute Geist, der: Absolute spirit
Absolute Idee, die: Absolute idea
Absolute Wesen, das: Absolute essence
Absolute Wissen, das: Absolute knowing
Abstrakt: *Abstract*/concrete
Abstrakte Recht: Abstract right
Allgemein: Universal
Älteste Systemprogramm, das: Earliest system-program
An sich: In itself
Andere, das: Other
Anerkennung, die: Recognition
Anfang, der: Beginning
Anmerkungen, die: Remarks
Anschauung, die: Intuition
Anthropologie: Anthropology
Antinomien, die: Antinomies
Architektur, die: Architecture
Armut, die: Poverty
Atomismus, das: Atomism
Attraktion: Attraction
Aufheben: Sublate

Aufklärung, die: Enlightenment
Äussere, das: Inner/*outer*
Äussere Staatsrecht, das: International law
Äusserlichkeit, die: External relations

Bacchantische Taumel, der: Bacchanalian revel
Begierde, die: Desire
Begriff, der: Concept, Notion
Beobachtende Vernunft, die: Observing reason
Beschaffenheit, die: *See* Determination
Besonder: Particular
Bestimmung, die: Determination
Beweise vom Dasein Gottes, die: *See* God
Bewusstsein, das: Consciousness
Bildung, die: Culture
Bürgerliche Gesellschaft, die: Civil society

Chemische Prozess, der: Chemical process
Chemismus, der: Chemism

Dasein: *Dasein*
Denken, das: Thinking
Dialektische Vernunft, die: Dialectic
Ding, das: Thing
Drama, das: Drama

Eigenschaft, die: *See* Thing
Eigentum, das: Property
Einbildung, die: Imagination
Eins, das: One
Einsicht, die reine: Insight
Einzelne, das: Singular
Empirismus, der: Empiricism
Endlich, Endlichkeit, die: Finite, finitude
Entfremdung, die: Alienation
Epos, das: Epic
Erfahrung, die: Experience
Erhabene, das: Sublime
Erinnerung, die: Recollection
Erkennen, das: Cognition
Erkenntnistheorie, die: Epistemology
Erscheinung, die: Appearance
Etwas: Something
Existenz, die: Existence

Familie, die: Family
Freiheit, die: Freedom
Für das Bewusstsein: For consciousness
Für es: For consciousness
Für sich: For itself
Für uns: For us
Fürsichsein, das: Being for self
Fürstliche Gewalt, die: Monarch

Ganze, das: *Whole*/part
Gedächtnis, die: Memory
Gegensatz, der: Opposition

Geist, der: Spirit
Geistige Tierreich, das: Spiritual animal kingdom
Geoffenbarte Religion, die: Christianity
Geschichte der Philosophie, die: History of philosophy
Gesetz, das: Law
Gesetz des Herzens, das: Law of the heart
Gesetzgebende Gewalt, die: Legislature
Gesetzgebende Vernunft, die: Law-giving reason
Gesetzprüfende Vernunft, die: Law-testing reason
Gewissen, das: Conscience
Glaube, der: Faith
Gott, der: God
Grenze, die: Limit
Grösse, die: Magnitude, Quantity
Grund, der: Ground

Handlung, die: Action
Herrschaft und Knechtschaft: Master-slave

Idealismus, der: Idealism
Idee, die: Idea
Identität, die: Identity
Individuum, das: Individual
Innere, das: *Inner*/outer
Intelligenz, die: Intelligence
Internationale Gesellschaft für Dialektische Philosophie: International Society for Dialectical Philosophy
Internationale Hegel Gesellschaft: International Hegel Society

Internationale Hegel Vereinigung: International Hegel Association

Jahrbuch für Wissenschaftliche Kritik: Journal for Scientific Criticism
Jenaer Systementwürfe: Jena Drafts for a System
Jenseits, das: Beyond

Kapitalismus, der: Capitalism
Kausalität, die: Causality
Kirchenväter, die: Church fathers
Klassische Kunstform, die: Classical art
Knotenlinie, die: Nodal line
Komödie, die: Comedy
Konkret: Abstract/*concrete*
Körper, der: Body
Korporation, die: Corporations
Kraft, die: Force
Kreis von Kreisen, der: Circle of circles
Krieg, der: War
Kritische Philosophie, die: Kant's critical philosophy
Kritisches Journal der Philosophie: Critical Journal of Philosophy
Kunst, die: Art
Kunst-Religion, die: Religion in the form of art

Leben, das: Life
Leib, der: Body
Leidenschaften, die: Passions
List der Vernunft, die: Cunning of reason
Logik, die: Logic

Lust, die: Pleasure
Lyrische, das: Lyric

Malerei, die: Painting
Mann, der: Man
Mass, das: Measure
Mechanik, die: Mechanics
Mechanismus, der: Mechanism
Metaphysik, die: Metaphysics
Methode, die: Method
Möglichkeit, die: Possibility
Moralität, die: Morality
Musik, die: Music

Natur, die: Nature
Natürliche Religion, Naturreligion, die: Natural religion
Naturrecht, das: Natural law
Negation der Negation, die: Negation of negation
Nichts, das: Nothing
Notwendigkeit, die: Necessity
Nützlichkeit, die: Utility

Objektive Geist, der: Objective spirit
Objektivität, die: Objectivity
Offenbare Religion, die: Christianity
Organik, die: Organics
Organismus, der: Organism

Person, die: Person
Pflicht, die: Duty
Phänomenologie, die: Phenomenology
Philosophie, die: Philosophy
Physik, die: Physics
Physiognomie, die: Physiognomy
Poesie, die: Poetry

Polizei, die: Police
Psychologie, die: Psychology

Qualität, die: Quality
Quantität, die: Quantity, magnitude
Quantitative Verhältnis, die:
Ratio
Quantum: Quantum

Raum, der: Space
Recht, das: Right
Rechtszustand, der: Legal status
Reflexion, die: Reflection
Regierungsgewalt, die: Executive
Reine Einsicht, die: Insight, pure
Religion, die: Religion, Philosophy
of religion
Repulsion: Repulsion
Romantik, die: Romanticism
Romantische Kunstform, die:
Romantic art

Sache selbst, die: *Sache selbst*
Schädellehre, die: Phrenology
Schluss, der: Syllogism
Schöne, das: Beauty
Schöne Seele, die: Beautiful soul
Seele, die: Soul
Sein, das: Being
Selbstbewusstsein, das: Self-
consciousness
Sinnliche Gewissheit, die: Sense
certainty
Sittlichkeit, die: Ethical life
Skeptizismus, der: Skepticism
Skulptur, die: Sculpture
Spekulative Satz, der: Speculative
proposition
Spekulative Vernunft, die: Specu-
lative reason

Sprache, die: Language
Staat, der: State
Stände, die: Classes
Stoizismus, der: Stoicism
Subjektive Geist, der: Subjective
spirit
Subjektivität, die: Subjectivity
Substantialität, die: Substan-
tiality
Symbolische Kunstform, die:
Symbolic art
System, das: System

Teile, die: Whole/*Part*
Teilung der Arbeit, die: Division
of labor
Teleologie, die: Teleology
Tierische Organismus, der:
Zoology
Tod, der: Death
Totalität, die: Totality
Tragödie, die: Tragedy
Transcendentale Idealismus, der:
Transcendental idealism
Tugend, die: Virtue

Übergehen, das: Transition
Übergreifen, das: Overreach
Unendlich, Unendlichkeit, die:
Infinite, infinity
Unglückliche Bewusstsein, das:
Unhappy consciousness
Unmittelbar: Immediate
Unmittelbare Wissen, das: Imme-
diate knowing
Unrecht, das: Wrong
Unterschied, der: Difference
Urteil, das: Judgment

Vegetabilische Natur, die: Botany
Verfassung, die: Constitution
Verhältnis, das quantitative: Ratio
Verkehrte Welt, die: Inverted world
Vermittlung, die: Mediation
Vernunft, die: Reason
Verrücktheit, die: Insanity
Verschiedenheit, die: Diversity
Verstand, der: Understanding
Vertrag, der: Contract
Vollendete Religion, die: Christianity
Vorstellung, die: Representation

Wahlverwandtschaft, die: Elective affinity
Wahre als Subjekt, das: Truth as subject
Wahrheit, die: Truth

Wahrnehmen, das: Perception
Wechselwirkung, die: Reciprocity
Weib, das: Woman
Weltgeschichte, die: World history
Werden, das: Becoming
Wert, der: Value
Wesen, das: Essence
Widerspruch, der: Contradiction
Wille, der: Will
Willkur, die: *See* Will
Wirklichkeit, die: Actuality
Wirklichkeit des Vernünftigen, die: Actuality of the Rational
Wissen, das: Knowledge
Wissenschaft, die: Science

Zahl, die: Number
Zeit, die: Time
Zufälligkeit, die: Contingency
Zusätze, die: Additions

Bibliography

There was some interest in Hegelian philosophy in both Great Britain and America during the latter half of the 19th, and into the beginning of the 20th century. But John Findlay's *Hegel: A Re-examination* in 1958 initiated a veritable explosion of works in English, not only in critical studies, but also in translations of original texts and of studies by French, German, and other scholars. This bibliography tries to do some justice to this rich range of material.

While the bibliography includes Hegel's first editions, the editions of his collected works, and editions of his lectures, only a few untranslated secondary sources in foreign languages have been cited, usually where they have had a significant effect on the development of Hegelian thought. Every effort has been made to cite the first publication, even where a work has been reprinted several times and where it is currently available under another publisher. For translations, the original date of publication is indicated in parentheses.

Because the editions of Hegel's lectures, using manuscripts and student transcripts that come from a number of different semesters, reflect a variety of editorial principles, the sources of translations have been indicated. Unfortunately, of the editions that follow a single lecture course, only one set of lectures on natural law, those on the philosophy of religion, and a part of the lectures on the history of philosophy have appeared in English.

Much of the important work on Hegel has appeared in articles. To keep the bibliography within manageable bounds, articles that appear in anthologies (of which there are many) have not been listed separately. This means that some important scholars' names are underrepresented in the list of authors. Anthologies are ordered in the alphabetical listing by title rather than by editor, since this indicates clearly where there are a number of authors and maintains the convention that the names of editors and translators appear after the title of the work.

The final section of the bibliography, listing philosophical works by "Hegelians," is selective. As suggested in the introduction, the title "Hegelian" can be extended very broadly or it can be restricted quite severely, depending on one's critical sensibilities. The inclination here is to be broad-church, so texts have been selected from a variety of subsequent traditions with the intention of offering a taste rather than trying to be comprehensive.

Hegel's writing is notoriously dense. For someone who wants to read Hegel for the first time, the *Lectures on the Philosophy of History* and the *Lectures on the Philosophy of Religion* are the most accessible. Then the student may want to venture into the *Phenomenology of Spirit* and the *Philosophy of Right*. The *Science of Logic* is more abstract and can be approached more easily by way of the *Encyclopedia Logic*, which includes additions from the lectures. Nonetheless, it is essential reading for anyone who wants to understand the systematic foundation for all Hegelian philosophy.

The secondary literature is extensive. Kurt Steinhauer's *Hegel Bibliography: Background Material on the International Reception of Hegel within the Context of the History of Philosophy* presents a fairly thorough listing of works in all languages up to 1975, together with indexes of keywords and of authors, editors, and translators. A second part prepared in collaboration with H.-D. Schluter appeared in 1998. Frederick G. Weiss's "Hegel: A Bibliography of Books in English Arranged Chronologically," in *The Legacy of Hegel*, covers the period to 1971. Joseph C. Flay has prepared a bibliography on Hegel and the history of philosophy in *Hegel and the History of Philosophy* and others on Hegel's aesthetics and logic in *Art and Logic in Hegel's Philosophy*. These are limited to English, French, German, and Italian authors. Also useful is the bibliography in his own *Hegel's Quest for Certainty*. Henry S. Harris's *Hegel's Ladder II: The Odyssey of Spirit* concludes with an 84-page bibliography, which ranges widely, though primarily focused on the *Phenomenology of Spirit*.

In his commentary to *Hegel: The Letters*, Clark Butler fills in the details of Hegel's life, although by organizing the letters thematically he does not maintain a consistent temporal sequence. Jacques D'Hondt's *Hegel in His Time* corrects long-standing prejudices about Hegel's relation to the Prussian regime during his years in Berlin. More recently, Terry Pinkard has published *Hegel: A Biography*.

For the philosophical development that led from Kant to Hegel, Frederick Beiser's *The Fate of Reason* covers the early stages. Though varying in quality, the essays in *The Emergence of German Idealism*, edited by Michael Baur and Daniel O. Dahlstrom, cover much of the period. *Between Kant and Hegel*, translated by George di Giovanni and Henry S. Harris, provides some of the key texts.

A good overview of Hegelianism can be found in Stephen Crites's article by that name in *The Encyclopedia of Philosophy* (1967). The critical decades just after Hegel's death are discussed in John Toews's scholarly study: *Hegelianism: The Path toward Dialectical Humanism, 1805–1841*.

The best short introduction to Hegel remains Edward Caird's *Hegel*, originally published in 1883. John Findlay's *Hegel: A Re-examination* initiated the renaissance of Hegelian studies in the Anglo-Saxon world. Charles Taylor's *Hegel* is best when discussing political philosophy, and Stephen Houlgate's *Freedom, Truth, and History* provides a readable and perceptive introduction, with a focus on art and religion. Also useful is Raymond Plant's *Hegel: An Introduction*. Alexandre Kojève's *Introduction to the Reading of Hegel*, which derives its interpretation from the master–slave dialectic, has been influential, particularly in French thought. Walter Stace's *The Philosophy of Hegel* made sense of his systematic claims for several generations of puzzled students. The *Cambridge Companion to Hegel* has articles by a number of leading scholars on all aspects of Hegel's thought.

Of the journals, *Hegel-Studien* contains the results of recent scholarship on the manuscripts and lectures, as well as significant articles. Its supplementary volumes (*Beihefte*) contain both scholarly monographs and the proceedings of congresses of the International Hegel Association, which are organized around specific themes. The *Owl of Minerva* and the *Bulletin of the Hegel Society of Great Britain* have provided a forum for much current work being done in the English-speaking world.

The authoritative study of the early writings is Henry S. Harris's *Hegel's Development*. Volume 1, *Towards the Sunlight*, covers Hegel's time in Stuttgart, Tübingen, Bern, and Frankfurt. Volume 2, *Night Thoughts*, reviews the various projects of the Jena years up to the *Phenomenology*.

The culmination of Harris's research can be found in *Hegel's Ladder*, a two-volume study of the *Phenomenology of Spirit*, which not only offers an analysis of every paragraph, but also discusses its significance for his overall project and the background Hegel had in mind. Other useful commentaries on this work are Joseph Flay's *Hegel's Quest for Certainty*, Jean Hyppolite's *Genesis and Structure of Hegel's Phenomenology of Spirit*, Kenneth Westphal's *Hegel's Epistemological Realism*, and Merold Westphal's *History and Truth in Hegel's Phenomenology*.

The *Science of Logic* has received less attention. John M. E. McTaggart's *A Commentary on Hegel's Logic* reads it from the perspective of British idealism. Jean Hyppolite's *Logic and Existence* provides a theoretical introduction. John Burbidge's *On Hegel's Logic* attempts to discern the logical sequence in eight of its chapters. For the shorter *Encyclopedia Logic*, the commentaries of Errol E. Harris (*An Interpretation of the Logic of*

Hegel) and Geoffrey Mure (*A Study of Hegel's Logic*) can be used with profit.

Hegel's philosophy of nature has been even more ignored than the logic. Michael Petry's translation is a valuable resource, containing in its notes detailed references to the sources Hegel used and the science of his time. John Burbidge's *Real Process* is limited to Hegel's discussions of chemistry. Three sets of conference proceedings—*Hegel and Newtonianism* (edited by Michael Petry), *Hegel and the Philosophy of Nature* (edited by Stephen Houlgate), and *Hegel and the Sciences* (edited by R. S. Cohen and M. W. Wartofsky)—offer an introduction to some of the current work in this field.

Michael Petry's translation of the *Philosophy of Subjective Spirit* provides for this part of the *Encyclopedia* the same kind of thorough documentation that he offered for the philosophy of nature. In addition, it contains two sets of student transcripts from Hegel's lectures.

While Karl-Heinz Ilting's *Vorlesungen über Rechtsphilosophie 1818–1831* initiated the publication of a number of student transcripts from Hegel's lectures on the *Philosophy of Right*, only one has been translated. Shlomo Avinieri's *Hegel's Theory of the Modern State* and Eric Weil's *Hegel and the State* are two classic studies of this part of his philosophy. Also useful are Adriaan Peperzak's *Philosophy and Politics*, Joachim Ritter's *Hegel and the French Revolution*, Charles Taylor's *Hegel and Modern Society*, and William H. Walsh's *Hegelian Ethics*.

For the philosophy of history, the student can turn to George Dennis O'Brien's *Hegel on Reason and History*; for aesthetics, William Desmond's *Art and the Absolute* and Jack Kaminsky's *Hegel on Art* can be read with profit. Emil Fackenheim's *The Religious Dimension of Hegel's Thought* was one of the first in English to focus on the lectures on religion; but Stephen Crites's *Dialectic and Gospel in the Development of Hegel's Thinking*, Walter Jaeschke's *Reason in Religion*, Philip Merklinger's *Philosophy, Theology, and Hegel's Berlin Philosophy of Religion, 1821–1827*, Dale Schlitt's *Hegel's Trinitarian Claim*, Raymond Williamson's *Introduction to Hegel's Philosophy of Religion,* and James Yerkes' *The Christology of Hegel* should also be noted.

Of the subsequent philosophers who have drawn on Hegel for inspiration mention will be made of only some of the more important: Francis H. Bradley, Robin G. Collingwood, Benedetto Croce, John Dewey, Søren Kierkegaard, Nishida Kitaro, Karl Marx, and Josiah Royce.

HISTORY

Hegel's Biography

D'Hondt, Jacques. *Hegel in His Time* (1968). Translated by John Burbidge, Nelson Roland, and Judith Levasseur. Peterborough, Ontario: Broadview, 1988.

———. *Hegel Secret* (Secret Hegel). Paris: Presses Universitaire de France, 1968.

Haym, Rudolf. *Hegel und seine Zeit: Vorlesungen über Entstehung und Entwicklung, Wesen und Werth der Hegelschen Philosophie* (Hegel and His Time: Lectures Concerning the Emergence and Development, Essence and Value of the Hegelian Philosophy). Berlin: Gärtner, 1857.

Hegel, G. W. F. *Briefe von und an Hegel* (Letters from and to Hegel). Edited by Johannes Hoffmeister. Hamburg: Meiner, 1952–54.

———. *Hegel: The Letters*. Translated by Clark Butler and Christiane Seiler. Bloomington: Indiana University Press, 1984.

Hegel in Bericht seiner Zeitgenossen (Hegel in Accounts of His Contemporaries). Edited by Georg Nicolin. Hamburg: Meiner, 1970.

Kaufmann, Walter. *Hegel: Reinterpretation, Texts and Commentary*. Garden City, N.Y.: Doubleday, 1965.

Mueller, Gustav E. *Hegel: The Man, His Vision and Work*. (1959) New York: Pageant, 1968.

Pinkard, Terry. *Hegel: A Biography*. Cambridge: Cambridge University Press, 2000.

Rosenkranz, Karl. *G. W. F. Hegels Leben* (G. W. F. Hegel's Life). Berlin: Duncker & Humblot, 1844.

Walker, Nicholas. "Hegel in the Mirror of Biography: On the Biographical Hegel-Literature from Rosenkranz to Althaus." *Bulletin of the Hegel Society of Great Britain* 27/28 (1993): 1–11.

Background to Hegel

Beiser, Frederick C. *The Fate of Reason: German Philosophy from Kant to Fichte*. Cambridge, Mass.: Harvard University Press, 1987.

di Giovanni, George, and Henry S. Harris. *Between Kant and Hegel: Texts in the Development of Post-Kantian Idealism*. Albany: State University of New York Press, 1985.

The Emergence of German Idealism. Edited by Michael Baur and Daniel O. Dahlstrom. Washington, D.C.: Catholic University of America Press, 1999.

Fackenheim, Emil L. *The God Within: Kant, Schelling, and Historicity*. Toronto: University of Toronto Press, 1996.

Kroner, Richard. *Von Kant bis Hegel* (From Kant to Hegel). Tübingen: Mohr, 1921.

Hegelianism

Avinieri, Shlomo. "Hegel and the Emergence of Zionism." *Bulletin of the Hegel Society of Great Britain* 6 (Autumn/Winter 1982): 12–18.

Baugh, Bruce. "Limiting Reason's Empire: The Early Reception of Hegel in France." *Journal of the History of Ideas* 31 (1993): 259–75.

Brazill, William. *The Young Hegelians*. New Haven, Conn.: Yale University Press, 1970.

Burbidge, John W. "Hegel in Canada." *Owl of Minerva* 25, no. 2 (Spring 1994): 215–19.

Butler, Judith. *Subjects of Desire: Hegelian Reflections in Twentieth-Century France*. New York: Columbia University Press, 1987.

Crites, Stephen D. "Hegelianism." *Encyclopedia of Philosophy*. New York: Macmillan, 1967: 3: 451–59.

Easton, Lloyd. *Hegel's First American Followers: The Ohio Hegelians*. Athens: Ohio University Press, 1966.

Harris, Henry S. "The Hegel Renaissance in the Anglo-Saxon World since 1945." *Owl of Minerva* 15, no. 1 (Fall 1983): 77–106.

Hegel and British Idealism. Bulletin of the Hegel Society of Great Britain 31 (Spring/Summer 1995).

Hook, Sidney. *From Hegel to Marx*. London: Gollancz, 1936.

Janicaud, Dominique. "Recent French Scholarship." *Owl of Minerva* 7, no. 3 (March 1976): 1–4.

Löwith, Karl. *From Hegel to Nietzsche* (1941). Translated by David E. Green. London: Constable, 1965.

Mackintosh, Robert. *Hegel and Hegelianism*. Bristol: Thoemmes, 1990.

Magazzeni, Gianni. "Hegel's Political Philosophy in Italy." *Bulletin of the Hegel Society of Great Britain* 7 (Spring/Summer 1983): 28–32.

Marcuse, Herbert. *Reason and Revolution: Hegel and the Rise of Social Theory*. New York: Oxford University Press, 1941.

McLellan, David. *The Young Hegelians and Karl Marx*. London: Macmillan, 1969.

Muirhead, John H. *The Platonic Tradition in Anglo-Saxon Philosophy*. London: Allen & Unwin, 1931.

Nakano Hajimu. "Hegel Studies in Japan." *Owl of Minerva* 8, no. 4 (June 1977): 2–6.

Nuzzo, Angelica. "An Outline of Italian Hegelianism (1832–1998)." *Owl of Minerva* 29, no. 2 (Spring 1998): 165–205.

Panasiuk, Ryszard. "Hegel in Poland." *Bulletin of the Hegel Society of Great Britain* 5 (Spring/Summer 1982): 6–13.

Régnier, Marcel. "Hegel in France." *Bulletin of the Hegel Society of Great Britain* 8 (Autumn/Winter 1983): 10–20.

Rockmore, Tom. "Aspects of French Hegelianism." *Owl of Minerva* 24, no. 2 (Spring 1993): 191–206.

Schacht, Richard. *Hegel and After: Studies in Continental Philosophy between Hegel and Sartre*. Pittsburgh: University of Pittsburgh Press, 1975.

Schutte, Ofelia M. "The Master–Slave Dialectic in Latin America: the Social Criticism of Zea, Freire, and Roig." *Owl of Minerva* 22, no. 1 (Fall 1990): 5–18.
Simchoni, Avital. "British Idealism: Its Political and Social Thought." *Bulletin of the Hegel Society of Great Britain* 3 (Spring/Summer 1981): 16–31.
Thulstrup, Niels. *Kierkegaard's Relation to Hegel* (1967). Translated by George L. Stengran. Princeton, N.J.: Princeton University Press, 1980.
Toews, John E. *Hegelianism: The Path toward Dialectical Humanism, 1805–1841.* Cambridge: Cambridge University Press, 1980.
Vesjak, Boris. "Hegelianism in Slovenia: A Short Introduction." *Bulletin of the Hegel Society of Great Britain* 34 (Autumn/Winter 1996): 1–12.
Watson, David. "Hegelianism in the United States." *Bulletin of the Hegel Society of Great Britain* 6 (Autumn/Winter 1982): 18–28.
Xue, Hua, and Xue-Mei Xue. "Information on Hegel Studies and Editions in China." *Owl of Minerva* 18, no. 1 (Fall 1986): 92–95.

HEGEL'S PHILOSOPHY

General

Collected Works

Hegel, G. W. F. *Gesammelte Werke* (Collected Works). Edited by the North Rhine–Westphalia Academy of Sciences. Hamburg: Meiner, 1968–.
———. *Sämtliche Werke* (Complete Works). Edited by Georg Lasson. Leipzig: Meiner, 1907–40.
———. *Sämtliche Werke* (Complete Works). Jubilee edition edited on the basis of the Werke of 1832–45 by Hermann Glockner. Stuttgart: Frommann, 1927–40.
———. *Vorlesungen: Augewählte Nachschriften und Manuskripte* (Lectures: Selected Transcripts and Manuscripts). Hamburg: Meiner, 1983–.
———. *Werke* (Works). Edited on the basis of the Werke of 1832–45 by Eva Moldenhauer and Kurt Markus Michel. Frankfurt am Main: Suhrkamp, 1969–70.
———. *Werke: Vollständige Ausgabe durch einen Verein von Freunden des Verewigten* (Works: Complete Edition by an Association of Friends of the Immortal). Berlin: Duncker & Humblot, 1832–45; 2d ed., 1840–47.

Selections

Hegel: The Essential Writings. Edited by Frederick G. Weiss. New York: Harper & Row, 1974.
Hegel: Selections. Edited by Michael J. Inwood. New York: Macmillan, 1989.
Hegel: Selections. Edited by Jacob Loewenberg. New York: Scribner's, 1929.
The Hegel Reader. Edited by Stephen Houlgate. Oxford: Blackwell, 1998.
The Philosophy of Hegel. Edited by Carl J. Friedrich. New York: Modern Library, 1954.

Secondary Sources

Acton, Harry Burrows. "Hegel, Georg Wilhelm Friedrich." *Encyclopedia of Philosophy*. New York: Macmillan, 1967: 3: 435–51.

Adorno, Theodor. *Hegel: Three Studies* (1963). Translated by S. W. Nicholson. Cambridge, Mass.: MIT Press, 1993.

Berthold-Bond, Daniel. *Hegel's Grand Synthesis*. Albany: State University of New York Press, 1989.

Beyond Epistemology: New Studies in the Philosophy of Hegel. Edited by Frederick G. Weiss. The Hague: Nijhoff, 1974.

Bloch, Ernst. *Subjekt-Objekt: Erläuterungen zu Hegel* (Subject-Object: Comments on Hegel). Berlin: Aufbau, 1951.

Butler, Clark. *G. W. F. Hegel*. Boston: Twayne, 1977.

Caird, Edward. *Hegel*. Edinburgh: Blackwood, 1883.

The Cambridge Companion to Hegel. Edited by Frederick C. Beiser. Cambridge: Cambridge University Press, 1993.

Croce, Benedetto. *What Is Living and What Is Dead of the Philosophy of Hegel*. Translated from the third Italian edition (1912) by Douglas Ainslie. London: Macmillan, 1915.

Cunningham, G. Watts. *Thought and Reality in Hegel's System*. London: Longman's, 1910.

Derrida, Jacques. *Glas* (1974). Translated by John P. Leavey and Richard Rand. Lincoln: University of Nebraska Press, 1986.

Feminist Interpretations of G. W. F. Hegel. Edited by Patricia J. Mills. University Park: Pennsylvania State University Press, 1996.

Findlay, John N. *Hegel: A Re-examination*. London: Allen & Unwin, 1958.

Gadamer, Hans-Georg. *Hegel's Dialectic: Five Hermeneutical Studies* (1971). Translated by P. Christopher Smith. New Haven, Conn.: Yale University Press, 1976.

Hegel. Edited by Michael Inwood. Oxford Readings in Philosophy. Oxford: Oxford University Press, 1985.

Hegel: A Collection of Critical Essays. Edited by Alasdair MacIntyre. Garden City, N.Y.: Doubleday, 1972.

Hegel: Critical Assessments. Edited by Robert Stern. London: Routledge, 1993.

Hegel and Modern Philosophy. Edited by David Lamb. London: Croom Helm, 1987.

A Hegel Symposium. Edited by Don Carlos Travis. Austin: University of Texas Press, 1962.

Houlgate, Stephen. *Freedom, Truth, and History: An Introduction to Hegel's Philosophy*. London: Routledge, 1991.

Inwood, Michael. *Hegel*. London: Routledge & Kegan Paul, 1983.

——. *A Hegel Dictionary*. Oxford: Blackwell, 1992.

Kainz, Howard. *G. W. F. Hegel: The Philosophical System*. New York: Twayne, 1996.

———. *Paradox, Dialectic, and System: A Contemporary Reconstruction of the Hegelian Problematic*. University Park: Pennsylvania State University Press, 1987.

Kaufmann, Walter. *Hegel: Reinterpretation, Texts and Commentary*. Garden City, N.Y.: Doubleday, 1965.

Kojève, Alexandre. *Introduction to the Reading of Hegel* (1947). Edited by A. Bloom; translated by J. H. Nichols. New York: Basic Books, 1969.

Lamb, David. *Hegel—From Foundation to System*. The Hague: Nijhoff, 1980.

The Legacy of Hegel: Proceedings of the Marquette Hegel Symposium, 1970. Edited by Joseph J. O'Malley, Keith W. Algozin, Howard P. Kainz, and Lee C. Rice. The Hague: Nijhoff, 1973.

Maker, William. *Philosophy without Foundations*. Albany: State University of New York Press, 1994.

McCumber, John. *The Company of Words: Hegel, Language, and Systematic Philosophy*. Evanston, Ill.: Northwestern University Press, 1993.

Mure, Geoffrey R. G. *An Introduction to Hegel*. Oxford: Oxford University Press, 1940.

———. *The Philosophy of Hegel*. London: Oxford University Press, 1965.

New Studies in Hegel's Philosophy. Edited by Warren E. Steinkraus. New York: Holt, Rinehart & Winston, 1971.

Pippin, Robert B. *Hegel's Idealism: The Satisfactions of Self-Consciousness*. Cambridge: Cambridge University Press, 1989.

Plant, Raymond, *Hegel: An Introduction*. London: Allen & Unwin, 1973.

Rose, Gillian. *Hegel Contra Sociology*. London: Athlone, 1981.

Rosen, Stanley. *G. W. F. Hegel: An Introduction to the Science of Wisdom*. New Haven, Conn.: Yale University Press, 1974.

Russell, Bertrand. "Hegel." *History of Western Philosophy*. New York: Simon & Schuster, 1945.

Selected Essays on G. W. F. Hegel. Edited by Lawrence S. Stepelevich. Atlantic Highlands, N.J.: Humanities, 1993.

Singer, Peter. *Hegel*. Oxford: Oxford University Press, 1983.

Soll, Ivan. *An Introduction to Hegel's Metaphysics*. Chicago: University of Chicago Press, 1969.

Stace, Walter T. *The Philosophy of Hegel: A Systematic Exposition*. London: Macmillan, 1924.

Stirling, J. Hutchison. *The Secret of Hegel: Being the Hegelian System in Origin, Principle, Form, and Matter*. London: Longman, Roberts & Green, 1865.

Taylor, Charles. *Hegel*. Cambridge: Cambridge University Press, 1975.

Journals

Bulletin of the Hegel Society of Great Britain
Hegel-Jahrbuch. Proceedings of the Internationale Hegel Gesellschaft

Hegel-Studien (in association with the Hegel Commission of the North Rhine-Westphalia Academy of Sciences)
Idealistic Studies
Jahrbuch für Hegelforschung
Owl of Minerva. Journal of the Hegel Society of America

Bibliographies

Flay, Joseph C. "Bibliography." *Hegel and the History of Philosophy*. Edited by Joseph J. O'Malley, Keith W. Algozin, and Frederick G. Weiss. The Hague: Nijhoff, 1974: 194–236.

———. "Bibliography." *Art and Logic in Hegel's Philosophy*. Edited by Warren E. Steinkraus and Kenneth Schmitz. Atlantic Highlands, N.J.: Humanities, 1980: 238–70.

———. *Hegel's Quest for Certainty*. Albany: State University of New York Press, 1984: 413–39.

Harris, Henry S. *Hegel's Ladder II: The Odyssey of Spirit*. Indianapolis: Hackett, 1997: 784–868.

Steinhauer, Kurt, and H.-D. Schluter. *Hegel Bibliography: Background Material on the International Reception of Hegel within the Context of the History of Philosophy*. Munich: Saur, 1980, 1998.

Weiss, Frederick G. "Hegel: A Bibliography of Books in English Arranged Chronologically." *The Legacy of Hegel*. Edited by Joseph J. O'Malley, Keith W. Algozin, Howard P. Kainz, and Lee C. Rice. The Hague: Nijhoff, 1973: 298–308.

Early Writings

Editions and Translations

Between Kant and Hegel: Texts in the Development of Post-Kantian Idealism. Translated by George di Giovanni and Henry S. Harris. Albany: State University of New York Press, 1985.

Hegel, G. W. F. *The Difference between Fichte's and Schelling's System of Philosophy*. Translated by Henry S. Harris and Walter Cerf. Albany: State University of New York Press, 1977.

———. *The Difference between the Fichtean and Schellingian Systems of Philosophy*. Translated by Jere P. Surber. Reseda, Calif.: Ridgeview, 1978.

———. *Early Theological Writings*. Translated by Thomas M. Knox and Richard Kroner. Chicago: University of Chicago Press, 1948.

———. *Faith and Knowledge*. Translated by Walter Cerf and Henry S. Harris. Albany: State University of New York Press, 1977.

———. "G. W. F. Hegel: *Philosophical Dissertation on the Orbits of the Planets* (1801). Preceded by the 12 Theses Defended on August 27, 1801." Translated, with foreword and notes, by Pierre Adler. *Graduate Faculty Philosophy Journal* 12, nos. 1&2 (1987): 269–309.

——. *Hegel and the Human Spirit: A Translation of the Jena Lectures on the Philosophy of Spirit (1805) with commentary*. Translation and commentary by Leo Rauch. Detroit, Mich.: Wayne State University Press, 1983.

——. "Hegel's Habilitationsthesen." A translation with introduction and annotated bibliography by Norbert Waszek. In *Hegel and Modern Philosophy*, edited by David Lamb. London: Croom Helm, 1987.

——. *Hegel's Political Writings*. Translated by Thomas M. Knox. London: Oxford University Press, 1964.

——. *Hegels Theologische Jugendschriften* (Hegel's Early Theological Writings). Edited by Hermann Nohl. Tübingen: Mohr, 1907.

——. *The Jena System, 1804–5: Logic and Metaphysics*. Translated by John W. Burbidge, George di Giovanni, Henry S. Harris, et al. Montreal: McGill-Queen's University Press, 1986.

——. *Natural Law: The Scientific Ways of Treating Natural Law, Its Place in Moral Philosophy, and Its Relation to the Positive Sciences of Law*. Translated by Thomas M. Knox. Philadelphia: University of Pennsylvania Press, 1975.

——. *System of Ethical Life and First Philosophy of Spirit*. Edited and translated by Henry S. Harris and Thomas M. Knox. Albany: State University of New York Press, 1979.

——. *Three Essays, 1793–1795: The Tübingen Essay, Berne Fragments, The Life of Jesus*. Translated by Peter Fuss and John Dobbins. Notre Dame, Ind.: University of Notre Dame Press, 1984.

Secondary Sources

Cook, Daniel. "Language and Consciousness in Hegel's Jena Writings." *Journal of the History of Philosophy* 10 (1972): 197–211.

Dickey, Laurence. *Hegel: Religion, Economics, and Politics of the Spirit, 1770–1807*. Cambridge: Cambridge University Press, 1987.

Dilthey, Wilhelm. *Die Jugendgeschichte Hegels* (Hegel's Early History). Berlin: Reimer, 1905.

Dokumente zu Hegels Entwicklung (Documents on Hegel's Development). Edited by Johannes Hoffmeister. Stuttgart: Frommann, 1936.

Hance, Allen S. "The Rule of Law in *The German Constitution*." *Owl of Minerva* 22, no. 2 (Spring 1991): 159–74.

Häring, Theodor L. *Hegel: Sein Wollen und sein Werk* (Hegel: His Willing and His Work). Leipzig: Teubner, 1929–38.

Harris, Henry S. *Hegel's Development. Volume 1: Toward the Sunlight, 1770–1801*. Oxford: Oxford University Press, 1972.

——. *Hegel's Development. Volume 2: Night Thoughts, Jena, 1801–1806*. Oxford: Oxford University Press, 1983.

Hegel on Ethical Life, Religion, and Philosophy. Edited by A. Wylleman. Dordrecht: Kluwer, 1989.

Lukács, György. *The Young Hegel* (1947). Translated by Rodney Livingstone. London: Merlin, 1975.

Rauch, Leo. "Hegel and the Emerging World: The Jena Lectures on Naturphilosophie (1805–6)." *Owl of Minerva* 16, no. 2 (Spring 1985): 175–81.

Wahl, Jean. *Le Malheur de la conscience dans la philosophie de Hegel* (The Unhappiness of Consciousness in the Philosophy of Hegel). Paris: Rieder, 1929.

Phenomenology of Spirit

Editions and Translations

Hegel, G. W. F. *Hegel's Phenomenology of Spirit*. Selections translated and annotated by Howard P. Kainz. University Park: Pennsylvania State University Press, 1994.

———. *The Phenomenology of Mind*. Translated by James B. Baillie. London: Sonnenschein, 1910.

———. *The Phenomenology of Spirit*. Translated by Arnold V. Miller. Oxford: Oxford University Press, 1977.

———. *System der Wissenschaft. 1. Theil. Die Phänomenologie des Geistes* (System of Science. Pt. 1: The Phenomenology of Spirit). Bamberg: Goebhardt, 1807.

Kaufmann, Walter. *Hegel: Texts and Commentary*. Garden City, N.Y.: Doubleday, 1966.

Secondary Sources

Absolute Knowing. Owl of Minerva 30, no. 1 (Fall 1998).

De Nys, Martin. "The Motion of the Universal: Hegel's Phenomenology of Consciousness." *Modern Schoolman* 56 (1978–79): 301–20.

———. "Sense Certainty and Universality: Hegel's Entrance into the *Phenomenology*." *International Philosophical Quarterly* 18 (1978): 445–65.

Dove, Kenley. "Hegel's Phenomenological Method." *Review of Metaphysics* 23, no. 4 (June 1970): 615–41.

Dulckheit, Katharina. "Can Hegel Refer to Particulars?" *Owl of Minerva* 17, no. 2 (Spring 1986): 181–94.

Flay, Joseph C. *Hegel's Quest for Certainty*. Albany: State University of New York Press, 1984.

Forster, Michael N. *Hegel's Idea of a Phenomenology of Spirit*. Chicago: University of Chicago Press, 1998.

Harris, Henry S. *Hegel: Phenomenology and System*. Indianapolis, Ind.: Hackett, 1995.

———. *Hegel's Ladder I: The Pilgrimage of Reason*. Indianapolis, Ind.: Hackett, 1997.

———. *Hegel's Ladder II: The Odyssey of Spirit*. Indianapolis, Ind.: Hackett, 1997.

Hegel's Phenomenology of Spirit: A Reappraisal. Edited by Gary K. Browning. Dordrecht: Kluwer, 1997.

Heidegger, Martin. *Hegel's Concept of Experience* (1950). New York: Harper & Row, 1970.

——. *Hegel's Phenomenology of Spirit* (1980). Translated by Parvis Emad and Kenneth May. Bloomington: Indiana University Press, 1988.

Hoffheimer, Michael H. "The Idea of Law (Recht) in Hegel's *Phenomenology*." *Clio* 21 (1992): 345–67.

Hyppolite, Jean. *Genesis and Structure of Hegel's Phenomenology of Spirit* (1946). Translated by Samuel Cherniak and John Heckman. Evanston, Ill.: Northwestern University Press, 1974.

Jamros, Daniel P. *The Human Shape of God: Religion in Hegel's Phenomenology*. New York: Paragon, 1994.

Kainz, Howard P. *Hegel's Phenomenology, Part 1: Analysis and Commentary*. Tuscaloosa: University of Alabama Press, 1976.

——. *Hegel's Phenomenology, Part 2: The Evolution of Ethical and Religious Consciousness to the Dialectical Standpoint*. Athens: Ohio University Press, 1983.

Kline, George L. "The Dialectic of Action and Passion in Hegel's *Phenomenology of Spirit*." *Review of Metaphysics* 23, no. 4 (June 1970): 679–89.

Lauer, Quentin. *A Reading of Hegel's Phenomenology of Spirit*. New York: Fordham University Press, 1976.

Loewenberg, Jacob. *Hegel's Phenomenology: Dialogues on the Life of Mind*. La Salle, Ill.: Open Court, 1965.

Ludwig, Walter D. "The Method of Hegel's *Phenomenology of Spirit*." *Owl of Minerva* 23, no. 2 (Spring 1992): 165–75.

Maker, William. "Hegel's *Phenomenology* as an Introduction to Science." *Clio* 10 (1981): 381–97.

Marx, Werner. *Hegel's Phenomenology of Spirit* (1971). Translated by Peter Heath. New York: Harper & Row, 1975.

Method and Speculation in Hegel's Phenomenology. Edited by Merold Westphal. Atlantic Highlands, N.J.: Humanities, 1982.

Navickas, Joseph L. *Consciousness and Reality: Hegel's Philosophy of Subjectivity*. The Hague: Nijhoff, 1976.

Norman, Richard. *Hegel's Phenomenology: A Philosophical Introduction*. London: Sussex University Press, 1976.

Okrent, Mark B. "Consciousness and Objective Spirit in Hegel's *Phenomenology*." *Journal of the History of Philosophy* 18 (1980): 39–55.

The Phenomenology of Spirit Reader: Critical and Interpretative Essays. Edited by Jon Stewart. Albany: State University of New York Press, 1998.

Pinkard, Terry. *Hegel's Phenomenology: The Sociality of Reason*. Cambridge: Cambridge University Press, 1994.

Rauch, Leo, and David Sherman. *Hegel's Phenomenology of Self-Consciousness: Text and Commentary*. Albany: State University of New York Press, 1999.

Robinson, Jonathan. *Duty and Hypocrisy in Hegel's Phenomenology of Mind*. Toronto: University of Toronto Press, 1977.

Rockmore, Tom. *Cognition: An Introduction to Hegel's Phenomenology of Spirit.* Berkeley: University of California Press, 1997.

———. *Hegel's Circular Epistemology.* Bloomington: Indiana University Press, 1986.

Russon, John. *The Self and Its Body in Hegel's Phenomenology of Spirit.* Toronto: University of Toronto Press, 1997.

Schacht, Richard. "A Commentary on the Preface to Hegel's *Phenomenology of Spirit.*" *Philosophical Studies* (U.S.A.) 23 (1972): 1–31.

Shklar, Judith. *Freedom and Independence: A Study of the Political Ideas of Hegel's Phenomenology of Mind.* Cambridge: Cambridge University Press, 1976.

Simpson, Peter. *Hegel's Transcendental Induction.* Albany: State University of New York Press, 1998.

Solomon, Robert. *In the Spirit of Hegel: A Study of G. W. F. Hegel's Phenomenology of Spirit.* Oxford: Oxford University Press, 1983.

Verene, Donald. *Hegel's Recollection: A Study of Images in the Phenomenology of Spirit.* Albany: State University of New York Press, 1985.

Ware, Robert Bruce. *Hegel: The Logic of Self-Consciousness and the Legacy of Subjective Freedom.* Edinburgh: Edinburgh University Press, 1999.

Westphal, Kenneth. *Hegel's Epistemological Realism: A Study of the Aim and Method of Hegel's Phenomenology of Spirit.* Dordrecht: Kluwer, 1989.

Westphal, Merold. *History and Truth in Hegel's Phenomenology.* Atlantic Highlands, N.J.: Humanities, 1979.

Williams, Robert R. *Recognition: Fichte and Hegel on the Other.* Albany: State University of New York Press, 1992.

Science of Logic

Editions and Translations

Hegel, G. W. F. *Hegel's Science of Logic.* Translated by Walter H. Johnston and Leslie G. Struthers. London: Allen & Unwin, 1929.

———. *Hegel's Science of Logic.* Translated by Arnold V. Miller. London: Allen & Unwin, 1969.

———. *Wissenschaft der Logik.* 1. Theil: *Die objektive Logik;* 1. Abtheilung: *Die Lehre vom Sein* (Science of Logic, Part 1: The Objective Logic; 1st Section: The Doctrine of Being). Nürnberg: Schrag, 1812.

———. *Wissenschaft der Logik.* 1. Theil: *Die objektive Logik;* 2. Abtheilung: *Die Lehre vom Wesen* (Science of Logic, Part 1: The Objective Logic; 2nd Section: The Doctrine of Essence). Nürnberg: Schrag, 1813.

———. *Wissenschaft der Logik.* 2. Theil: *Die subjektive Logik: Die Lehre vom Begriff* (Science of Logic, Part 2: The Subjective Logic: The Doctrine of the Concept). Nürnberg: Schrag, 1816.

——. *Wissenschaft der Logik*. 1. Theil: *Die objektive Logik;* 1. Abtheilung: *Die Lehre vom Sein* (Science of Logic, Part 1: The Objective Logic; 1st Section: The Doctrine of Being). 2d rev. ed. Stuttgart: Cotta, 1832.

Secondary Sources

Ahlers, Rolf. "The Absolute as the Beginning of Hegel's Logic." *Philosophical Forum* 6 (1974–5): 288–300.

Art and Logic in Hegel's Philosophy. Edited by Warren E. Steinkraus and Kenneth Schmitz. Atlantic Highlands, N.J.: Humanities, 1980.

Baillie, James B. *The Origin and Significance of Hegel's Logic*. London: Macmillan, 1901.

Baur, Michael. "Sublating Kant and the Old Metaphysics: A Reading of the Transition from Being to Essence in Hegel's *Logic*." *Owl of Minerva* 29, no. 2 (Spring 1998): 139–64.

Biard, J., D. Buvat, J.-F. Kervegan, J.-F. Kling, A. Lacroix, André Lécrivain, and Michel Slubicki. *Introduction à la Lecture de la "Science de la Logique" de Hegel* (Introduction to the Reading of Hegel's *Science of Logic*). 3 vols. Paris: Aubier, 1981, 1983, 1987.

Burbidge, John W. *Hegel on Logic and Religion*. Albany: State University of New York Press, 1992.

——. *On Hegel's Logic: Fragments of a Commentary*. Atlantic Highlands, N.J.: Humanities, 1981.

Butler, Clark. *Hegel's Logic: Between Dialectic and History*. Evanston, Ill.: Northwestern University Press, 1997.

Cave, George P. "The Dialectic of Becoming in Hegel's Logic." *Owl of Minerva* 16, no. 2 (Spring 1985): 147–60.

Dahlstrom, Daniel O. "Hegel's Science of Logic and Idea of Truth." *Idealistic Studies* 13 (1983): 33–49.

di Giovanni, George. "Reflection and Contradiction: A Commentary on Some Passages of Hegel's Science of Logic." *Hegel-Studien* 8 (1973): 131–62.

Essays on Hegel's Logic. Edited by George di Giovanni. Albany: State University of New York Press, 1990.

Ferrini, Cinzia. "On the Relation between 'Mode' and 'Measure' in Hegel's *Science of Logic*: Some Introductory Remarks." *Owl of Minerva* 20, no. 1 (Fall 1988): 21–49.

Harris, William T. *Hegel's Doctrine of Reflection*. New York: Appleton, 1881.

——. *Hegel's Logic: A Book on the Genesis of the Categories of Mind*. Chicago: Griggs, 1890.

Hartnack, Justus. *Hegel's Logic* (1995). Translated by Lars Aagaard-Mogensen. Indianapolis, Ind.: Hackett, 1998.

Hibben, John G. *Hegel's Logic: An Essay in Interpretation*. New York: Scribner, 1902.

Hoffmeyer, John F. *The Advent of Freedom: The Presence of the Future in Hegel's Logic*. Cranbury, N.J.: Associated Universities Press, 1994.

Houlgate, Stephen. "Necessity and Contingency in Hegel's *Science of Logic*." *Owl of Minerva* 27, no. 1 (Fall 1995): 37–49.

Hyppolite, Jean. *Logic and Existence* (1932). Translated by Leonard Lawlor and Amit Sen. Albany: State University of New York Press, 1997.

Johnson, Paul. *The Critique of Thought: A Re-examination of Hegel's Science of Logic*. Aldershot, England: Gower, 1988.

Lachterman, David. "Hegel and the Formalization of Logic." *Graduate Faculty Journal* 12, nos. 1–2 (1980): 153–89.

———. *Studies in Hegelian Dialectic*. Cambridge: Cambridge University Press, 1896.

Marcuse, Herbert. *Hegel's Ontology and the Theory of Historicity* (1932). Translated by Seyla Benhabib. Cambridge, Mass.: MIT Press, 1987.

McTaggart, John M. E. *A Commentary on Hegel's Logic*. Cambridge: Cambridge University Press, 1910.

Mueller, Gustav E. "The Hegelian Legend of 'Thesis-Antithesis-Synthesis.'" *Journal of the History of Ideas* 19 (1958): 411–14.

Pinkard, Terry. *Hegel's Dialectic: The Explanation of Possibility*. Philadelphia: Temple University Press, 1988.

Rockmore, Tom. "Foundationalism and Hegelian Logic." *Owl of Minerva* 21, no. 1 (Fall 1989): 41–50.

Rosen, Michael. *Hegel's Dialectic and Its Criticism*. Cambridge: Cambridge University Press, 1982.

Rowe, William V. "Essence, Ground, and First Philosophy in Hegel's *Science of Logic*." *Owl of Minerva* 18, no. 1 (Fall 1986): 43–56.

Sarlemijn, Andries. *Hegel's Dialectic* (1971). Translated by P. Kirschenmann. Dordrecht: Reidel, 1975.

Schmitz, Kenneth L. "Hegel's Attempt to Forge a Logic for Spirit." *Dialogue* 10 (1971): 653–72.

White, Alan. *Absolute Knowledge: Hegel and the Problem of Metaphysics*. Athens: Ohio University Press, 1983.

Encyclopedia of the Philosophical Sciences

Editions and Translations

Hegel, G. W. F. *Encyclopädie der Philosophischen Wissenschaften im Grundrisse* (Encyclopedia of the Philosophical Sciences in Outline). Heidelberg: Oßwald, 1817.

———. *Encyclopädie der Philosophischen Wissenschaften im Grundrisse* (Encyclopedia of the Philosophical Sciences in Outline). 2d expanded ed. Heidelberg: Oßwald, 1827.

———. *Encyclopädie der Philosophischen Wissenschaften im Grundrisse* (Encyclopedia of the Philosophical Sciences in Outline). 3d rev. ed. Heidelberg: Oßwald, 1830.

——. *Encyclopedia of the Philosophical Sciences in Outline and Critical Writings* (1817 ed.). Translated by Steven A. Taubeneck and others. New York: Continuum, 1990.

Encyclopedia Logic

Editions and Translations

Hegel, G. W. F. *The Encyclopaedia Logic* (1830). Translated by Theodore F. Geraets, Wallis A. Suchting, and Henry S. Harris. Indianapolis, Ind.: Hackett, 1991.
——. *The Logic of Hegel* (1830). Translated by William Wallace. Oxford: Oxford University Press, 1874.
——. *Vorlesungen über Logik und Metaphysik: Heidelberg, 1817* (Lectures on Logic and Metaphysics: Heidelberg, 1817). Edited by Karen Gloy. *Vorlesungen 11.* Hamburg: Meiner, 1992.

Secondary Sources

Harris, Errol E. *An Interpretation of the Logic of Hegel.* Lanham, Md.: University Press of America, 1983.
Mure, Geoffrey R. G. *A Study of Hegel's Logic.* Oxford: Oxford University Press, 1950.
Wallace, William. *Prolegomena to the Study of Hegel's Philosophy and Especially of His Logic.* Oxford: Oxford University Press, 1894.

Encyclopedia Philosophy of Nature

Editions and Translations

Hegel, G. W. F. *Hegels Jenaer Naturphilosophie.* Edited by Klaus Vieweg. Munich: Fink, 1998.
——. *Hegel's Philosophy of Nature* (1830). Translated by Michael J. Petry. London: Allen & Unwin, 1970.
——. *Hegel's Philosophy of Nature* (1830). Translated by Arnold V. Miller. Oxford: Oxford University Press, 1970.
——. *Naturphilosophie: Band I: Die Vorlesungen von 1819/20* (Philosophy of Nature: Vol. 1: The Lectures of 1819–20). Edited by Manfred Gies. Naples: Bibliopolis, 1982.

Secondary Sources

Alexander, Samuel. "Hegel's Conception of Nature." *Mind* 11 (1886): 495–523.
Buchdahl, Gerd. "Hegel's Philosophy of Nature." *British Journal for the Philosophy of Science* 23 (1972): 257–66.

Burbidge, John W. "Hegel's Hat Trick." *Bulletin of the Hegel Society of Great Britain* 39 (Spring/Summer 1999): 46–63.

————. *Real Process: How Logic and Chemistry Combine in Hegel's Philosophy of Nature*. Toronto: University of Toronto Press, 1996.

Harris, Errol E. *The Spirit of Hegel*. Atlantic Highlands, N.J.: Humanities, 1993.

Harris, William T. "Philosophy of Nature." *Journal of Speculative Philosophy* 5 (1871): 274–82.

Hegel and Newtonianism. Edited by Michael J. Petry. Dordrecht: Kluwer, 1993.

Hegel and the Philosophy of Nature. Edited by Stephen Houlgate. Albany: State University of New York Press, 1998.

Hegel and the Sciences. Edited by Robert S. Cohen and Marx W. Wartofsky. Dordrecht: Kluwer, 1984.

Hegel's Metaphysics of Nature. Bulletin of the Hegel Society of Great Britain 26 (Autumn/Winter 1992).

Hegels Philosophie der Natur: Beziehungen zwischen empirischer and spekulativer Naturerkenntnis (Hegel's Philosophy of Nature: Relations between an Empirical and a Speculative Cognition of Nature). Edited by Rolf-Peter Horstmann and Michael J. Petry. Stuttgart: Klett-Cotta, 1986.

Lucas, George R., Jr. "A Re-interpretation of Hegel's Philosophy of Nature." *Journal of the History of Philosophy* 22 (1984): 103–13.

Peterson, Mark C. E. "Animals Eating Empiricists: Assimilation and Subjectivity in Hegel's *Philosophy of Nature*." *Owl of Minerva* 23, no. 1 (Fall 1991): 49–62.

————. "The Role of Practical and Theoretical Approaches in Hegel's *Philosophy of Nature*." *Owl of Minerva* 27, no. 2 (Spring 1996): 155–65.

Stallo, John B. *General Principles of the Philosophy of Nature, with an Outline of Some of Its Recent Developments among the Germans*. Boston: Crosby & Nichols, 1848.

Webb, T. R. "The Problem of Empirical Knowledge in Hegel's *Philosophy of Nature*." *Hegel-Studien* 15 (1980): 171–86.

Encyclopedia Philosophy of Spirit

Editions and Translations

Hegel, G. W. F. *The Berlin Phenomenology*. Translated by Michael J. Petry. Dordrecht: Reidel, 1981.

————. *Hegel's Philosophy of Mind* (1830). Translated by William Wallace with the *Zusätze* (additions) translated by Arnold V. Miller. Oxford: Oxford University Press, 1971.

————. *The Philosophy of Mind* (1830). Translated by William Wallace. Oxford: Oxford University Press, 1894.

————. *Philosophy of Subjective Spirit* (1830 with the 1822 and 1825 lectures). Translated by Michael J. Petry. Dordrecht: Reidel, 1978.

———. *Vorlesungen über die Philosophie des Geistes: Berlin 1827/28* (Lectures on the Philosophy of Spirit: Berlin 1827/28). Edited by Franz Hespe and Burkhard Tuschling. *Vorlesungen 13*. Hamburg: Meiner, 1994.

Secondary Sources

Berthold-Bond, Daniel. *Hegel's Theory of Madness*. Albany: State University of New York Press, 1995.

Clark, Malcolm. *Logic and System: A Study of the Transition from "Vorstellung" to Thought in the Philosophy of Hegel*. The Hague: Nijhoff, 1971.

Cook, Daniel. *Language in the Philosophy of Hegel*. The Hague: Mouton, 1973.

De Vries, Willem. *Hegel's Theory of Mental Activity*. Ithaca, N.Y.: Cornell University Press, 1988.

Greene, Murray. *Hegel on the Soul: A Speculative Anthropology*. The Hague: Nijhoff, 1972.

Harris, Errol E. "Hegel's Anthropology." *Owl of Minerva* 25, no. 1 (Fall 1993): 5–14.

Hegel's Philosophy of Spirit. Edited by Peter G. Stillman. Albany: State University of New York Press, 1987.

Hegel: The Absolute Spirit. Edited by Theodore F. Geraets. Ottawa: University of Ottawa Press, 1984.

Lucas, Hans-Christian. "The 'Sovereign Ingratitude' of Spirit toward Nature: Logical Qualities, Corporeity, Animal Magnetism, and Madness in Hegel's 'Anthropology.'" *Owl of Minerva* 23, no. 2 (Spring 1992): 131–50.

McCumber, John. "Hegel on Habit." *Owl of Minerva* 21, no. 2 (Spring 1990): 155–65.

Olson, Alan M. *Hegel and the Spirit*. Princeton, N.J.: Princeton University Press, 1992.

Peperzak, Adriaan. "'Second Nature': Place and Significance of the Objective Spirit in Hegel's *Encyclopaedia*." *Owl of Minerva* 27, no. 1 (Fall 1995): 51–66.

Pillow, Kirk. "Habituating Madness and Phantasying Art in Hegel's *Encyclopedia*." *Owl of Minerva* 28, no. 2 (Spring 1997): 183–215.

Winfield, Richard. "Conceiving Reality without Foundations: Hegel's Neglected Strategy for *Realphilosophie*." *Owl of Minerva* 15, no. 2 (Spring 1984): 183–98.

Philosophy of Right

Editions and Translations

Hegel, G. W. F. *The Ethics of Hegel*. Selections from his *Rechtsphilosophie* translated by J. MacBride Sterrett. Boston: Ginn, 1893.

———. *Grundlinien der Philosophie des Rechts, oder Naturrecht und Staatswissenschaft im Grundrisse* (Principles of the Philosophy of Right, or Natural Law and Political Science in Outline). Berlin: Nicolai, 1820.

———. *Hegel's Philosophy of Right*. Translated by Samuel W. Dyde. London: Bell, 1896.

———. *Hegel's Philosophy of Right*. Translated by Thomas M. Knox. Oxford: Oxford University Press, 1942.

———. *Hegel's Philosophy of Right*. Translated by Hugh Barr Nisbett; edited by Allen Wood. Cambridge: Cambridge University Press, 1991.

———. *Lectures on Natural Right and Political Science. The First Philosophy of Right. Heidelberg, 1817–18* (Becker et al., ed.). Translated by J. Michael Stewart and Peter C. Hodgson. Berkeley: University of California Press, 1995.

———. *Philosophie des Rechts: Die Vorlesungen von 1819/20* (Philosophy of Right: The Lectures of 1819/20). Edited by Dieter Henrich. Frankfurt: Suhrkamp, 1983.

———. *The Philosophy of Law*. Translated by Jacob Loewenberg. New York: German Publications Society, 1914.

———. *Political Writings*. Edited by Laurence Dickey. Cambridge: Cambridge University Press, 1999.

———. *Vorlesungen über Naturrecht und Staatswissenschaft: Heidelberg, 1817/18* (Lectures on Natural Law and Political Science: Heidelberg, 1817/18). Edited by Claudia Becker and others. *Vorlesungen 1* (Lectures 1). Hamburg: Meiner, 1983.

———. *Vorlesungen über Rechtsphilosophie, 1818–31* (Lectures on the Philosophy of Right, 1818–31). Edited by Karl-Heinz Ilting. Stuttgart-Bad Cannstatt: Frommann-Holzboog, 1972–74.

Secondary Sources

Avinieri, Shlomo. *Hegel's Theory of the Modern State*. Cambridge: Cambridge University Press, 1972.

Beck, Lewis W. "The Reformation, the Revolution, and the Restoration in Hegel's Political Philosophy." *Journal of the History of Philosophy* 14 (1976): 51–61.

Bellamy, Richard. "Hegel and Liberalism." *History of European Ideas* 8 (1987): 693–708.

Brod, Harry. *Hegel's Philosophy of Politics*. Boulder, Colo.: Westview, 1992.

Browning, Gary K. *Hegel and the History of Political Philosophy*. New York: St. Martin's, 1999.

Carritt, Edgar F. "Hegel's Sittlichkeit." *Proceedings of the Aristotelian Society* 36 (1935–6): 223–36.

Cullen, Bernard. *Hegel's Social and Political Thought: An Introduction*. Dublin: Gill & Macmillan, 1979.

Dahlstrom, Daniel O. "The Dialectic of Conscience and the Necessity of Morality in Hegel's *Philosophy of Right*." *Owl of Minerva* 24, no. 2 (Spring 1993): 181–89.

Drydyk, Jay. "Hegel's Politics: Liberal or Democratic?" *Canadian Journal of Philosophy* 16 (1986): 99–122.

Foster, Michael B. *The Political Philosophies of Plato and Hegel*. Oxford: Oxford University Press, 1935.

Franco, Paul. *Hegel's Philosophy of Freedom*. New Haven, Conn.: Yale University Press, 1999.

Hardimon, Michael. *The Project of Reconciliation: Hegel's Social Philosophy*. Cambridge: Cambridge University Press, 1993.

Hegel and Legal Theory. Edited by Drucilla Cornell, M. Rosenfeld, and D. J. Carlson. London: Routledge, 1991.

Hegel on Economics and Freedom. Edited by William Maker. Macon, Ga.: Mercer University Press, 1987.

Hegel's Philosophy of Action. Edited by Lawrence S. Stepelevich and David Lamb. Atlantic Highlands, N.J.: Humanities, 1983.

Hegel's Political Philosophy: Problems and Perspectives. Edited by Zbigniew A. Pelczynski. Cambridge: Cambridge University Press, 1971.

Hegel's Political Philosophy. Edited by Walter Kaufmann. New York: Atherton, 1970.

Hegel's Social and Political Thought. Edited by Donald P. Verene. Atlantic Highlands, N.J.: Humanities, 1980.

Hoffheimer, Michael H. "Hegel's Criticism of Law." *Hegel-Studien* 27 (1992): 27–52.

Kelly, George. *Hegel's Retreat from Eleusis: Studies in Political Thought*. Princeton, N.J.: Princeton University Press, 1978.

———. *Idealism, Politics, and History*. Cambridge: Cambridge University Press, 1969.

Lakeland, Paul. *The Politics of Salvation: The Hegelian Idea of the State*. Albany: State University of New York Press, 1989.

MacGregor, David. "The State at Dusk." *Owl of Minerva* 21, no. 1 (Fall 1989): 51–64.

Mitias, Michael. *Moral Foundation of the State in Hegel's Philosophy of Right: Anatomy of an Argument*. Amsterdam: Rodopi, 1984.

Patten, Alan. *Hegel's Idea of Freedom*. Oxford: Oxford University Press, 1999.

Peperzak, Adriaan. "The Foundations of Ethics according to Hegel." *International Philosophical Quarterly* 23, no. 4 (1983): 349–65.

———. *Philosophy and Politics: A Commentary on the Preface to Hegel's Philosophy of Right*. The Hague: Nijhoff, 1987.

Pinkard, Terry. "Freedom and Social Categories in Hegel's Ethics." *Philosophy and Phenomenological Research* 47 (1986): 209–32.

Popper, Karl. *The Open Society and Its Enemies*. Vol. 2. *The High Tide of Prophecy: Hegel, Marx, and the Aftermath*. London: Paul, 1945.

Reyburn, Hugh. *The Ethical Theory of Hegel: A Study of the Philosophy of Right*. Oxford: Oxford University Press, 1921.

Ritter, Joachim. *Hegel and the French Revolution: Essays on the Philosophy of Right* (1969). Translated by Richard D. Winfield. Cambridge, Mass.: MIT Press, 1982.

Rosenzweig, Franz. *Hegel und der Staat* (Hegel and the State). Munich: Oldenbourg, 1920.

Smith, Steven. *Hegel's Critique of Liberalism: Rights in Context*. Chicago: University of Chicago Press, 1989.

The State and Civil Society: Studies in Hegel's Political Philosophy. Edited by Zbigniew A. Pelczynski. Cambridge: Cambridge University Press, 1984.

Steinberger, Peter. *Logic and Politics: Hegel's Philosophy of Right*. New Haven, Conn.: Yale University Press, 1988.

Taylor, Charles. *Hegel and Modern Society*. Cambridge: Cambridge University Press, 1979.

Tunick, Mark. *Hegel's Political Philosophy: Interpreting the Practice of Legal Punishment*. Princeton, N.J.: Princeton University Press, 1992.

Walsh, William H. *Hegelian Ethics*. London: Macmillan, 1969.

Waszek, Norbert. *The Scottish Enlightenment and Hegel's Account of "Civil Society."* Dordrecht: Kluwer, 1988.

Weil, Eric. *Hegel and the State* (1950). Translated by Mark A. Cohen. Baltimore, Md.: Johns Hopkins University Press, 1998.

Williams, Robert R. *Hegel's Ethics of Recognition*. Berkeley: University of California Press, 1998,

Winfield, Richard. *Law in Civil Society*. Lawrence, Kans.: University Press of Kansas, 1995.

———. *Reason and Justice*. Albany: State University of New York Press, 1988.

Wood, Allen. *Hegel's Ethical Thought*. Cambridge: Cambridge University Press, 1990.

Philosophy of History

Editions and Translations

Hegel, G. W. F. *Introduction to the Philosophy of History* (Karl Hegel, ed.). Translated by Leo Rauch. Indianapolis: Hackett, 1988.

———. *Lectures on the Philosophy of History* (Karl Hegel, ed.). Translated by John Sibree. London: Bohn, 1857.

———. *Lectures on the Philosophy of World History: Introduction* (Hoffmeister, ed.). Translated by Hugh B. Nisbet, with an introduction by Duncan Forbes. Cambridge: Cambridge University Press, 1975.

———. *Reason in History: A General Introduction to the Philosophy of History* (Karl Hegel, ed.). Translated by Robert S. Hartman. New York: Library of Liberal Arts, 1953.

———. *Die Vernunft in der Geschichte* (Reason in History). Edited by Johannes Hoffmeister. Hamburg: Meiner, 1955.

———. *Vorlesungen über die Philosophie der Geschichte* (Lectures on the Philosophy of History). Edited by Karl Hegel. Berlin: Duncker & Humblot, 1840.

———. *Vorlesungen über die Philosophie der Weltgeschichte* (Lectures on the Philosophy of World History). Edited by Georg Lasson. Leipzig: Meiner, 1917–20.

——. *Vorlesungen über die Philosophie der Weltgeschichte: Berlin, 1822/23* (Lectures on the Philosophy of World History: Berlin, 1822/23). Edited by Karl-Heinz Ilting, Karl Brehmer, and Hoo Nam Seelmann. *Vorlesungen 12*. Hamburg: Meiner, 1996.

Secondary Sources

Bal, Karol. "Hegel's Philosophy of History—Between Dialectics and Metaphysics." *Dialectics and Humanism* 1 (1974): 331–38.

D'Hondt, Jacques. *Hegel: Philosophe de l'Histoire Vivante* (Hegel: Philosopher of Living History). Paris: Presses Universitaires de France, 1966.

Fillion, Réal R. "Realizing Reason in History: How Cunning Does It Have to Be?" *Owl of Minerva* 23, no. 1 (Fall 1991): 77–92.

Grier, Philip T. "The End of History and the Return of History." *Owl of Minerva* 21, no. 2 (Spring 1990): 131–44.

History and System: Hegel's Philosophy of History. Edited by Robert L. Perkins. Albany: State University of New York Press, 1984.

Houlgate, Stephen. "World History as the Progress of Consciousness: An Interpretation of Hegel's Philosophy of History." *Owl of Minerva* 22, no. 1 (Fall 1990): 69–80.

Morris, George S. *Hegel's Philosophy of the State and of History*. Chicago: Griggs, 1892.

O'Brien, George Dennis. *Hegel on Reason and History*. Chicago: Chicago University Press, 1975.

Wilkins, B. T. *Hegel's Philosophy of History*. Ithaca, N.Y.: Cornell University Press, 1974.

Aesthetics

Editions and Translations

Hegel, G. W. F. *Hegel's Aesthetics: Lectures on Fine Art* (Hotho's 2d ed.). Translated by Thomas M. Knox. Oxford: Oxford University Press, 1975.

——. *Introduction to Hegel's Philosophy of Fine Arts*. Translated by Bernard Bosanquet. London: Paul, Trench, 1886.

——. *The Philosophy of Art: Being the Second Part of Hegel's Aesthetik*. Translated by William M. Bryant. New York: Appleton, 1879.

——. *The Philosophy of Fine Arts* (Hotho's 1st ed.). Translated by Francis P. B. Osmaston. London: Bell, 1920.

——. *Vorlesungen über Asthetik: Berlin, 1820/21: Eine Nachschrift* (Lectures on Aesthetics: Berlin, 1820/21: A Transcript). Edited by Helmut Schneider. Frankfurt: Lang, 1995.

——. *Vorlesungen über die Aesthetik* (Lectures on Aesthetics). Edited by Heinrich Gustav Hotho. Berlin: Duncker & Humblot, 1835–38.

————. *Vorlesungen über die Philosophie der Kunst: Berlin, 1823* (Lectures on the Philosophy of Art: Berlin, 1823). Edited by Annemarie Gethmann-Siefert. Hamburg: Meiner, 1998.

Secondary Sources

Art and Logic in Hegel's Philosophy. Edited by Warren E. Steinkraus and Kenneth Schmitz. Atlantic Highlands, N.J.: Humanities, 1980.

Bradley, Andrew Cecil. "Hegel's Theory of Tragedy." *Hibbert Journal* 2 (1903–04): 662–80.

Bryant, William M. "Hegel's Aesthetics." *Journal of Speculative Philosophy* 13 (1879): 399–403.

Bungay, Stephen. *Beauty and Truth: A Study of Hegel's Aesthetics*. Oxford: Oxford University Press, 1986.

Desmond, William. *Art and the Absolute: A Study of Hegel's Aesthetics*. Albany: State University of New York, 1986.

————. "Gothic Hegel." *Owl of Minerva* 30, no. 2 (Spring 1999): 237–52.

Donougho, Martin. "The Woman in White: On the Reception of Hegel's Antigone." *Owl of Minerva* 21, no. 1 (Fall 1989): 65–89.

Etter, Brian. "Beauty, Ornament, and Style: The Problem of Classical Architecture in Hegel's Aesthetics." *Owl of Minerva* 30, no. 2 (Spring 1999): 211–35.

————. "The Sounds of the Ideal: Hegel's Aesthetics of Music." *Owl of Minerva* 26, no. 1 (Fall 1994): 47–58.

Harries, Karsten. "Hegel on the Future of Art." *Review of Metaphysics* 27 (1973–74): 677–96.

Harris, H. S. "The Resurrection of Art." *Owl of Minerva* 16, no. 1 (Fall 1984): 5–20.

Hofstadter, Albert. "Art: Death and Transfiguration. A Study in Hegel's Theory of Romanticism." *Review of National Literatures* 1 (1970): 149–64.

Houlgate, Stephen. "Hegel and the 'End' of Art." *Owl of Minerva* 29, no. 1 (Fall 1997): 1–21.

Kainz, Howard P. "Hegel's Theory of Aesthetics in the *Phenomenology*." *Idealistic Studies* 2 (1972): 81–94.

Kaminsky, Jack. *Hegel on Art: An Interpretation of Hegel's Aesthetics*. Albany: State University of New York Press, 1962.

Kedney, John S. *Hegel's Aesthetics: A Critical Exposition*. Chicago: Griggs, 1892.

Knox, Israel. *The Aesthetic Theories of Kant, Hegel, and Schopenhauer*. New York: Columbia University Press, 1936.

Magnus, Kathleen Dow. "Spirit's Symbolic Self-Presentation in Art: A Reading of Hegel's Aesthetics." *Owl of Minerva* 30, no. 2 (Spring 1999): 155–207.

Müller, Gustav E. "The Function of Aesthetics in Hegel's Philosophy." *Journal of Aesthetics and Art Criticism* 5 (1946): 49–53.

Taft, Richard. "Art and Philosophy in the Early Development of Hegel's System." *Owl of Minerva* 18, no. 2 (Spring 1987): 145–62.

Winfield, Richard D. *Systematic Aesthetics*. Gainesville: University Press of Florida, 1995.

Wyss, Beat. *Hegel's Art History and the Critique of Modernity: The "Sorrow of Perfect" in the Aesthetics of German Idealism and Modern Art Criticism*. Cambridge: Cambridge University Press, 1999.

Philosophy of Religion

Editions and Translations

Hegel, G. W. F. *The Christian Religion* (Lasson, ed.). Edited and translated by Peter C. Hodgson. Missoula, Mont.: Scholars Press, 1979.

———. *Lectures on the Philosophy of Religion* (Marheineke, ed.). Translated by Ebenezer B. Speirs and J. Burdon Sanderson. London: Paul, Trench, 1885.

———. *Lectures on the Philosophy of Religion* (Jaeschke, ed.). Translated by Peter C. Hodgson, Robert F. Brown, and J. Michael Stewart. Berkeley: University of California Press, 1984–87.

———. *Lectures on the Philosophy of Religion: The Lectures of 1827* (Jaeschke, ed.). Translated by Peter C. Hodgson, Robert F. Brown, and J. Michael Stewart. Berkeley: University of California Press, 1988.

———. *Vorlesungen über die Philosophie der Religion* (Lectures on the Philosophy of Religion). Edited by Philipp Marheineke. Berlin: Duncker & Humblot, 1832.

———. *Vorlesungen über die Philosophie der Religion* (Lectures on the Philosophy of Religion). Edited by Walter Jaeschke. *Vorlesungen 3–5*. Hamburg: Meiner, 1983–85.

Secondary Sources

Black, Edward. "Religion and Philosophy in Hegel's Philosophy of Religion." *Monist* 60 (1977): 198–212.

Crites, Stephen. *Dialectic and Gospel in the Development of Hegel's Thinking*. University Park: Pennsylvania State University Press, 1998.

Dupré, Louis. "The Despair of Religion." *Owl of Minerva* 16, no. 1 (Fall 1984): 21–30.

Fackenheim, Emil L. *The Religious Dimension of Hegel's Thought*. Bloomington: Indiana University Press, 1967.

Hegel and the Philosophy of Religion. Edited by Darrel E. Christensen. The Hague: Nijhoff, 1970.

Hodgson, Peter C. *God in History: Shapes of Freedom*. Nashville, Tenn.: Abingdon, 1989.

———. "The Metamorphosis of Judaism in Hegel's Philosophy of Religion." *Owl of Minerva* 19, no. 1 (Fall 1987): 41–52.

Jaeschke, Walter. *Reason in Religion* (1986). Translated by J. Michael Stewart and Peter C. Hodgson. Berkeley: University of California Press, 1990.

Kung, Hans. *The Incarnation of God* (1970). Translated by J. R. Stephenson. New York: Crossroad, 1987.

Lauer, Quentin. *Hegel's Concept of God*. Albany: State University of New York Press, 1982.

Merklinger, Philip M. *Philosophy, Theology, and Hegel's Berlin Philosophy of Religion, 1821–1827*. Albany: State University of New York Press, 1993.

Min, Anselm. "Hegel on the Foundation of Religion." *International Philosophical Quarterly* 14 (1974): 79–99.

New Perspectives on Hegel's Philosophy of Religion. Edited by David Kolb. Albany: State University of New York Press, 1992.

O'Regan, Cyril. *The Heterodox Hegel*. Albany: State University of New York Press, 1994.

Reardon, Bernard M. G. *Hegel's Philosophy of Religion*. London: Macmillan, 1977.

Rocker, Stephen. *Hegel's Rational Religion: The Validity of Hegel's Argument for the Identity in Content of Absolute Religion and Absolute Philosophy*. Cranbury, N.J.: Fairleigh Dickinson University Press, 1995.

Schlitt, Dale M. *Divine Subjectivity: Understanding Hegel's Philosophy of Religion*. Cranbury, N.J.: Scranton University Press, 1990.

———. *Hegel's Trinitarian Claim: A Critical Reflection*. Leiden: Brill, 1984.

Schmitz, Kenneth L. "Hegel's Philosophy of Religion: Typology and Strategy." *Review of Metaphysics* 23, no. 4 (June 1970): 717–36.

Shanks, Andrew. *Hegel's Political Theology*. Cambridge: Cambridge University Press, 1991.

Williamson, Raymond K. *Introduction to Hegel's Philosophy of Religion*. Albany: State University of New York Press, 1984.

Yerkes, James. *The Christology of Hegel*. Albany: State University of New York Press, 1983.

History of Philosophy

Editions and Translations

Hegel, G. W. F. *Hegel's Introduction to the Lectures on the History of Philosophy* (Hoffmeister, ed.). Translated by Thomas M. Knox and Arnold V. Miller. Oxford: Oxford University Press, 1985.

———. *Lectures on the History of Philosophy (The Lectures of 1825–1826)* (Garniron and Jaeschke, ed.). Translated by Robert F. Brown and J. Michael Stewart. Berkeley: University of California Press, 1990–.

———. *Lectures on the History of Philosophy* (Michelet, ed.). Translated by Elizabeth S. Haldane and Frances H. Simpson. London: Paul, Trench, 1892–96.

———. *Vorlesungen über die Geschichte der Philosophie* (Lectures on the History of Philosophy). Edited by Pierre Garniron and Walter Jaeschke. *Vorlesungen 6–9* (Lectures 6–9). Hamburg: Meiner, 1986–96.

———. *Vorlesungen über die Geschichte der Philosophie* (Lectures on the History of Philosophy). Edited by Johannes Hoffmeister. Leipzig: Meiner, 1938–40.

——. *Vorlesungen über die Geschichte der Philosophie* (Lectures on the History of Philosophy). Edited by Karl L. Michelet. Berlin: Duncker & Humblot, 1833–36.

Lauer, Quentin. *Hegel's Idea of Philosophy* (Hoffmeister, ed.). New York: Fordham University Press, 1971.

Secondary Sources

Butler, Clark. "Empirical versus Rational Order in the History of Philosophy." *Owl of Minerva* 26, no. 1. (Fall 1994): 29–34.

Gray, J. Glenn. *Hegel's Hellenic Ideal*. New York: Columbia University Press, 1941.

Hegel and the History of Philosophy. Edited by Joseph J. O'Malley, Keith W. Algozin, and Frederick G. Weiss. The Hague: Nijhoff, 1974.

Hegel on the Modern World. Edited by Ardis B. Collins. Albany: State University of New York Press, 1995.

Hegel's Critique of Kant. Edited by Stephen Priest. Oxford: Oxford University Press, 1987.

Hudson, Jay William. "Hegel's Conception of an Introduction to Philosophy." *Journal of Philosophy, Psychology, and Scientific Method* 6 (1909): 345–53.

Kainz, Howard P. *An Introduction to Hegel: The Stages of Modern Philosophy*. Athens: Ohio University Press, 1996.

Weiss, Frederick G. *Hegel's Critique of Aristotle's Philosophy of Mind*. The Hague: Nijhoff, 1969.

Other Writings

Bryant, William M. *Hegel's Educational Ideal*. Chicago: Werner, 1896.

Hegel, G. W. F. *The Philosophical Propaedeutic*. Translated by Arnold V. Miller; edited by Michael George and Andrew Vincent. Oxford: Blackwell, 1986.

HEGELIAN PHILOSOPHY

Germany

Adorno, Theodor. *Negative Dialectics* (1966). Translated by E. B. Ashton. New York: Seabury, 1973.

Bauer, Bruno. *The Trumpet of the Last Judgement against Hegel the Atheist and Antichrist* (1841). Translated by Lawrence S. Stepelevich. Lewiston, N.Y.: Mellen, 1989.

Baur, Ferdinand Christian. *Ferdinand Christian Baur on the Writing of Church History*. Edited and translated by Peter C. Hodgson. New York: Oxford University Press, 1968.

Engels, Friedrich. *Dialectics of Nature*. Translated by Clemens Dutt. Moscow: Foreign Languages, 1954.

Erdmann, Johann Eduard. *A History of Philosophy* (1866). Translated by W. S. Hough. London: Sonnenschein, 1890–92.

——. *Outlines of Logic and Metaphysics* (1841). Translated by B. C. Burt. London: Sonnenschein, 1896.

Feuerbach, Ludwig. *The Essence of Christianity* (1841). Translated by Marian Evans (George Eliot). London, 1854.

——. *Principles of the Philosophy of the Future* (1843). Translated by Manfred H. Vogel. Indianapolis, Ind.: Bobbs-Merrill, 1966.

Marx, Karl. *Critique of Hegel's "Philosophy of Right."* Translated by Annette Jolin and Joseph O'Malley. Cambridge: Cambridge University Press, 1970.

——. *Economic and Political Manuscripts of 1844.* Edited by Dirk J. Struik. New York: n.p., 1964.

Marx, Karl, and Friedrich Engels. *The German Ideology.* Moscow: Foreign Languages, 1968.

Rosenzweig, Franz. *The Star of Redemption* (1930). Translated by William W. Hallo. New York: Holt, Rinehart & Winston, 1971.

Strauss, David F. *The Life of Jesus Critically Examined.* Translated by Peter C. Hodgson. Ramsey, N.J.: Sigler, 1994.

The Young Hegelians: An Anthology. Edited by Lawrence S. Stepelevich. Cambridge: Cambridge University Press, 1983.

England

Baillie, James B. *The Idealistic Construction of Experience.* London: Macmillan, 1906.

Bosanquet, Bernard. *A History of Aesthetics.* London: Sonnenschein, 1892.

——. *Logic or The Morphology of Knowledge.* Oxford: Oxford University Press, 1888.

——. *The Philosophical Theory of the State.* London: Macmillan, 1899.

——. *The Principle of Individuality and Value.* London: Macmillan, 1912.

——. *The Value and Destiny of the Individual.* London: Macmillan, 1913.

Bradley, Francis H. *Appearance and Reality.* London: Sonnenschein, 1893.

——. *Ethical Studies.* Oxford: Oxford University Press, 1876.

——. *The Principles of Logic.* London: Kegan Paul, Trench, Trübner, 1883.

Collingwood, Robin G. *An Essay on Metaphysics.* Oxford: Oxford University Press, 1940.

——. *The Idea of History.* Oxford: Oxford University Press, 1946.

——. *The Idea of Nature.* Oxford: Oxford University Press, 1945.

——. *The Principles of Art.* Oxford: Oxford University Press, 1938.

——. *Speculum Mentis.* Oxford: Oxford University Press, 1924.

Green, Thomas Hill. *The Works of Thomas Hill Green.* London: Longmans Green, 1885–88.

McTaggart, John M. E. *Studies in Hegelian Cosmology.* Cambridge: Cambridge University Press, 1901.

Mure, Geoffrey R. G. *Idealist Epilogue.* Oxford: Oxford University Press, 1978.

North America

Blanshard, Brand. *The Nature of Thought*. London: Allen & Unwin, 1939.

Cooper, Barry. *The End of History: An Essay on Modern Hegelianism*. Toronto: University of Toronto Press, 1984.

Desmond, William. *Beyond Hegel and Dialectic*. Albany: State University of New York Press, 1992.

———. *Desire, Dialectic, and Otherness: An Essay on Origins*. New Haven, Conn.: Yale University Press, 1987.

Dewey, John. *Essays in Experimental Logic*. Chicago: University of Chicago Press, 1916.

———. *Experience and Nature*. LaSalle, Ill.: Open Court, 1925.

———. *Human Nature and Conduct*. New York: Holt, 1922.

———. *Logic: The Theory of Inquiry*. New York: Holt, 1938.

———. *Reconstruction in Philosophy*. New York: Holt, 1920.

Fackenheim, Emil L. *Encounters between Judaism and Modern Philosophy*. New York: Basic Books, 1973.

———. *To Mend the World: Foundations of Future Jewish Thought*. New York: Schocken, 1982.

Fukuyama, Francis. *The End of History and the Last Man*. New York: Free Press, 1992.

Harris, E. E. *Nature, Mind, and Modern Science*. London: Allen & Unwin, 1954.

Hegel and His Critics: Philosophy in the Aftermath of Hegel. Edited by William Desmond. Albany: State University of New York Press, 1989.

Royce, Josiah. *The Religious Aspect of Philosophy*. Boston, 1885.

———. *The Spirit of Modern Philosophy*. Boston: Houghton, Mifflin, 1892.

———. *The World and the Individual*. New York: Macmillan, 1900–01.

Watson, John. *The Interpretation of Religious Experience*. Glasgow: Maclehose, 1912.

———. *The Philosophical Basis of Religion*. Glasgow: Maclehose, 1907.

Westphal, Merold. *Hegel, Freedom, and Modernity*. Albany: State University of New York Press, 1992.

Winfield, Richard D. *Freedom and Modernity*. Albany: State University of New York Press, 1991.

———. *The Just Economy*. New York: Routledge, 1988.

———. *The Just Family*. Albany: State University of New York Press, 1998.

———. *Overcoming Foundations: Studies in Systematic Philosophy*. New York: Columbia University Press, 1989.

———. *Stylistics: Rethinking the Artforms after Hegel*. Albany: State University of New York Press, 1996.

Europe

Cieszkowski, August von. *Selected Writings of August Cieszkowski*. Translated by André Liebich. Cambridge: Cambridge University Press, 1979.

Croce, Benedetto. *Philosophy, Poetry, History*. Translated by Cecil Sprigge. London: Oxford University Press, 1966.

Gentile, Giovanni. *The Philosophy of Art* (1944). Translated by Giovanni Gullace. Ithaca, N.Y.: Cornell University Press, 1972.

Kierkegaard, Søren. *Concluding Unscientific Postscript* (1846). Translated by David Swenson and Walter Lowrie. Princeton, N.J.: Princeton University Press, 1941.

———. *Philosophical Fragments* (1844). Translated by David F. Swenson. Princeton, N.J.: Princeton University Press, 1936.

Merleau-Ponty, Maurice. *Adventures of the Dialectic*. Translated by Joseph Bien. Evanston, Ill.: Northwestern University Press, 1973.

———. *Consciousness and the Acquisition of Language*. Translated by Hugh J. Silverman. Evanston, Ill.: Northwestern University Press, 1973.

———. *Phenomenology of Perception*. Translated by Colin Smith. London: Routledge, 1962.

Sartre, Jean-Paul. *Being and Nothingness* (1943). Translated by Hazel E. Barnes. New York: Philosophical Library, 1956.

———. *Critique of Dialectical Reason*. Translated by Alan Sheridan Smith; edited by Jonathan Rée (1961). London: NLB, 1976. 2d ed. translated by Quintin Hoare; edited by Arlette Elkaim-Sartre. London: Verso, 1991.

Zizek, Slavoi. *For They Know Not What They Do (Enjoyment as a Political Factor)*. London: Verso, 1991.

———. *The Sublime Object of Ideology*. London: Verso, 1989.

———. *Tarrying with the Negative: Kant, Hegel, and the Critique of Ideology*. Durham, N.C.: Duke University Press, 1993.

Asia

Nishida Kitaro. *Art and Morality*. Translated by David A. Dilworth and Valdo H. Viglielmo. Honolulu: University Press of Hawaii, 1973.

———. *Inquiry into the Good*. Translated by Masao Abe and Christopher Ives. New Haven, Conn.: Yale University Press, 1990.

———. *Intelligibility and the Philosophy of Nothingness: Three Philosophical Essays*. Translated by Robert Schinzinger. Tokyo: n.p., 1958.

———. *A Study of Good*. Translated by Valdo H. Viglielmo. Tokyo: n.p., 1960.

Tanabe Hajime. *Philosophy as Metanoetics*. Translated by Takeuchi Yoshinori with Valdo H. Viglielmo and James W. Heisig. Berkeley: University of California Press, 1986.

About the Author

John W. Burbidge (B.A., B.D., Ph.D., University of Toronto; M.A., Yale University) is professor emeritus of philosophy at Trent University. His books include *Being and Will; On Hegel's Logic; Hegel on Logic and Religion; Real Process: How Logic and Chemistry Combine in Hegel's Philosophy of Nature;* and *Within Reason.* Published articles include discussions of Friedrich W. J. Schelling, Charles Sanders Peirce, Emil Fackenheim, Henry S. Harris, historicity, and arguments from analogy. With others he has translated Jacques D'Hondt's *Hegel in His Time: Berlin, 1818–1831* and Hegel's *The Jena System, 1804–5: Logic and Metaphysics*; and he has edited Emil Fackenheim's *The God Within* and Wilfred Cantwell Smith's *Modern Culture from a Comparative Perspective.* He was president of the Hegel Society of America from 1988 to 1990 and in 1998 was elected fellow of the Royal Society of Canada.